Science 5–11

A Guide for Teachers

Second Edition

Alan Howe, Dan Davies, Kendra McMahon,
Lee Towler, Christopher Collier and Tonie Scott

LONDON AND NEW YORK

First edition published 2005 by David Fulton Publishers

This edition published 2009
by Routledge
2 Park Square, Milton Park, Abingdon, Oxon OX14 4RN

Simultaneously published in the USA and Canada
by Routledge
711 Third Avenue, New York, NY 10017 (8th Floor)

Routledge is an imprint of the Taylor & Francis Group, an informa business

Typeset in Bembo and Helvetica by RefineCatch Ltd, Bungay, Suffolk

British Library Cataloguing in Publication Data
A catalogue record for this book is available from the British Library

Library of Congress Cataloging-in-Publication Data
Science 5–11 : a guide for teachers / Alan Howe . . . [et al.].—2nd ed.
p. cm.
Includes bibliographical references.
1. Science—Study and teaching (Elementary)—Great Britain. 2. Science—Experiments. I. Howe, Alan (Alan Robin)
LB1585.5.G7S34 2009
372.3′50941—dc22 2008043454

ISBN 10: 0-415-48046-9 (hbk)
ISBN 10: 0-415-48045-0 (pbk)

ISBN 13: 978-0-415-48046-8 (hbk)
ISBN 13: 978-0-415-48045-1 (pbk)

Printed and bound by CPI Group (UK) Ltd, Croydon, CR0 4YY

SCIENCE 5–11

This new edition of the best-selling textbook *Science 5–11* provides a synthesis of ideas about teaching and learning that focuses on answering the question 'How best should I teach science?' Offering a practical and innovative guide which is ideal for students, trainee and practising teachers, the book provides full information on the appropriate science topics for key stage one and two, outlining the subject knowledge that a teacher needs, the curriculum requirements and the best ways to go about teaching, with an emphasis on practical science enquiry.

Fully updated to include:

- The possibilities for talk and discussion within science lessons
- How children might record their ideas and findings
- How ICT can be incorporated into lessons
- How science can be linked to other subjects in a creative and cross-curricular way
- Citizenship and education for sustainable development.

The authors draw on their expertise to identify approaches to teaching that are best used in different areas of science, and help readers understand key teaching issues by considering them in relation to specific contexts. With advice on lesson planning and a user-friendly structure, this book forms essential reading for all students and practising teachers in primary education.

Alan Howe has 15 years' experience of working with trainee teachers in primary science and is Co-Programme Leader for undergraduate Education Studies at Bath Spa University.

Dan Davies is Head of Applied Research and Consultancy at Bath Spa University and founder of the Centre for Research in Early Scientific Learning.

Kendra McMahon is Senior Lecturer in Primary Science at Bath Spa University and currently researching teaching science in the later primary years.

Lee Towler has recently retired from her post as Senior Lecturer in Primary Education at Bath Spa University.

Christopher Collier is Senior Lecturer in Primary Science at Bath Spa University and leads the BSU course for Primary Science Subject Leaders.

Tonie Scott is currently Headteacher at Bishop Henderson Primary School, Somerset.

Dedication

This book is dedicated to all the past members of the Bath Spa University primary education science team.

Contents

Acknowledgements

The authors would like to thank:
. . . the schools, teachers and children involved in the Improving Science Together Project funded by the AstraZeneca Science Teaching Trust; the staff and children at Batheaston Primary School, Bath; Bishop Henderson Primary School, Somerset; Bromley Heath Junior School, South Gloucestershire; Newbridge Junior School, Bath; Moorlands Infants' School, Bath; St Philip's Primary School, Bath and Chandag Infants' School, Keynsham.

Introduction

TEACHING IS one of the most rewarding professions imaginable. People become teachers for many reasons, but often it is because they believe they can inspire children to find learning fascinating. There are so many things to learn and so many ways to know; we think science offers teachers and learners a great deal in both respects. By being scientific we can satisfy our curiosity, ask new questions and make informed decisions in our lives. Science can focus our attention, stimulate our thinking and help us appreciate the wonders of the natural world. Through teaching science we can help children see new sights, think new thoughts and understand a little better why the world (and beyond) can be an enthralling place.

This book is organised somewhat differently from others on primary science currently available. In recent years there has been a renewed emphasis on teachers' own subject content knowledge, and many books aim to help teachers ensure their understanding is secure. Other books look at pedagogical knowledge (Shulman 1987) in detail and offer good advice regarding the many facets of teaching science: planning, assessment, progression and so on. However, for primary teachers in England and many other countries, daily classroom experience is of a science curriculum broken down into traditional disciplines (Sc2, 3 and 4 corresponding approximately to biology, chemistry and physics, respectively) and further subdivided into 'topics' – plants, forces, etc. Although this is a culturally imposed structure, as a team of teacher educators we have realised that each science topic offers teachers particular opportunities and particular challenges. In a sense, they all have their own pedagogies. For example, the teaching of 'forces' needs to be approached quite differently to 'humans and other animals', which requires a different pedagogy to teaching 'Earth and beyond'. Because these divisions sometimes do not equate to how children understand the world, we need to identify places where strong and productive links can be made between children's experiences and the science curriculum. We have, therefore, within each chapter, sought to provide the reader with a synthesis of content and pedagogy that is focused on answering the question 'How should I best teach this area of science?'

And how would a primary teacher know they were a 'good' science educator? We suggest the following criteria – they inform subsequent chapters. Good science teachers:

- have clear personal aims for science teaching
- have an understanding of the nature of science

- have an understanding of the 'processes of science' and how science creates knowledge – that ideas are tentative, and are based on interpretation of evidence
- have sufficient understanding of the 'big ideas' of science to see where learning is leading and to avoid giving misleading information
- value children's existing ideas
- have a knowledge of some common alternative ideas that children hold
- have a repertoire of teaching strategies they can use responsively and creatively
- feel excited about teaching science.

We intend this book to be a valuable starting point for anyone who wishes to teach science in a creative and inspiring way. Students in initial teacher training and primary teachers who are relatively new to the profession will find here a framework for teaching science that is both relevant and engaging for primary children. This framework is grounded in personal experience, theory and research, in line with our commitment to evidence-based practice. It will be introduced in the first chapter and developed in subsequent chapters as we consider what it means for teaching various topics within the primary science curriculum. We hope that the book will also be useful for those who are more experienced practitioners. Rather than present a prescriptive model for teaching science, we explain approaches and strategies that teachers can adopt, develop and use creatively with the children in their own classes. Teachers who have the additional responsibility of being science subject leaders or coordinators may also find it useful in helping them with supporting colleagues, and in reflecting on progression across the whole primary school. We focus on their role in chapter 12.

Organisation of chapters

In chapter 1 we consider the aims of primary science, introduce our view of the nature of science and explore the central role of scientific enquiry. There is also a full discussion of the importance of talk, specifically dialogue, between teachers and learners. Chapters 2–11 each take a topic, such as 'electricity', and explore in more depth the issues for teaching and learning in that topic. For ease of reference, each chapter will follow a similar pattern; the different sections are outlined below. The final chapter looks at the role of the *subject leader* in primary schools, considering what the job entails and the kinds of support a class teacher can expect from the post-holder.

Purpose of this chapter

A series of bullet points will set out the aims of the chapter for the reader.

Introduction

In the introduction to each chapter we will explain the relevance of the topic for primary children, and in terms of developing the 'big ideas' of science.

Progression from the early years to the beginning of secondary school

What are the key concepts that are to be developed within this conceptual area? What kinds of expectations might we have of children at various stages in their primary education and where is this leading? A table will summarise the subject knowledge related to those 'key ideas' for teachers to access at a glance, and we recommend sources that would support teachers in further developing their subject knowledge of these concepts.

Cross-curricular planning

Teachers are always keen to make learning as relevant and engaging as possible for their class. One way to achieve this is to teach in a way that creates links between different curriculum subjects. In this section we outline for each science topic the range of opportunities for cross-curricular planning. The context within which scientific ideas are presented is vitally important in motivating children and ensuring that the ideas connect with their own lives sufficiently to make sense. We also provide suggestions for how to introduce children to the topic in question in ways that will excite their interest and be meaningful and relevant for them.

Assessment for learning

In this section we select and exemplify those strategies for eliciting children's exciting ideas that are most appropriate for the topic. We also explore common alternative ideas that children may hold, preparing teachers for what they might encounter in their own classrooms. This will draw on a range of established research and literature. *Key questions* for formative assessment will be identified (these are *italicised* for ease of reference). The relationship between elicitation and formative and summative assessment will be considered in the context of the particular conceptual area.

Scientific enquiry

Here we focus on the particular aspects of scientific enquiry that could be developed through this topic, drawing on the categories developed by Goldsworthy *et al.* (2000a) during the Association for Science Education & King's College Science Investigations in Schools (AKSIS) research project: exploration, pattern-seeking, testing an explanation, identification and classification, fair testing, technology and reference enquiry. The intention is both to support the reader in understanding the different forms enquiry can take, and to suggest possibilities for enquiries as interventions. This section also addresses issues of assessment of scientific enquiry relevant to the conceptual area.

Developing children's understanding

In this section we provide a range of teaching strategies and activities that can support children's learning in the conceptual area and identify aspects of scientific enquiry, for example the use of models and analogies. We make suggestions for developing cross-curricular links and themes including: education for sustainable development (ESD), citizenship, creativity, thinking skills, information and communication technology (ICT), language and maths. These suggestions are intended to provide examples of useful interventions in supporting children in restructuring their ideas and include opportunities for application.

Using ICT to teach about . . .

In this section we outline some of the opportunities that arise to use ICT to enhance the teaching of each topic. We explore the appropriate use of a range of hardware (cameras, microscopes, dataloggers etc.), recommended software and resources available via the internet.

Classroom management

Primary teachers often find the organisational aspects of science, particularly practical work, a challenge. In this section we offer advice and raise awareness of health and safety issues relating to the conceptual theme.

In writing this book we have drawn on our wide range of experiences and expertise gathered from a variety of perspectives: as primary teachers, advisory teachers, university tutors and teacher trainers. We must also acknowledge that this book would not have been possible if we had not been fortunate enough to work within a science education community that is creative, dedicated and generous. We have drawn ideas together from past colleagues, students, trainees and teachers as well as from published sources. We hope we have acknowledged everyone and offended no one in the process.

CHAPTER

1

Science, learning and teaching

Purpose of this chapter

After reading this chapter you should have:

- reflected on the aims and purposes of teaching science in the primary school
- considered the nature of science
- an understanding of the processes that contribute to scientific enquiry
- an understanding of how children learn science
- considered approaches to teaching science.

What are the aims of primary science?

THE WAYS IN WHICH we teach science in our primary schools depend to a great extent on our beliefs about why we are doing it. What is it that makes it worthwhile? It is not the main aim of primary science to produce biochemists, engineers, doctors, ecologists, astronomers and wildlife photographers. Some adults will have a greater need for an understanding of particular aspects of science in their everyday lives than others, depending on their roles and interests, and primary science provides the foundation for this, but primary science has a much broader agenda. Primary-aged children are already beginning to position themselves in relation to different aspects of the curriculum and identify favourite things and perhaps label others as 'boring'. Lifelong views and interests can be initiated by powerful experiences during childhood, and so primary educators have a responsibility to ensure that children's experiences of science are positive. It is important that all social groups have access to all areas of science so that different perspectives are represented within the scientifically literate population, and no groups, for example women, are excluded by the ways in which science is presented. Stereotypes about scientists can be actively challenged. An important aim of science education as a whole is establishing 'scientific literacy' across the population. Science is not something scientists do in isolation from the rest of society. It requires funding, and so the providers of these funds must consider the research to be worthwhile. In many cases science is supported by public money, via taxation. Science is also subject to government regulation, such as ethical guidance for the use of animal experiments and standards for testing medicines. So it is not just scientists that need to make decisions about science and the directions in which science goes. In their roles as consumers, parents, citizens and voters, everyone has a stake in science and, arguably, a responsibility for it. In a scientifically literate society people would engage with science issues that affect society as a whole and take an active part through democratic processes and personal decisions. Primary-aged children are already developing viewpoints on issues that have an ethical as well as a scientific basis, such as how farm animals should be treated and how habitats should be protected.

But perhaps the most important aim of primary science is to foster children's appreciation of the world around us, to encourage a close observation of our physical environment, and to develop an understanding of how different aspects of it are related. And this is worthwhile just because it is fascinating, it is amazing, and experiencing this exploration enriches our lives. Arguably, this could be achieved just as well, if not better, through art, through literature, or perhaps through more everyday experiences such as going out for a walk. So what is it that makes the scientific study of the world a distinct and valuable approach?

What is science?

Science provides a way of making sense of the world, of responding to those 'why?' questions that children have, in a meaningful way. What is particular about science is the emphasis on evidence, on logic and on explanations that are rooted in physical properties. While we are not suggesting that other ways of understanding the world are unimportant, we consider that science provides a valuable way of answering some of those questions. It provides people with a means of engaging with the world in their everyday life, which is not fatalistic, or superstitious, but can be empowering.

Scientific knowledge is tentative; the explanations are the best we have at the moment, but there is always the possibility that these theories will be challenged or replaced in the light of new ideas and evidence. If children are to really understand science, this fundamental view of the nature of science must run through all of science teaching. Science is not standing still – ideas are changing, new evidence is being produced, and creative thinking generates new questions and explanations. Is using a mobile phone dangerous to our health? What are the possible impacts of light pollution? At any one time, scientists may disagree about explanations, and different studies may provide conflicting evidence.

Scientific knowledge could be defined as the ideas any individual constructs in their mind as a result of scientific processes. What mental images do you have about what happens to food after you have swallowed it? Where did these ideas come from? It is also the body of knowledge that is held by the scientific community as a whole, including the tensions and contradictions and uncertainties. This presents a particular challenge for teaching science – how is this tentativeness to be communicated, while at the same time acknowledging the value of the existing body of knowledge, and helping children to get to grips with ideas that have developed over thousands of years? If science is not a fixed body of knowledge, what content, what aspects of knowledge and understanding, should children learn? In fact, is there any point in learning any of it at all?

The time-scale for changes in the better-established concepts in science seems to be sufficiently long that there is a fairly stable body of knowledge that primary children can get to grips with that is likely to remain useful during their lifetime. The National Curriculum (NC) for England and Wales (DfEE/QCA 1999) is one attempt to select aspects that might be relevant and accessible for primary-aged children, and this book is largely based on that selection. Other authors (Millar and Osborne 1998) have emphasised the importance of the 'big ideas' in science – concepts such as particle theory, energy, evolution and the formation of the Earth – that unify different branches of science, and are powerful 'explanatory stories' in how, as a culture, we currently make sense of the world. We draw your attention to these big ideas in turn in subsequent chapters. The argument that science should be studied as one of the great cultural achievements of modern times is a compelling one.

There has been a recent trend towards people being more sceptical about scientists and having a lack of trust in their pronouncements. It is reasonable to be sceptical about the motivations of the funding bodies and to raise questions about who is defined as an 'expert'. Indeed, scientific attitudes include questioning what others say. However, the rejection of science might be partly due to unrealistic expectations of the kind of answers science can generate. It does not produce certainties, though findings have sometimes been presented as such. If teachers see scientific ideas as indisputable facts, and present them as such, they are misleading children and giving them a false understanding of the nature of science. Weighing evidence, understanding probability and assessing risk are all part of understanding how to make judgements and taking decisions based on scientific evidence. A critical understanding of how ideas are based on evidence requires an understanding of the processes of science, such as the use of controlled tests and the implications of sampling procedures. This critical understanding of science can begin in the primary school as children learn about scientitifc enquiry by making observations, carrying out tests and thinking about what they have found out.

In this book we present a view of science as a blend of skills, concepts and attitudes that should remain intertwined during teaching. If science is a combination of systematic, careful data collection, together with the insight and inspiration of individuals and of scientific communities that lead to new explanations, then science in school should reflect this creative and sometimes 'fuzzy' process rather than pretend science is a linear path from question to answer.

Learning in science – some theories

In order to make decisions about how to teach we need to think about how children learn. Constructivist theories of learning and, more recently, socio-cultural views of learning have significantly influenced approaches to science education. In this section we shall explore these and consider their implications for teaching primary science.

Constructivist theories view learning as a process by which an individual actively constructs ideas, rather than as a process of 'transmission' in which facts are poured into the mind of the learner. Versions of constructivism based on the work of Piaget emphasise the importance of interaction with the physical world and see young children as behaving like scientists – making and testing hypotheses about the environment: for example, 'This toy will fall to the floor if I drop it.'

In this view of learning science, the practical hands-on experiences become the most important element, and the teacher's role is to provide a rich environment for the child to explore. If we reflect on our own learning, few people would deny the power of handling objects, feeling and seeing something happen in giving us a depth of understanding. Interactionist theories such as this focus on the interaction 'between hand and mind' (Davies and Ward 2003). Different kinds of play contribute to children's learning in science. Going around a garden smelling flowers or examining different pebbles could be defined as exploratory play. Working out how to make a swing go higher with friends in the playground might be problem-solving play. More symbolic play might include dressing up a doll to go outside in the rain.

There is a great deal of evidence (Driver et al. 1985, SPACE Project – various authors 1989–1998) that children construct their own ideas and explanations about the world that are different from the scientific view. These are sometimes called 'alternative frameworks', sometimes less respectfully labelled as 'misconceptions'. If children are somehow innately motivated to make sense of the world around them, then it is not surprising that this would happen. This belief that children are developing ideas about the world, even in the absence of being 'taught', is an important one. The ideas that children construct are not random or thoughtless, but are logical interpretations, based on the limited knowledge and experience the child has. Although not every child will construct the same ideas, there are some common patterns in alternative frameworks, and being aware of these is useful to teachers. We outline some ways in which children think about scientific phenomena in subsequent chapters.

Social constructivist views of learning in science (Harlen and Qualter 2004, Ollerenshaw and Ritchie 1997) also emphasise the central role of practical investigations in developing children's ideas but, in addition, they stress the importance of learning with and from others – both peers and adults. They argue that children will develop their existing ideas when they encounter new evidence, which could be in the form of new physical experiences or new ideas from other people. This new evidence may confirm or conflict with their existing ideas, or develop new ideas, but if they are not to be rejected as meaningless then children must be able to make some sense of experiences by connecting them to their existing understanding. They may be able to make links without support, or it may need the intervention of someone else to help them. Ideas that do not make sense, or are not linked with other ideas, are those that are easily forgotten.

The above theories lead us to conclude that *talking* is a vital part of learning in science and a special kind of talk is particularly valuable – where meanings are negotiated through *dialogue* (more about this below). Talk should happen amongst children and between children and the teacher. Teacher's questioning is important as it helps the teacher to find out what children's ideas are and to try to get at the reasoning behind those ideas. The process of talking about observations and evidence and relating it to other experiences helps to make sense of the world.

In this view of learning, as well as recognising that ideas are developed within individual minds, a socio-cultural approach sets out to understand how ideas are developed between minds. Vygotsky (1978) proposed the existence of an individual and a social plane, 'intramental' and 'intermental' planes. His theory is that learning occurs when concepts developed on the social plane, the intermental plane, between people are then internalised by individuals to their 'intramental space'.

Other authors (such as Rogoff 1990) use the term appropriated instead of internalised to make the point that for the learner this is an active process that transforms the ideas of the social plane, not a copying process, which would take us back to a transmission view of learning.

Socio-cultural views of learning in science also stress the importance of the cultural context of learning. In this view, the way that people interact is thought to be important. For learning to occur, there needs to be a genuine two-way process of interpretation and meaning-making, where the ideas of all participants are respected and given equal value. During this exchange the ideas of each person may develop and change. One implication of this is that teachers need to beware of making assumptions about children's understanding of the language they use. The teacher needs to make an effort to understand children on their own terms, not just expect them to see things from the teacher's perspective. Bruner (1996) explains that to teach others we need to use our 'theory of mind' – we need to imagine what it is that another person is thinking.

Each person brings their own cultural position to the process of creating a dialogue, and this can present barriers to shared understanding. If a teacher presented putting sugar in tea as an example of dissolving, he might assume that people put sugar in a cup of tea after it was made, while in some African and Indian communities the common practice is to boil tea, sugar, water and milk together in a kettle. The scientific version of what dissolving means wouldn't change, but the way in which children made sense of the example might be different. A teacher might assume that the children understand that because they are doing science, the word 'table' is being used to refer to a chart for results, rather than a piece of furniture. Words with an everyday meaning can also have a particular scientitifc meaning: force, solid, and fruit are further examples of this.

In the classroom the teacher has a great deal of power in determining what counts as the 'right' knowledge. Children may come to accept the 'correct' teacher's view, but not really connect it with their own deeper understanding, so it becomes compartmentalised as 'school knowledge' and kept as separate from their everyday or common-sense views of the world. Another possibility, if the teacher's view is meaningless to the child in terms of their own existing knowledge and understanding, is either that they fail to 'get it right' in school, or that they learn to produce the 'right answer' by rote. So, for the teacher, the art is to make scientifically accepted ideas meaningful in terms of the child's existing ideas. In order to do this, the teacher needs to understand both the child's existing constructions and the scientific body of knowledge to be taught. Implementing these ideas is clearly a challenge for any teacher. The chapters of this book attempt to support teachers in this process of examining examples of children's ideas, presenting the ideas currently held by scientists, and providing a repertoire of teaching strategies that relate them.

This is not a 'top–down process': by helping children to engage with scientific ideas and language they can become part of science, rather than receivers of it. In each chapter we emphasise the importance of the context: is it interesting, meaningful and relevant? Might there be any aspects of the topic that are beyond the children's experience?

Children working together in groups, without an adult present, can come to a shared understanding about what they are doing and observing and how they are explaining their experiences. This can be very productive in that there is an immediate connection with existing ideas, and often children can help make sense of ideas to each other in terms of a shared language and set of experiences that a teacher would not have access to. With the teacher's dominant presence removed, children are free to have a more open-ended exploration of what is taking place. However, there is no guarantee that the understandings they reach will be in line with the scientific view! There may be dominant children in the group who are persuasive and convince the others that their explanations are correct when others may have ideas that fit better with accepted ideas and evidence.

The view taken in this book is not only that scientific processes are useful in supporting children's learning, and we strongly support the importance of providing first-hand experiences and extending the available evidence to children, but also that there are a range of other strategies that can be used to create a shared understanding of scientific concepts. Different areas of the curriculum present different challenges in terms of 'bridging the gap' between children's and scientific ideas and so require different teaching strategies (Leach and Scott 2002). This includes the use of analogies, introducing scientific models and discussing vocabulary. For the teacher, ensuring that they and the children 'stay on the same wavelength' is of central importance; they maintain a shared 'intermental space', so that new ideas can be introduced and developed in ways that are meaningful to the children.

Exploring dialogic talk and learning in science

Alexander (2008) uses the term *dialogic* to express a 'genuinely reciprocal' process of communication between teacher and pupil in which ideas are developed cumulatively over sustained sequences of interactions. Using dialogic talk can support children in coming to both understanding the scientific view and having their own viewpoints valued. Dialogic talk in which children's viewpoints are considered can be understood by contrasting it with authoritative talk in which children's ideas are only accepted if they are in line with the scientific:

> . . . either the teacher hears what the student has to say from the student's point of view, or the teacher hears what the student has to say only from the science point of view.
>
> (Mortimer and Scott 2003: 33)

Imagine if all a teacher's interactions with children were like this:

Teacher: Can you tell me something a plant needs to stay alive? Anna?
Anna: Water.
Teacher: Water, that's right. What else does it need? Max?
Max: Food.
Teacher: Food, not really no. Plants don't eat food, they make their own. What else do they need to stay alive? Sam?
Sam: They need air.
Teacher: Air. Right.

This kind of interaction might be useful for a brisk recap of information, but it is not about supporting new learning and deep understanding. It also conveys the hidden message that the teacher has all the answers. It is made up of 'IRE triads'; the teacher **initiates** with a question, the child **responds**, and the teacher **evaluates** their answer.

Instead of evaluating a child's response to a question: *Yes that's right*, and moving on, teachers can use children's ideas as starting points for further discussion: *What makes you say that? Can you give me an example? What do you mean by . . .? Would anyone else like to add to that?* This helps to develop an extended discussion in which children's ideas are explored and then different contributions are linked together to build up ideas.

Learning has emotional and social dimensions as well as the cognitive elements. If the classroom provides a safe environment in which children can express their views without fear of ridicule or of being ignored, then the teacher is more likely to be successful in eliciting their ideas and in finding out whether understanding is shared. If children are secure, they take responsibility for checking their own understanding by asking the teacher questions: 'Do you mean that . . .?', or they contribute: 'Oh yes, that's like . . .'. Children can help to explain new ideas to each other, 'You know, it's like when . . .', by accessing their shared culture in a way that teachers cannot. If the class as a whole accepts that changing your ideas is part of learning, this reduces fear of 'getting it wrong' and, at the same time, this also supports the idea that scientific knowledge is tentative and open to change. In this book we provide ideas for approaches to teaching that can help teachers to develop a culture in which questioning is valued and ideas are to be explored and developed together. The teacher plays the lead role in establishing this culture, by their example and by the ways in which they interact with children. You will find these 'open ended' and 'person-centred' openings to dialogue suggested for each topic in chapters 2 to 11.

This emphasis on dialogic talk and valuing children's ideas does not mean that the scientific ideas should not be introduced or discussed, but that this should happen in relation to the children's ideas. Mortimor and Scott (2003) suggest that teaching may involve cycles of talk in which there is a focus on exploring the children's ideas, then developing their ideas by relating them to the scientific ideas, followed by more authoritative summaries of the scientific point of view, then cycling back to a focus on the children's ideas. (See case studies 1 and 2 for examples of dialogic talk for different purposes.)

Case study 1: Living or non-living? Exploring children's ideas through dialogic talk

In this case study, we illustrate how the way a teacher began a topic helped to establish a class culture of open discussion and sharing of ideas. This transcript has been annotated by the class teacher and her comments are shown in italics.

I wanted to find out what the children (9–10 years old, class size 37) knew about the characteristics of living things and set our topic on plants in this broader context. The children sat on the floor in a circle around a varied collection of objects, including some living plants. Initially, we classified the collection into living and non-living and discussed some of the characteristics of living things.

The opening question was an 'invitation to participate' that had two functions. Firstly it handed over control of the direction of the conversation to the children and secondly it signalled to them that their ideas were going to be explored, not tested.

T: We're going to look at these things and think about whether they're living . . . whether they're non-living or anything else you've got to say about them to do with that . . . So does anyone want to start us off? Who's got something to say? Max?

Max: Well Miss, if it was a living, every living thing right, it has to have something to eat or to drink to live. Say like a table for instance, is non-living because it doesn't eat, it doesn't drink.

T: So what about a plant then? *(Max has used the words eat and drink, which we usually associate with animals rather than plants)*

Max: Well down in the soil, it's got that and they eat it through the roots.

T: I see. Does anyone else want to add anything about that?

Mike: Sometimes you can give them food, if they haven't got enough in the soil you can give them some food. *(This indicated to me there could be a widely held idea within the class that plants get their food through their roots)*

T: I see, You can actually buy something called plant food can't you? . . . (*Acknowledging that there was evidence to support this idea.)* Paul?

Paul: Well another thing about how plants live, is when we breathe out oxygen, they get it, when we breathe in . . . Carbon dioxide, they get it.

T: Is that the right way round? *(A number of children had appeared to be concerned about Paul's idea and I assumed I knew why)*

?: No! No!

T: Shh I'm really glad you mentioned those two gases. *(Valuing his contribution)* Just listen again to what you said. Donna, do you want to pick up on that? Not at the moment, we'll come back to you. Tom, do you?

Tom: Plants take in the carbon dioxide and make it into oxygen.

T: They certainly take in carbon dioxide and what they do with it, we'll think about more as we go through the term. *(Tom's response had indicated an area that would need intervention and I signalled this to them.)*

Edited extract from McMahon (2009)

The children could make distinctions between living and non-living and could identify a number of characteristics of living things. It also enabled me to identify the common alternative concept that plants get their food from the soil. Some of the children had been introduced to the idea that plants use carbon dioxide and expel oxygen, but they seemed to see it as the opposite of breathing rather than being about plants making food. Although not every child had been able to express their ideas, I had begun to build up a picture of the range of ideas held by the class.

The teacher encouraged the children to respond to each other's suggestions – creating an environment in which different ideas can be considered, rather than expecting everyone to agree. There is a balance to be struck here between valuing everyone's contributions while simultaneously marking all ideas as start points that could be changed. The underlying message that needs to come across is 'We all have something to contribute and we all have something to learn.'

Case study 2: Do seeds need light to germinate? Interpreting results through dialogic talk

Discussing results of scientitifc enquiries with children can be challenging for teachers as they need to work with the actual results they observed, the associated 'correct' scientific explanations and the children's exisitng ideas, all at the same time. The intention is that this extract exemplifies some aspects of dialogic talk in science and provides a start point for reflecting on practice. This transcript has been annotated by the class teacher and her comments are shown in italics.

Dishes containing 10 cress seeds on moist filter paper had been placed under transparent, translucent and opaque covers. The results showed small differences between the number of seeds that germinated in each dish. We first discussed whether we thought these differences were meaningful and decided they might just be because of the odd 'dud' seed. Then I reminded the class of the prediction we had made beforehand.

T: Right just have a look at that for a moment. And think back to what we were trying to find out. Did we think it mattered how much light they had? . . . We did, didn't we?

?: Yes.

T: What did we predict would happen, perhaps especially to the opaque one? Ellen?

Ellen: We predicted it wouldn't grow.

T: We predicted that those wouldn't grow. Because we thought, well they haven't got any light so they won't grow, they won't germinate; they won't begin to grow . . . Look at those results. Is that what we found? *(Here I needed to draw the children's attention back to the data, helping them to interpret it and use it to challenge their constructs.)*

?: No.

T: No. That's not what we found at all.

Kate: *Gasps*

T: Kate?

Kate: It might not have been a fair test, Miss. *(I was interested to hear Kate criticise the test we had carried out as a possible interpretation that would mean she wouldn't have to change her ideas.)*

The children then suggested and discussed various possible problems with the test design, for example that one container may have been close to the window.

T: Mmm, it might not have been quite as accurate as we might have hoped, so that could be one explanation. Suppose it was accurate. Suppose it was a fair test. What would our results tell us? Sophie?

Sophie: That plants don't really need light that much so . . .

T: That's what our experiment's telling us isn't it? That they don't need light that much to get started on growing, to germinate. *(Here, I have decided on an interpretation of the experiment that I consider to be the correct one. It might have been better if I had continued to treat it as tentative.)*

Mike: They need water really.

T: Just water.

Adrian: And food really *(This was a missed opportunity to open a discussion on where seeds get their food.)*

T: What do plants use the light for? *(This was a critical question in getting the children to apply their developing understanding of photosynthesis to explain what they had observed.)*

?: Gasp.

T: Pete.

Pete: To make food.

T: To make food. Is there any reason, why seeds when they begin germinating might not need to make food? (long pause). What do you think, Carla?

Carla: Well, I think there's some food in there, like.

T: In where?

Carla: Like the seed like saves, like got a bit of food, already made like water and everything.

T: Sort of trapped inside the case.

Carla: Yes.

After a few more comments from the children that showed their acceptance of this idea, Tracey, a child with a statement of special educational needs for learning difficulties, made a vital connection between real life and our experimental set up.

T: Tracey, what do you want to say?

Tracey: When you plant seeds in the ground they can't get any light.

T: And you're saying when, if they're planted in soil, they couldn't get any light could they? (pause) Oh, that's a thought. So, maybe, they don't need light to start growing, because, if you bury a seed underground, which you often do when you plant it, it doesn't get light. Good point. Polly, you've been waiting patiently.

Polly: In the, haven't got leaves right . . . you can't get light, so you can't get food.

T: Aahh, so it's because the leaves aren't really there yet doing their job, the seed has to have the food ready instead. That's a really good thought, I like that.

Susan: There's no need to make food yet, because the food's in the seed.

Edited extract from McMahon (2009)

A feature of this case that makes it dialogic is the way that children initiate lines of discussion. Clearly the relationships within the class mean they feel comfortable in expressing their ideas. The children also listen to each other's ideas and build on them. The teacher is not always asking questions, but often takes the role of choosing who will speak from the different children who have something of their own to say – much like chairing a meeting. However, she does steer the discussion in particular directions and emphasises ideas that are in line with the ones she wants the children to learn by selecting, repeating and rephrasing them. It could be described as a 'scaffolded dialgue' (Alexander 2008) – it is not open ended, it has a clear objective, but the children's ideas and the data are used together to get there.

Within the CLIS-based teaching sequence this discussion serves as an intervention, as attention is drawn to evidence that conflicts with the children's previous ideas and through the discussion an alternative idea is introduced and, after some debate, accepted. There is also evidence of application of previous learning – that plants make their own food using sunlight – to this new context of seed germination.

Teaching – putting theory into practice

A model of teaching science that developed as a result of social constructivist theories of learning in science is presented below and is summarised in Figure 1.1. It is based on the Children's Learning in Science Project (CLISP) approach (Scott 1987) and builds on the work of Ollerenshaw and Ritchie (1997), among others. Here we have developed the model to take into acount some aspects of the socio-cultural perspective, so that we consider what the different stages might mean for the learning of the class as a group as well as for the learners as individuals. In the model, there are five different stages in a teaching sequence:

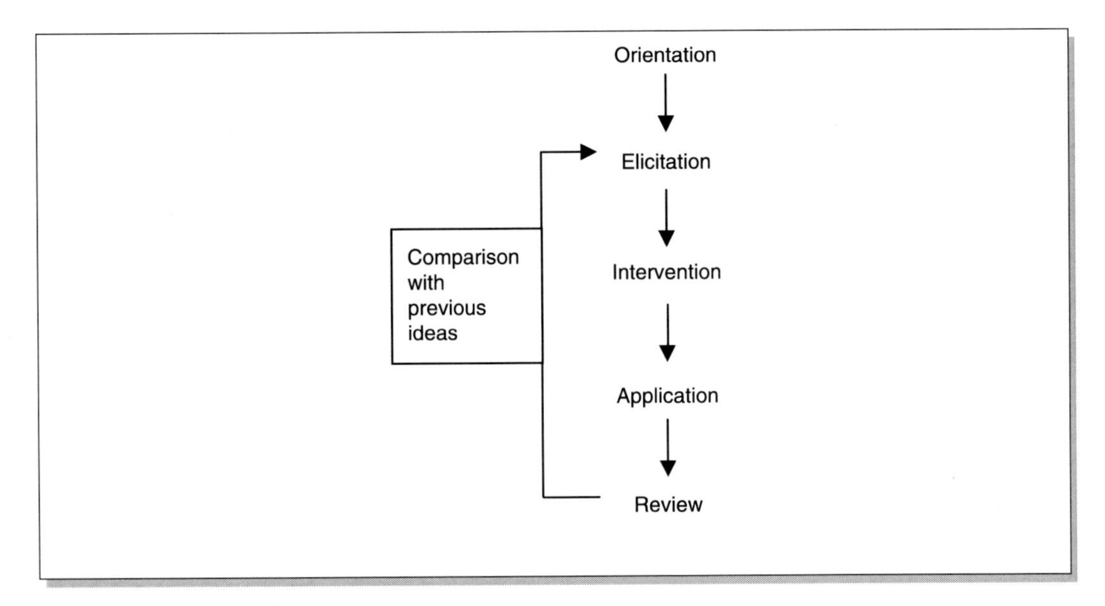

FIGURE 1.1 A constructivist teaching sequence

Orientation

Orientation is a process of setting the scene, of putting the topic into a context and of engaging the children's interest. Orientation might involve a provocation for learning that the teacher introduces: reading a story, or exploring a collection or discussing a local event, or it might be a response to something that the children have initiated. Talk might involve children in sharing their perspectives on a topic or relating it to their interests. The class as a whole can benefit from the breadth of ideas and questions that different children might bring. In a topic called 'clothes we wear' (planned to address understanding of the properties of materials) children could watch a short video clip of children doing an activity such as riding a bike and be asked what activities they enjoy and what clothes they would wear to do it. Children generally like to feel part of things, that they have something to contribute, and that the topic is meaningful for them. Planning a thoughtful orientation with time for the children to respond by talking together can help to establish a shared commitment to the topic for the class.

Elicitation

Orientation often merges into Elicitation. Elicitation is a process of clarifying and finding out the children's existing ideas. For the teacher this means that they gain an insight into the child's current understanding of the concept(s), which can inform their teaching. For the children, it is a process of becoming aware of their own ideas, of making them tangible, of 'structuring' them; this is the start of developing and possibly changing their ideas. They may begin to be aware that other children have somewhat different ideas or that they cannot explain something to their own satisfaction. Recording these ideas may be part of the process of clarifying them, and may be useful for both teacher and children to reflect on later. Different topic areas lend themselves to different ways of finding out and recording children's existing ideas, and these are known in science education as 'elicitation strategies'. These include:

- observing a child
- questioning
- sorting a collection
- annotated drawing
- floor books
- concept mapping
- concept cartoons
- true/false statements.

They are explained in more detail in Table 1.1 and are exemplified in the various chapters of this book.

Eliciting children's ideas is important at the start of a topic or unit of work as it can then inform medium-term planning for the class as a whole and identify groups or individuals who may need additional support or extension. However, it is not only for the start of the topic: it is important that teachers continue to provide children with opportunities to express their developing knowledge, and the elicitation strategies can be used at any point as part of formative assessment. They can also be used at the end of a topic, so that the children can think about what they have learned.

In this way, the elicitation is linked with review. Reviewing can take place at any point in a teaching sequence; it is a good idea to build in frequent opportunities for children to reflect on their ideas. In this book we support the use of elicitation strategies to help teachers gain insights into children's minds as an integral and ongoing part of their practice, rather than a one-off event at the start of a topic.

By seeing eliciation as a collaborative rather than solely an individual activity, a variety of ideas and views are made available on the social plane of the classroom for children to consider. The process of eliciation can be seen creating a shared pool of different ideas and experiences providing a rich starting point for everyone to learn from. Owning a range of ideas as a class might enable those ideas to be examined more critically – it is not a person being examined – it is the idea.

TABLE 1.1 Elicitation strategies

Elicitation strategy	Explanation
Observing a child	Observation is a powerful way of getting an insight into the ideas of young children: the way they handle objects, whether or not they show interest, what they can do alone or with help, what they do and for how long. Observing also includes listening carefully to what children are saying when they talk, in play or in groups.
Questioning and discussion	Talking with children is perhaps one of the most obvious ways of finding out their ideas. This can be questioning individuals or groups, or holding a whole-class discussion. However, closed questions will reveal little more than whether or not children know certain facts. It is more productive to ask open questions: *What can you tell me about . . .? Why do you think it does that . . .? Can you give me another example of that?* Active listening by the teacher is vital. Key questions are highlighted by italics throughout this book.
Sorting a collection	The ways in which children sort a collection of objects or pictures help us to understand how their ideas are organised, and the kinds of mental categories that they have developed.
Annotated drawing	Often a visual representation communicates an idea well. Annotating a drawing with labels or a few sentences to explain what it shows makes it even more helpful. This is not a formal 'diagram', but is a different way of representing the mental picture that a child holds. If a child's writing skills are limited, someone else can scribe their ideas on the drawing for them.
Floor books	Floor books got their name because they are books made out of large sheets of paper that an adult or children write on while sitting on the floor in a group. There are many possible variations on this format, but the important idea is that an adult (or child) records exactly what various children say, probably noting their name. See www.azteachscience.co.uk for a full explanation of how to create floor books with examples.
Concept mapping	Concept mapping is a way of representing connections and relationships between different ideas. Key words are either given or generated by the children and are joined with lines and phrases written along the line to explain how the key words are linked. The site www.azteachscience.co.uk explains one approach.
Concept cartoons	You can buy publications (Naylor and Keogh 2000) containing a series of cartoons in which a central problem is posed in the form of a cartoon, and the responses of different children are shown in speech bubbles around it. For example, one shows a drawing of a tub of ice cream that has just been taken out of the freezer and has droplets of moisture on the outside of the tub. The speech bubbles contain the children's suggestions about where the droplets have come from. They are very useful starting points for discussions, particularly with groups of children who are reluctant to express their own ideas or find it difficult to articulate them, as they can choose the idea that best matches their own. The websites www.azteachscience.co.uk and www.conceptcartoons.com have more information on using concept cartoons.

In each chapter we explore a relevant elicitation strategy, or strategies, and exemplify it (them). Many of the strategies can usefully be applied in a range of conceptual areas but, by exploring the benefits of each elicitation strategy for certain purposes, we hope that teachers will be able to make informed choices about which to use when.

Intervention

Having elicited children's ideas, the teacher can then decide how to help move the children's understanding forwards. Of course, different children in the class will have different starting points, and meeting the needs of the whole class can be quite challenging. Some may need to extend and develop existing ideas; others may have alternative ideas that need to be challenged and significantly restructured. Sometimes children's alternative ideas can be very resistant to change, as they keep hold of ideas that make sense to them, and a range of different teaching strategies may be needed to help the children learn the scientific version. The word intervention emphasises that this is an active process for the teacher, requiring careful analysis of the children's ideas and selection of appropriate kinds of activities.

In a social constructivist approach the most important intervention is to encourage children to test their ideas through the processes of scientific enquiry to extend, develop or replace them. This is not suggesting that children can 'discover' what has taken thousands of years of experimentation and thinking. The role of the teacher is crucial in helping to identify productive lines of enquiry and in making sure that children understand the relationship between their own ideas and any activities. In order to do this the teacher needs not only to know what the child's ideas are, but also to have an understanding of the thinking behind them. A child may say that a toy car eventually stops rolling along the floor because it has 'run out of energy', and then through exploring how different surfaces affect how the car travels, develop their understanding of the role of friction in slowing the car down.

Taking a socio-cultural view, the process of restructuring could be seen as a collaborative gathering of relevant experience and sources of evidence and a communal evalaution of the possibilities. It mirrors a view of scientists not as brilliant loners but as a community with a collective responsibility to criticise each other's interpretations of data, to look for exceptions to rules and to find the best possible explanations.

Other forms of intervention do not directly involve scientitifc enquiries. Ideas may be based on colloquial use of language such as a sign on a shop door saying 'No animals allowed here'. Discussion about what people mean by the term animal would be helpful in this case. Ideas may be based on limited experience, for example 'our food goes into our tummies and then into our arms and legs', in which case evidence such as models and drawings of what is inside our bodies and alternative ideas about what happens to food could be introduced. Challenges to existing ideas might come from various sources: other children, books, videos, visits, visitors or the teacher – 'The way I see it is that. . . . Does that make any sense to you?' The use of models and analogies can be very helpful in discussing ideas that are not immediately accessible to children.

Practical work may not always be in the form of a full investigation. (See Table 1.3 for a summary of alternatives.) Teachers can plan activities with a purpose in mind. For example, first-hand observation of their teeth might be combined with the teacher raising a question about why food needs to be broken into smaller bits. Children might go on to research different kinds of teeth. (Do birds have teeth? Are snake fangs teeth? Has everyone still got their baby teeth?)

Application

Children need to use new ideas in different contexts in order to take ownership of them and to be secure in their understanding of them. Also they need to see the value of the new ideas or they are likely to revert to previously useful ways of thinking. Opportunities for this may come through cross-curricular work. Design and technology (D&T) provides many opportunities to apply ideas about materials, electricity and sound. Children can be presented with problems to solve using their new understanding, such as working out how to separate out rubbish for recycling using their knowledge of the properties of materials. Sometimes ideas developed in one science topic can be applied in another – a child might draw on their understanding of a topic on light, and suggest using transparent, translucent and opaque materials to cover germinating seedlings to test the effect of different amounts of light on how they germinate. A class culture that values children's ideas and sees them as relevant can also help them to make connections between ideas rather than compartmentalise different aspects of their learning.

Review

Reviewing is sometimes seen as what is done at the end of an activity, but can be a much more continuous process. A better way of seeing review might be as part of the ongoing dialogue with and between children about their ideas. This thinking about thinking, or metacognition, is an important theme of other approaches to learning in science such as CASE (an acronym for Cognitive Acceleration in Science Education – more details in chapter 2).

In science children can think about both how their ideas might be different now from ones they held previously, and how the change in their ideas came about. Teachers might also talk about what *they* have learned. This is an important time for teachers to help children make the link between ideas and evidence, and how scientific knowledge is continually changing. Progress in learning science is partly moving from personal knowledge to a shared knowledge (Harlen 2006). The process of reviwing ideas collectively enables the class to decide which ideas are thought to be particularly significant, and give them the special status of shared knowledge. However, time for individuals to reflect on their personal learning is also important.

Scientific enquiry

An earlier section of this chapter considered what science is, establishing our view of it as a social enterprise in which evidence and ideas are generated. This view of scientific knowledge is linked with our view of children as constructing their own knowledge within social contexts. How can this be translated into what children actually do when they undertake a scientific enquiry in school?

The National Curriculum (NC) (DfEE/QCA 1999: 15) sees scientific 'method' as 'a spur to critical and creative thought'. How should we understand what is meant by scientific method? Doing science involves practising a range of skills that are sometimes referred to as 'process skills'

(Harlen and Qualter 2004) or 'processes'. These terms reflect the nature of science as a complex activity that is carried out through a combination of thinking and doing. Some process skills are *thinking skills* – hypothesising, interpreting and evaluating, while others are physical or motor skills, such as using measuring or magnifying equipment. Some of these involve manual dexterity – holding, pouring, cutting, and also have a conceptual component. For example, to use a hand lens, a thermometer or a newton meter requires a combination of physical manipulative skills and an understanding of what the tool does.

Scientific processes are often defined as distinct – exploring, questioning, predicting, hypothesising, planning, testing, observing, measuring, recording, interpreting, evaluating, concluding and communicating – and can be seen as processes that make up a whole enquiry. These processes often flow from one to the next, and the outcomes of one enquiry can feed into the next enquiry. However, these processes often become intertwined – in short, there is no neat sequence that is the 'scientific method'. Exploration can be thought of as a process within a scientific enquiry, but for young children, manipulating objects and materials and using different senses to find out about them is an enquiry in itself. Older children will make observations, generate hypotheses to explain observed phenomena and then seek evidence to support or refute these hypotheses. Process skills contribute both to the evidence base and the stimulus for generating new hypotheses. Being scientific therefore leads to conceptual development. Treating the processes as distinct may lead children to a simplistic view of science as a set of standard procedures that have to be gone through, that produce an idea at the other end, rather than a complex relationship between creative thinking and production of evidence. We take the view that in understanding the holistic nature of things, it is often helpful to think about the various aspects that make it up, and so we sometimes discuss the processes as separate, while understanding that they are actually parts of a whole process (McMahon and Davies 2003).

Attitudes towards science will fundamentally affect engagement with it. Curiosity with a questioning attitude is a springboard of science, so the primary curriculum has a clear role in encouraging this through the way in which science is taught throughout primary school. Beginning an exploration into uncharted territory requires courage as well as curiosity. Other scientific attitudes – attention to detail, accuracy and willingness to accept evidence – are also important.

In the NC for England and Wales, scientific enquiry (Sc1) is seen as learning about 'ideas and evidence' and three strands of 'investigative skills': planning; obtaining and presenting evidence; and considering evidence and evaluating, with different processes grouped within a strand.

The *planning* strand could involve initial explorations and discussions about the children's previous experiences that lead to hypothesising and raising questions. Children might talk about their experiences of growing sunflowers and other plants, they might observe and sort collections of seeds and wonder about what they grow into. This might lead into the suggestion (a hypothesis) that: *The biggest seeds will grow into the biggest plants.* For younger children, planning might involve deciding to try planting different seeds and seeing what happens. Older children would be expected to think more about the planning of their test: as well as the size of the seed, *what different things might affect how tall the plants grow* (identifying variables), how they can make sure these don't interfere with finding out about the effect of the size of seed (planning a fair test), and how many seeds should be planted (repeating measurements). Children may disagree about their predictions: *I don't think it will make any difference. I think the biggest seeds will grow into the tallest plants.*

'Fair testing' means only changing one factor in a situation while keeping all the other factors the same, to try to isolate what is causing the observed effect. Fair tests often involve some abstraction from the everyday context in order to control the variables, and so it can be difficult, especially for younger children, to understand and make sense of what is going on. A starting point might be to make simple comparisons between two scenarios: *I've heard you can grow potatoes in a bucket – let's see which is better, in a bucket or in our vegetable patch.* In general, understanding of fair testing is developed from Year 2 onwards, but it is not until the later years of primary education that children should be expected to plan a fair test independently. Sometimes teachers struggle to help younger children carry out a fair test, when an exploration would provide a much richer and more meaningful experience.

The next strand, *obtaining and presenting evidence*, is about carrying out the test, in this case, planting the seeds and making new decisions that they had not previously thought of, such as: *Shall we put netting over the flowerbed to keep the birds off?* or *Shall we bury them all in the same depth of soil?* They may have planned to take photographs or to measure the plants every day, but decide that twice a week is going to be enough as the plants are growing more slowly than they predicted. Presenting the results might take the form of a display of photographs, or children might use tables of results to draw graphs.

It is easy to think that having carried out the test and collected some data, the enquiry is finished, but the last strand, *considering evidence and evaluating*, is an important and often neglected part of the process. Children need to think about what they have found out: *did the size of the seed make a difference to how big the plant was?* Interpreting data often raises more questions: perhaps there was no clear pattern in how tall the plants were, but *Did some have more leaves than others?* or *Did they have thicker stems? Why did some not grow at all? Did they need more water than the others?* The 'fairness' of the test could be evaluated: *maybe those plants nearest the wall didn't get enough sunlight. Was there a different way we could have gotten the information, perhaps using books about plants, or reading seed packets?* If we see children as being scientists, then they can be scientists who discuss ideas, listen to those of others and perhaps argue about findings and how to interpret them at science 'conferences'.

The purpose of an enquiry is to find out more about something – to learn something. For primary children, carrying out enquiries is an important way of developing their conceptual understanding. But through carrying out an enquiry children also learn what it means to 'do science' – they learn about the nature of science and about the relationship between ideas and evidence.

Teachers sometimes feel a tension between wanting children to carry out their own investigations and wanting them to find out certain information (for example, about the relationship between layers of insulation and how quickly an ice cube melts), so that their understanding of particular topics is developed (Driver 1983). Decisions about how much the focus of an enquiry should be directed by the teacher and how much by the interests of the child are not easy. There are times when teachers can see how an investigation might challenge or extend the ideas of a whole class in a certain direction and they may frame the enquiry more closely. On other occasions they may help an individual child or small group to test their own hypotheses in order to help them see limitations in their ideas. At other times, opportunities can be given for children to follow their own lines of enquiry within a topic, without a predefined direction.

There may be occasions when children carry out practical activities that are not complete enquiries but have other purposes such as demonstrating a particular phenomeon or practising a measuring skill. These are summarised in Table 1.2.

TABLE 1.2 Types of practical work

Type of practical work	Description and purpose	Type of questioning
Exploratory activities	Semi-structured handling or playing with objects or a collection, e.g. a tank of water and a collection of toys, various magnets and different materials. For young children this exploration may be an end in itself; for older children it may be used to engage their interest in a new topic, allow them to play with new resources or stimulate their raising of questions.	To focus attention: *Have you seen what happens when . . .?* To challenge thinking: *Why do you think that . . .?* To prompt further action: *I wonder what would happen if . . .?*
Sorting activities	Children can be asked to sort a collection of objects in order to elicit their ideas, to broaden their experience, to apply new understanding or to develop criteria.	*How are the objects similar?* *How are they different?* *How can we sort these?* *Can we sort these differently?*
Specific skill or process focus activities	Children can be taught a specific skill, such as how to use a tape measure or how to write measurements in a table of results. They could be learning about a specific scientific process such as raising questions and how to phrase them, or how to make generalisations from results. This focused teaching could be in preparation for an enquiry, or because it becomes evident that children are finding a skill or process difficult.	*How many questions can we think of?* *Can we ask a question in a different way?* *Which questions could we answer by looking/reading/ carrying out a fair test?*
Illustrative activities	Sometimes teachers will set up an activity to illustrate a particular concept, for example for children to try heating a range of different materials. Another form of illustrative activity might be a teacher demonstration, which is particularly useful when it would be too dangerous for children to carry out by themselves, such as burning materials, or to engage the children's interest, e.g. a bicarbonate of soda and water 'volcano'. If 'recipe' style instructions have been provided for children then it is the teacher who has made the decisions and carried out most of the process of the enquiry rather than the children, so this is an 'illustrative activity' rather than a 'full investigation'.	*What do you notice?* *What else did you notice?* *What will happen now?* *Why did that happen?*
Full enquiry	Described on pages 19–20. Different kinds of enquiry are detailed in Table 1.3.	

The AKSIS project (Goldsworthy *et al.* 2000a) noted how sometimes there is a mismatch between what a child sees as the purpose of practical work and the teacher's view. They give an example of an enquiry in which a teacher saw the main purpose as being to learn about certain investigative skills, but the child saw the purpose as to find out about how fast people can run. They recommend that teachers make the learning intentions and their expectations clear to children. The important message here is that teachers need to be clear in their own minds about what they want children to learn from practical work and to share this with the children.

Different ways to enquire scientifically

A central feature of this book is that it acknowledges that different areas of content knowledge emphasise different processes of science. So, rather than treating the 'processes of science' as homogeneous and generally applicable, we have identified how teachers can emphasise different approaches to 'doing science' when they teach different topics.

We have suggested that science can be considered to be a combination of conceptual knowledge and the processes that generate that knowledge. In the current English National Curriculum (DfEE/QCA 1999), this is shown by the requirement that Sc1 (scientific enquiry) is 'taught through' Sc2 (life processes and living things), Sc3 (materials and their properties) and Sc4 (physical processes). These divisions reflect how knowledge in science is sometimes compartmentalised and how different traditions and approaches have developed in different scientific fields. The processes of science are common to constructing biological, chemical and physical knowledge – all involve hypothesising, making observations and interpreting data.

However, there are ways of applying those processes that are specific to particular disciplines. Studying the feeding behaviour of a python might involve observation in the natural habitat during which the scientist aims to avoid disturbing the natural environment. Developing a new plastic might require systematic control of different variables, for example, temperature or the ratios of various chemical additives, in a laboratory environment. Data collection methods depend on the degree to which it is possible or desirable to control variables, so, for example, in biological sciences it is more common to use random sampling as a means of providing a form of controlled testing. All enquiries take a systematic, rigorous approach, but the methods and strategies are quite different and particular to the field of study.

For children to carry out a full enquiry they would go through the process of raising questions or predicting and hypothesising, or both, deciding how to answer the question, perhaps through a survey or fair test, collecting data through observations or measurements, and interpreting their results to draw conclusions and suggest explanations. Children can do this independently when the subject matter is within their conceptual understanding and when they have experienced the enquiry process before. It is a challenging undertaking, and children may find it difficult to keep focused on the original question and take a systematic approach. For this reason, teachers often provide 'scaffolding' in the form of some kind of framework, for example 'planning boards' (Goldsworthy and Feasey 1998). Another teaching strategy is to break the investigation into stages, with support through discussion at each step. Alternatively, the teacher might take some of the decisions, while leaving children to make other decisions. It is important, however, that over time children do have experience of taking control of all the aspects of an enquiry, and that sometimes they should control the whole enquiry. It is worth noting here that this does not necessarily mean that every step has to be 'written up'. Not only can this be very boring for children if it takes the same format every time, but it also takes a considerable amount of precious science time. Varying which part of the enquiry process is recorded and creative thinking about how this is done are important in maintaining children's enthusiasm.

The AKSIS project (Goldsworthy *et al.* 2000a) noted how the 'fair test' has become the dominant feature of scientific enquiry in primary schools in recent years, and it recommends an approach to teaching that supports children learning to find the appropriate kind of enquiry for the kind of question that is being asked and identifying the types of scientific enquiry (shown in Table 1.3). As different kinds of enquiry are often associated with different topics in science, in this book we are using these categories as a way of exploring the full range of enquiries that children can do in primary school, emphasising different ones in different chapters.

We have used the enquiry categories shown in Table 1.3 within this book to help explore how to teach the processes of science. In each chapter we have identified aspects of scientific enquiry that are most relevant to that topic area. Although this categorisation is helpful, it is not meant to be prescriptive. For example, although we have emphasised observation in the chapter on plants, it may also be appropriate to answer a question on plants through a pattern-finding approach or a fair test. Although we focus on question-raising particularly in chapters 2 and 10, children should be encouraged to raise questions in other areas too. By explaining these different approaches in context we hope that they will be made more meaningful to the reader and will offer guidance on how children can be supported in developing them. Some areas of the curriculum offer opportunities that others do not, and by noting these we hope teachers will be able to provide a rich experience of science for children.

As a note of caution, much modern science involves work across the traditional subject disciplines. For example, understanding the possible impact of overhead power cables on health has involved doctors specialising in childhood leukaemia, epidemiologists (scientists who study the incidence and distribution of diseases) and statisticians, as well as physicists with expertise in electromagnetic fields. We have made sure that we identify links within and beyond the science curriculum in each chapter.

Planning

How can teachers take account of theories of learning in science in their planning? Although the constructivist teaching sequence has been presented as a clear set of stages, as with the processes of science which it parallels, in reality it is rather messier: perhaps there will be several cycles of reviewing and interventions, and the boundaries between, say, orientation and elicitation, or elicitation and intervention, may not be so clear. Also, although the sequence might appear to be a framework for teaching over a period of several weeks, it could equally take one lesson, or be a five-minute interaction with a child.

Medium-term plans need to be seen as a framework that sets out key learning objectives and possible pathways and activities that might support children's learning, but these need to be changed, developed, amended, removed or added to in response to the children. Beginning a topic with orientation activities and elicitation of children's existing ideas establishes a context and starting

TABLE 1.3 Types of scientific enquiry (based on Goldsworthy et al 2000a)

Type of enquiry	Explanation	Example
Exploration	Observe (observation includes all senses), possibly using particular equipment to record the observations or to take measurements.	Study of the changes that occur to a habitat over a period of time, observing what happens when an ice cube is left on the windowsill.
Classifying and identifying	Match the item with a name, put it in a pre-existing category, or create groups and categories yourself. This may be part of another enquiry or an end in itself. Classifying and identifying can be the starting point for generating hypotheses and making creative links between aspects of phenomena.	Deciding what different objects are made from. Noting characteristics of animals that live in desert environments could lead to ideas about how they survive.
Fair test	Carry out an enquiry by altering one variable (factor) and observing or measuring the effect while keeping other variables (factors) the same. This is appropriate when it is possible (and ethical) to control the different variables and when the purpose of the enquiry is to explore relationships between the variables.	*Is it true that the hotter the water, the faster the sugar dissolves?*
Pattern-seeking	Conduct a survey or a keep a record of lots of examples and look for patterns in the data collected. This is particularly appropriate when variables cannot be controlled, such as when investigating living things. The outcomes are often descriptive, and may describe correlations, but provide weaker evidence for establishing a cause and effect relationship.	Are there fewer different kinds of plants living under trees than in the hedgerows?
Making things or developing systems	Make something, or design a system to solve a problem. This approach has overlaps with technology; sometimes by applying our understanding in a problem-solving context, the limits of the understanding are pushed, and the process might stimulate further exploration.	Designing a switch to go into an electrical circuit. Designing a 'magnetic fishing game' could develop children's understanding about which materials are magnetic and which are not and about differing strengths of magnets.

TABLE 1.3 (Continued)

Type of enquiry	Explanation	Example
Investigating models	Test out a particular explanation, which might be your own or someone else's, and see if it works and makes sense. This may involve constructing a fair test, but it has a different starting point. This kind of enquiry is useful for supporting children's development of scientific concepts, challenging their ideas by presenting them with alternatives.	If children have an idea that electricity gets 'used up' around a circuit, this could be challenged directly by helping them to think through the logic of their explanation: *Does this mean a series of bulbs in a circuit would get dimmer and dimmer?* And then try it out and see.
Reference	Find a secondary source of information to answer the question: a book, a person or a website. This involves making a judgement about the reliability of the source and possibly looking for different versions and explanations.	*Mr Lucas said that a spider isn't an animal – how can we check?*

points. In this book we intend to help teachers develop a repertoire of possible interventions to choose from and to support them in finding their own creative responses to children's needs. Medium-term planning may identify opportunities for cross-curricular links and focus points that are fixed in advance, such as planned visits. Opportunities for focused assessment should be identified at the medium-term planning stage. For example, the topic may present opportunities to develop and assess certain aspects or types of scientific enquiry. Being aware in advance of what resources are available or need to be prepared is also important.

A lesson plan needs to identify a particular learning objective or objectives. This will be linked to the medium-term plan, but will also depend on ongoing assessment of the children's understanding and skills. The objective will help inform the teacher's decisions about how the lesson will be structured. Science lessons may have a distinct beginning, middle and end, but the lesson structure and timing can be varied and need not follow a prescribed format.

It is a good idea for science lessons to have a clear beginning that engages the children's interest and attention, maybe by looking at an unfamiliar object or image, or posing a question. Links can be made to previous learning, perhaps providing the children with feedback on the last lesson and discussing the new learning objective. Often there may be one learning objective that has a conceptual content and one that is more concerned with process skills. Including a learning objective concerned with scientific attitudes would help children to understand what kinds of thinking and behaviour help them to 'be scientists'. Some examples of learning objectives are set out below:

- 'I am looking for children who can tell me what a seed needs in order to germinate.'
- 'I am looking for children who notice something about the plant (that no one else has observed).'
- 'I am looking for children who show they are curious by asking questions about this collection.'

Watson *et al.* (2000) stress the importance of making sure that children understand the purpose of the lesson and revisiting this during the lesson. However, this should be done in such a way as to retain the spirit of enquiry and be open to unforseen possibilities.

The middle section of a lesson can be hugely varied: children may be working independently or in groups for most of the time, or there may be short bursts of activity and group discussion interspersed with frequent whole-class discussions. The children may all be doing similar activities or they may be doing very different kinds of work. The teacher may rotate their time around every group or plan to spend more time with certain children. The work may take place in the classroom or might involve working outdoors.

Having a distinct 'ending' to a lesson ensures that children are given time to reflect on what they have learned and helps their ideas take shape. Sharing thoughts and experiences contributes to the collaborative culture and is a real opportunity for children to learn from each other. The teacher can help to signal particularly significant ideas and support the children in making links with their existing ideas.

Differentiating lessons to meet the needs of different children in the class is a challenge. Finding out children's existing ideas means that activities can be planned to move children forward, and these may need to be different for different children. But not all differentiation has to be based on activities. Children can be grouped together so that they challenge each other's ideas. Teachers may plan to spend more time with groups or individuals, talking about aspects of the work. Much differentiation is 'on the spot' as teachers respond to children's actions and comments during the course of a lesson. Developing a dialogic approach to teaching supports this ongoing response to children's learning.

It is important to note that children who are low attainers in other areas of the curriculum, for example in English, may be high attainers in science. A child may need support with recording their ideas or in accessing information, while still thriving on a high level of conceptual challenge. In such a situation, differentiation could be achieved through using analogies to explain concepts in different ways (see chapters 7 and 8 for examples). A child with high mathematical attainment could be challenged to apply this through investigative work involving sophisticated data-handling, but we must not make assumptions about their understanding of the scientific concepts. Some children may need more structure, or scaffolding, for carrying out a scientific enquiry, while others may benefit from the opportunity to become more independent and to take more decisions themselves.

There are inevitable tensions between the theory and the practice of teaching and between what is ideal and what can be achieved. While we believe each child will have an individual understanding of the world and therefore particular learning needs, we also recognise that teachers have to teach large groups of children with limited time and resources. We have been mindful of this while writing this book, and this is reflected particularly in the classroom-management sections, where we offer advice on how approaches suggested in each chapter might be put into practice.

All lesson-planning should involve a risk assessment. This simply means that thought needs to be given to any possible sources of risk and that action needs to be taken to minimise any danger. This may involve discussing safety issues with children, or it may mean checking that certain materials are suitable to use in a primary classroom. We have identified any specific areas of risk associated with the topics in each chapter. Detailed guidance is provided in the publication *Be Safe!*

Health and Safety in Primary School Science and Technology (ASE 2001), and a copy of this should be kept in all schools.

Summary

In this chapter we have reflected on the aims of primary science – to support children in developing a sense of 'awe and wonder' about the world and in gaining a 'scientific literacy'. We considered how these are informed by views about the nature of science. The ways in which we approach teaching science depend on ideas about how children learn. Social constructivist theories of learning stress the importance of understanding the existing ideas a child has, because these will affect how they make sense of any new experiences. The child is seen as actively making sense of the world rather than as a passive receiver of knowledge. Drawing on socio-cultural theory helps us to understand that the meanings children construct about the world are rooted in their experience within a culture and how language shapes our thinking as well as hands-on, physical encounters with objects and phenomena. The role of dialogic talk in learning in science is introduced and exemplified through some short case studies. Children can learn about the nature of science and scientific processes through carrying out enquiries of their own. These enquiries can lead to development of their understanding of concepts, but other teaching strategies may also be helpful. The CLIS teaching sequence has been developed to take account of socio-cultural approaches and provides general guidance on how to approach the teaching of a new topic.

Discussion points

1. What were your own experiences of science at school?
2. What messages about the nature of science did you come away with?
3. What examples of children's alternative ideas have you come across?

Further reading

Alexander (2008), *Towards Dialogic Teaching: Rethinking classroom talk*: this booklet summarises research and theory behind Alexander's version of dialogic teaching and provides guidance for developing in the classroom.

Davies and Howe (2003), *Teaching Science and Design and Technology in the Early Years*: this book focuses on children aged 3–7 and shows how science-rich activities contribute to their learning. It advises practitioners how to build on children's early experiences and ideas about science, first through play and then through more structured teaching.

Harlen and Qualter (2004), *The Teaching of Science in Primary Schools*: this book provides an accessible discussion of learning and teaching in science, taking a social-constructivist perspective. It takes different asepcts of the teaching of science such as 'Teachers' and children's questions', 'Ways of helping the development of process skills', and considers them in depth, drawing on relevant research.

Ollerenshaw and Ritchie (1997), *Primary Science: Making It Work*: again, taking a social-constructivist perspective, this book develops the CLIS teaching sequence from a primary persepctive. By developing in-depth case studies of teachers and groups of children, and how learning has been supported through practical enquiry and dialogue, it helps to explain how theory can be put into practice.

CHAPTER

Materials and their properties

Purpose of this chapter

After reading this chapter you should have:

- an understanding of how the study of the properties of materials will progress from early childhood to the beginning of secondary education
- a knowledge of key concepts, and strategies for developing children's understanding of these concepts
- an appreciation of an approach to science education that begins with exploring children's existing ideas in order to develop or challenge their understanding
- an understanding of how thinking skills can be developed through the teaching of science.

Introduction

THE STUDY OF MATERIALS and their properties is fundamental to science – it helps us understand so many aspects of our natural and manufactured worlds. Ideas about planet Earth, rocks, soil, the weather, food, clothes and life itself all make more sense if we know something about materials and their properties.

We have all learned through experience to identify some of the properties of common materials. We know which material is more likely to make a warm coat, an effective sunshade or mop up a spill. We will know that picking up a metal spoon that has been left in the saucepan is to invite a nasty burn. It is less likely that we stop to consider the reason why – that metals tend to be good conductors of heat energy. That we consciously think about how the structure and arrangements of the atoms that compose the metal make it a good conductor of heat seems even less credible. One of the biggest 'big ideas' of science is the *particulate nature of matter*, meaning that all materials are made from tiny particles or *atoms* that bond to each other in various ways. This idea, which has taken scientists over 2,000 years of thinking and experimenting to develop, helps to describe the structure and composition of materials, which in turn determines their properties, explaining why diamond is hard and the graphite in our pencils is soft. It also helps us understand phenomena such as conduction, evaporation, melting and dissolving. In this chapter we identify different approaches that enable us to teach about the properties of materials in response to current theories of learning in science. In chapter 3 we explain the essential ideas and concepts that underpin our understanding of the particulate nature of materials, and you are referred to this chapter for further details.

Progression from the early years to the beginning of secondary school

From the moment of birth children experience, and soon begin to interact with, the materials that compose the world around them. Splashing in the bath, tracing the way in which water disappears down the plughole, dropping toys and listening to the satisfying noises they make when they hit the floor and 'finger-painting' with food on their high-chair tray all provide playful means of finding out about the natural and made world in which they live. In the Foundation Stage, developing their knowledge and understanding of the world involves helping children to recognise that everything in the world around them is made up of an amazing variety of natural and manufactured materials and that these materials behave in different ways.

> Each piece of wood, each pebble, each fruit will have a unique shape, colour and texture to explore – providing children with natural materials will do more to foster curiosity than providing a toy or resource that evidently has a specific purpose usually predetermined by the adult mind. The toddler squeezing mud through his fingers in the garden or crunching through leaves in the park is exploring natural materials.
>
> (Howe 2004: 1)

Activities that allow children to explore and play with a range of materials, together with careful questioning by adults, will help them appreciate some of the properties of the materials and develop their vocabulary. Play with sand, water, clay, dough, 'feely bags', papers, glues, fabrics, toys, wood and metal objects and finger-painting provide opportunities for this kind of exploration.

Questioning will focus on how the material looks, feels, how it can be changed and similarities and differences: is it hard, soft, rough, smooth, transparent, bendy, stretchy, shiny?

In one Nursery class a casual question, 'Why is your teddy made from fur fabric?' led to several weeks of fun and a number of the children becoming engrossed in speculating and discovering why Wellington boots are good for rainy days, pencils are made from wood, glass is good for windows and towels are good for drying oneself.

At Key Stage 1 (KS1) (Sc3, 1a–d, 2a–b) children need to continue developing their observation of materials, to recognise and name familiar materials, but also to be able to sort them into groups based on their observable characteristics and uses.

At Key Stage 2 (KS2) (Sc3, 1a–e, 2a–g, 3a–e) the sorting of materials entails learning to group and classify materials on the basis of more scientific properties, such as electrical or thermal conductivity.

The key concepts taught at KS1 and KS2 are identified in Table 2.1, along with some notes to inform the teacher's understanding.

In Key Stage 3 (KS3) (Sc3, 1a–h, 2a–i, 3a–g) children are introduced to the way in which the particle theory of matter can be used to explain the properties of solids, liquids and gases.

TABLE 2.1 Materials and their properties: progression of key concepts

Key concepts	NC references	Teachers' background knowledge
Materials can be classified according to their origin, type, properties or uses	KS1 Sc3 1a, b, c KS2 Sc3 1a	The term material has a very specific scientific use. It refers to the form of matter from which substances are made. Usually this matter is in solid form but it can also be in the form of a liquid or gas. These are known as states of matter. Materials can be classified according to their origin, type, properties or uses. However they are classified, they all originate from the resources of the Earth. In some cases, the materials are natural and can be used with little or no modification, whilst in other cases the natural (or raw) material needs to be manufactured or processed in some way before being used to make something else. Natural materials include: ■ those from the biological environment: wood, vegetable fibres, animal fibres and products ■ those from the physical world: rocks, soil, air, water. Soil is made up of the weathered remains of bedrock and contains the mineral nutrients needed for plant growth mixed with humus – the decaying remains of dead organisms. Soil also contains water from rainfall and air from the atmosphere. Other geological raw materials are the result of processes that have been operating in and on the crust of the Earth for millions of years. They include permeable rocks such as chalk and sandstone and non-permeable or 'hard' rock such as marble or granite. Limestone, sand, gravel and clay, as well as fossil fuels such as coal and oil, are extracted from the Earth's crust and used for a variety of purposes. Rocks fall into one of three groups (igneous, metamorphic or sedimentary) depending on the processes that formed them. Igneous rocks are formed by the melting and subsequent cooling of geological materials, and are characterised by randomly-orientated, angular, interlocking grains. Metamorphic rocks are formed by heat and pressure acting on an existing rock so that over a long period of time the rock recrystallises with grains often in a banded or layered orientation. Sedimentary rocks result from material at the Earth's surface being broken down, transported, deposited and then compacted and cemented into rock, so that grains are often rounded and non-interlocking. Manufactured materials are made from raw materials which have been processed in a variety of ways and include: ■ metals from ores: for example, iron, copper, lead, tin, zinc and aluminium

TABLE 2.1 (Continued)

Key concepts	NC references	Teachers' background knowledge
		■ alloys: steel (carbon and iron), brass (copper and zinc) ■ ceramics and glass: bricks, tiles, earthenware, pottery, china, glassware ■ polymers: natural fibrous materials such as hair, skin or rubber, and synthetic materials such as plastics made from products of the oil industry ■ composites: combinations of materials such as chipboard, fibreglass or reinforced concrete.
Properties and characteristics of materials	KS1 Sc3 1d KS2 Sc3 1a–d	Each material has its own characteristics and these are important when we try to distinguish between materials and choose materials for particular purposes. The uses we put materials to depend upon their particular properties. The properties can be measured as the materials react to a variety of influences and they include: ■ mechanical properties such as hardness, strength, elasticity, toughness, stiffness ■ thermal properties such as conductivity (how well a material will conduct heat) ■ electrical properties such as conductivity ■ chemical properties such as reactivity and solubility ■ optical properties such as transparency, reflectivity, refractivity ■ magnetic properties.
Properties of materials determine how we use them	KS1 Sc3 1d	Materials used for making objects and structures are chosen because they exhibit particular properties; for example glass because it is transparent and has heat insulation properties. Other factors need to be taken into account: cost, aesthetic qualities and availability might be considered. Materials that are becoming scarce, such as oil or hardwood timber, have increased the need for alternatives to be developed.

Cross-curricular planning

It is important that children are actively engaged in interpreting new information.

> If we want to help them make sense of their educational experiences we must ensure that we place new tasks in contexts that will enhance their meaning for young children. This often means actively making links with what children already know and presenting the activity in the context of a story or game.
>
> (Whitebread 2003: 14)

In our model of teaching outlined in chapter 1, the first stage – orientation – is aimed at introducing a topic, developing interest and motivation through familiarising children with the objects to be explored and allowing them to think about what they know and questions they would like to ask. It also provides time to 'play' or 'fiddle' with new or unusual items. One starting point is the use of a collection of objects to introduce different concept areas of science – a collection of toys to focus on forces (chapter 6) or torches to begin exploring electricity (chapter 7), for example. Collections of 'rubbish', building materials, paper tissues, wools, sugars or metal objects could all serve as starting points for work with different emphases. A small display of objects accompanied by a question board will encourage children to begin thinking about a new topic, about what it is they know and about what they would like to know, discussing it and raising questions that can be 'posted' on the question board. Young children can have their comments and questions scribed for them.

Teaching of rocks and soils lends itself very well to developing meaningful links between home and school. For example the collections referred to above could be expanded by encouraging children to bring their own samples from home. Harlen and Qualter (2004) describe a case study in a Year 5 class in which the teacher encouraged children to contribute soil samples from their gardens at home. In doing so, the teacher made an important link with the children's experience and made the subsequent study of soil properties seem real.

During the teaching of materials and their properties, clear cross-curricular links can be made with mathematics, and in particular, ways of sorting data. Venn diagrams are often an appropriate way to sort collections of objects by property, particularly when the collection includes objects made from more than one material. For example, a pair of scissors made from both metal and plastic could be sorted in the intersecting group when distinguishing between dull and shiny materials. Other ways of sorting data that can be taught through collections include Carroll diagrams and branching databases.

Assessment for learning

Taking note of what children say and the questions they ask is the beginning of the elicitation process that enables teachers to make a formative assessment of where children are in their present understanding. A class or group may work with a carefully selected collection of objects that represent a range of materials and properties. Key questions might include:

Can you use your senses (except taste in most cases!) to find out about the materials?
Can you group the materials?
Can you identify materials such as metals and plastics?
Can you explore the collection and ask questions? (For example, Does it float or sink? Is it magnetic? Will electricity pass through it?)

Children's ideas about materials

Everyday usage of the word 'materials' usually refers specifically to fabric, and this is probably the understanding of the term that young children will bring to school. The SPACE project (Russell *et al.* 1991) found that, when asked to identify and sort objects according to what they are made of, young children in the Foundation Stage and KS1 are inclined to describe them by referring to a particular property, often what the material feels like. Some children confuse smoothness with softness and suggest that smooth materials feel soft. A few children describe observations made with senses other than touch: for example, some describe what noises the materials make or what the materials look like in terms of colour, shape or size. Many children describe the material in terms of how it is used. At KS2 they are more able to identify the material from which objects are made, such as metal, plastic, wood, soil, stone or polystyrene, and the uses to which objects could be put, for example, food, building materials, and things to write on are common responses. Some children describe how objects are perceived to have observable properties in common: hard, soft, shiny, bendy or that they feel the same.

Natural objects are identified in the sense of not having been subjected to any manufacturing process; however, the converse 'manufactured' is notable by its absence. Commonly at Upper KS2, classifying on observational criteria implies a more active, manipulative approach suggesting the need for an empirical test such as scratching, cutting or filing to determine 'hardness'.

Children's ideas about what constitutes a rock are based around characteristics such as roughness, hardness, size and heaviness, the inference being that rocks are rough, hard, large and heavy. A good deal of confusion exists about the differences between rocks, stones and pebbles so that a smooth sample of sandstone may be rejected as an example of a rock because it is not jagged. Furthermore:

> Children lack a conceptual framework within which to consider and compare the attributes of rock.
>
> (Russell *et al.* 1993: 142)

When asked to relate properties of materials to their uses, KS1 children generate about one suggestion per material and Upper KS2 children twice that number. Functional properties are by far the most common: 'Wood is good 'cos it's strong, if it's out in the rain it won't rot for a long time.' Less frequent responses concern manufacturing, aesthetic and (rarely) economic properties. Seldom do descriptions of materials include labels such as 'solid' or 'liquid'. When asked to draw some solids, the preference is for 'hard' objects such as stones to be chosen, and some children choose solids they associate with 'strength', such as weights. Drawings of liquids often include washing-up detergent, indicating that they are perhaps thinking of the word 'liquid' on the label rather than of the properties of the detergent.

Summative assessment (assessment of learning)

The QCA (2003a) document *Assessing Progress in Science, Key Stage 1 and 2: Materials* provides information for teachers about how children's responses to elicitation activities correspond to National Curriculum level statements. At NC level 1 it is expected that children can name familiar substances such as stone and wood, and describe these in terms of their properties, for example by observing that cotton wool feels soft. At NC level 2 children can identify some of the materials from which objects are made, e.g. wood, metal or plastic. In addition, at NC level 2 children label groups of objects made from the same material as such, and they will identify differences between objects in terms of their properties. At NC level 3 children would be expected to indicate why the properties of the material from which an object is made make it suitable for its purpose, e.g. the strength of wood makes it suitable to be used as a ruler. Describing the differences between the properties of materials and explaining how these differences are used to classify substances for example as solids, liquids and gases is consistent with NC level 4. Specifically at NC level 5, children would be expected to use metallic properties such as electrical conductivity to distinguish metals from other solids (DfEE/QCA 1999).

Scientific enquiry

As discussed in chapter 1, teaching scientific-enquiry skills and processes that generate knowledge should be focused and relevant to the topic area being taught. The focus in this chapter is on the skills and processes of observing, sorting, classifying and predicting that we have already identified as essential in developing an understanding of materials. These types of enquiry are included within the categories of exploration, identification and classification developed by the AKSIS project (Goldsworthy *et al.* 2000a). It is suggested that, particularly for the Foundation Stage and Year 1, the emphasis should be on exploration, handling materials to look for physical properties, similarities and differences, and ways in which they can be used and changed.

Sorting has traditionally been an activity developed with younger children and, particularly with use of Venn diagrams and Carroll diagrams for sorting, has clear links with the mathematics curriculum. However, the development of the skills of observation, sorting and classifying should be ongoing throughout primary education if we are to ensure that these skills become increasingly sophisticated and that properties identified include more scientific ones such as malleability, strength and transparency.

Sorting games based upon collections of objects can be used in a variety of ways to develop both the skills and an understanding of the properties of materials, helping children to become aware of the variety of materials that form the world around them and fulfilling the requirements of the NC.

We have collected, over time, ideas for a number of sorting games used by teachers and trainee teachers in the classroom to add motivation and fun. These are described in Box 2.1. These games need to be planned with care and have recognition given to the development of the vocabulary that is required. Classroom management should be considered – whilst a whole-class introduction is worthwhile, small groups working to handle and sort their collection allows for greater participation. A useful and cheap starting point is to put together a collection of (clean) household packaging, with a variety of cartons, yoghurt pots, plastic bottles, bottle tops, corks, rubber bands, polystyrene, bubble wrap and anything else to hand. A collection designed to sort metal and plastic objects into two groups could include a metal ruler, spoon, scissors with plastic handle, plastic coat hanger with a metal hook, etc. Plastic 'PE' hoops can be used to show each group – metal and plastic. A trainee teacher working with a Year 1 class on such a task found the children were at first puzzled by how to sort a pair of scissors made from metal and plastic but soon decided that they could fit in both groups. One child realised that if the hoops were overlapped, the scissors could be placed in both groups.

Question raising is an important scientific skill and one highlighted in the NC: Sc1 2a 'Pupils should be taught to ask questions' (DfEE/QCA 1999). Some of the games outlined in Box 2.1 provide opportunities for children to practise raising questions.

BOX 2.1 Sorting and classifying games

These games can be adapted for children of various ages and stages of development from the Foundation Stage to the end of KS2. They are designed to develop the skills and language of sorting and classifying.

Sorting into groups

Give out a group of objects and ask children to sort them. For Nursery and KS1, keep the number of objects small, no more than ten. There is no need to tell them what to sort for – they will have their own interesting (and often unexpected) ideas. This gives you an insight into their thinking, not whether they can sort according to your criteria!

You may need to demonstrate. Stick to two groups initially, e.g. is . . . red, is not . . . red. Young children usually choose colour, shape and size as a starting point. You may need to introduce the concept of 'bigger than', 'smaller than'.

Coloured PE hoops can be used for the sorting and overlapped for items that fit both groups, thus introducing Venn diagrams.

Guess the criterion

With the children in a circle, look at the collection of objects. Talk about what's there and the characteristics of one or two objects, particularly any unfamiliar ones. Begin to sort into two groups, and ask the children to guess the criterion you are using. Then ask one child to sort them while other children try to guess the criterion s/he has used. This can be repeated many times with different criteria.

It is a good idea to start with a small collection and divide it into two groups, gradually increasing the size of the collection and number of groups over a period of time. Children can work in small groups, each with a collection to sort.

With very young children ask them to 'whisper' their criterion to you: this ensures they don't change it when the right answer is given!

Guess which object

Choose one object from the collection, but do not reveal which it is. Children ask questions based on various criteria to try to discover which object it is, e.g. is it made from wood? If the answer is no, remove all wooden objects and further questions centre on those that are left. Only allow yes or no answers. Choose a child to select the object while others try to find out which one has been selected.

Give us a clue

Select an object from a collection but do not reveal choice. Provide clues one at a time until children identify the object.

Mystery object

Put one object from the collection into a closed box or bag without giving the children a chance to see which it is. Pass the box round the children and give them the opportunity to feel, shake and listen before asking one question about its hidden contents. Continue until object is identified. A small group each with a box ensures the children's interest is maintained.

Spot the criterion

Split the class into groups and give each group a small collection and a coloured pencil. Ask each group to sort their collection in three different ways and to record these ways on a sheet of paper. They then sort using a fourth criterion, leave the objects so arranged but without recording the criterion. Each group moves to the next collection and tries to guess the final criterion used by the previous group. They then record in a different colour their own three ideas for sorting and leave the objects sorted in a fourth way.

This can be continued as long as is thought appropriate. It allows you to find out a great deal about how the children are thinking, and each group's responses can be easily identified. This activity could be used at the start and end of a topic and help the teacher to assess changes in the children's thinking.

Adding to a collection

Select an object and choose a criterion but do not reveal it. Children take it in turns to add one more object, which is accepted or rejected depending on whether it fits the chosen criterion. Children have to identify the criterion being used.

Domino game

This game can be used to identify similarities or differences (differences are easier to begin with). Each child holds an object from a collection. One child is asked to place their object on the floor; the others are then asked if their object is different in any way from the object on the floor. One child is asked to place their object alongside the first and the criterion is recorded. Children are then asked for an object, which is different from the second object on the floor. The process continues until all objects are on the floor. The game can be made more difficult by insisting that criteria can only be used once, e.g. shape, size, texture, material, etc.

Finding similarities

Children work with a partner, examine at least three collections and select one object from each which they think has something in common. They share with the whole class their items and the similarity between them.

Making a key

Children work in groups, each with a small collection of 5–10 objects and a large sheet of paper. They are asked to develop an identification key using yes/no questions. Groups move round and try each others' identification keys.

Label-it

On post-it notes, write single words that would describe a property or attribute of the object, e.g. shiny, hard, red. Stick the labels on appropriate objects. Can we move the labels to different objects in the room? Can we add more words?

Word bank

Using the word bank made above, sort the words in a variety of ways, e.g. nouns, adjectives, those that can be both (e.g. glass), alphabetically, etc.

Grids and Carroll diagrams

Chalk a matrix (e.g. 2×2) on the floor. Put four real objects down the side. Use the word bank again as headings of the table. Use ticks or crosses to record the properties of the objects (see below).

	Shiny	Red	Clear
Cup	✓		
Box		✓	
Tin			

This can be developed by using a Carroll diagram that shows two criteria and the alternative 'not' category.

BOX 2.1 (Continued)

	Transparent	Not transparent
Flexible		
Not flexible		

Objects can then be placed in the appropriate sector of the diagram, as in Figure 2.1.

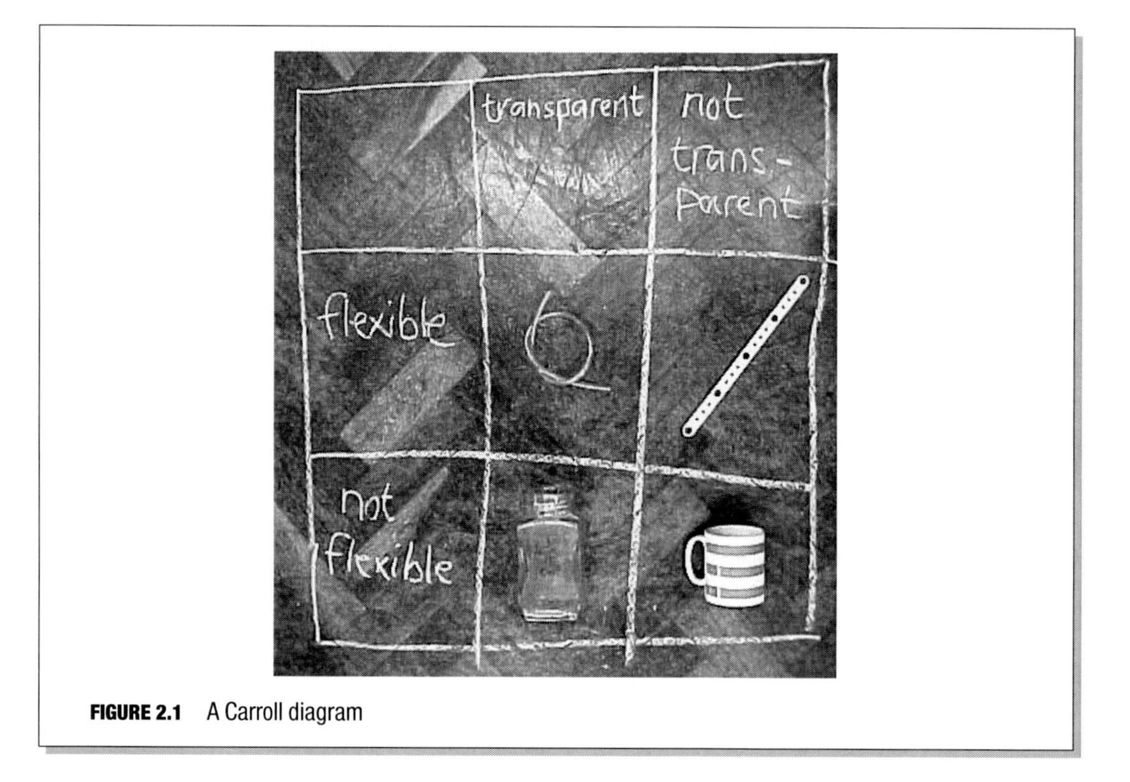

FIGURE 2.1 A Carroll diagram

Other sorts of questions can also be raised during a sorting and classifying activity or game. Questions can be categorised according to how they might be answered:

- What colour is it? What texture is it? (Answer by observation)
- Which object will float or sink? Which material allows light through? (Answer by exploration)
- Which material is hardest? Which is most flexible? (Answer by comparison and fair testing)
- How is it made? Where does it come from? (Answer by research through secondary sources).

Children are fond of asking questions that are not easily answered. It may be worth pointing out that science does not have an answer to some questions or that there may be an answer, but Teacher doesn't know! Rather than seeing this as a problem, this could be an opportunity to value children's contributions by emphasising that genuine questions are worth asking even if they cannot be answered.

Children will need practice in raising and phrasing questions that can be investigated through 'fair testing'. For example, a child could initially ask 'Which fabric is best for making a hat?' This would need to be modified to 'Which fabric is the most opaque?' if the intention was to carry out a fair test.

'Materials' provides many opportunities from Year 2 onwards for fair-testing investigations. It is important that such investigations take place in an appropriate context to ensure science is seen as having relevance to everyday life – examples are given in Table 2.2.

We can see from the activities suggested above that the science of materials provides good opportunities for the development of vocabulary and the skills of speaking and listening. As children observe, sort and classify materials they will use both words in common use such as hard, soft, absorbent, waterproof and, later, more 'scientific' terms such as density, compressibility, elasticity. When reporting or discussing how water, bread or clay change when heated or cooled, children will be developing their scientific language as they describe events, observations and experiences.

Mathematical skills will also need to be developed, for keeping accurate measurements of volume, of temperature as water cools and for the use of Venn diagrams in sorting materials. Tables will be necessary to record observations of how heat changes materials and a bar graph used to record masses of various solids that can dissolve in the same volume of water. As with so much science in primary school, the development of mathematical and scientific skills will go hand in hand.

TABLE 2.2 Suggestions for 'fair test' investigations

Material property	Context	Possible investigation
Waterproofness	Which materials are suitable for an umbrella or raincoat?	Dropping water onto samples, observing if water soaks into the material, sits on the surface or passes through to an absorbent layer beneath.
Transparency	Which material is suitable for a sunshade?	Using a light meter or sensor to determine which sample allows least light through.
Absorption	Which material is best for mopping up spills? (DfEE/QCA 1998 Unit 3c)	Decide what the 'best' paper kitchen roll means. Examine the paper samples closely to determine the factors or variables involved (e.g. pattern, thickness, layers).
Tensile strength	Which cord or thread is best for tying a parcel?	Use a newton meter or a range of weights to conduct a 'pull' test.
Hardness	Which material is best for a floor-covering in a kitchen? (DfEE/QCA 1998 Unit 3c) Which rocks or building materials will be most resistant to weathering? (DfEE/QCA 1998 Unit 3c)	Develop a 'rub' test or scratch test to determine hardness. Consider other tests relevant to the context, e.g. reaction to vinegar to mimic acid rain. Discuss how to combine the results from different tests.

Developing children's understanding

Properties of materials

Through the use of games such as those in Box 2.1, children will not only learn to identify and name many common materials, but will also realise that each material has its own characteristics and that the uses we can make of materials depend upon their particular properties. Children at KS2 can, with support, develop a variety of tests to determine the properties of materials. Some of the more important properties of materials that could be investigated include transparency (see chapter 6), density, hardness, strength, elasticity, stiffness and flexibility, compressibility, thermal and electrical conductivity and magnetic properties. Such tests might include:

- a simple circuit used to test for conductivity
- using a magnet to find out which materials are attracted
- a torch to test which materials allow light to pass through
- a scratch test to see which material can be marked by another
- a 'pull test' to see which materials will stretch or are elastic
- a 'bend test' to see which materials are flexible or stiff
- a squeeze test to find out which materials can be compressed.

The setting up of all these tests will contribute to the development of the skills of fair testing. Finding out the elasticity of various thicknesses of rubber band, the hardness of different woods, the absorbency of paper towels or the permeability of different materials can be accomplished in various ways and can provide scope for children to think about how best to test for properties and how to carry out their tests to arrive at valid and reliable results. Arguments that develop in the process of sorting can be useful to develop the motivation for exploring further. A heated debate ensued from one session of sorting into will/will not float. One child was positive that a conker would sink because 'I threw one into the canal when I was walking with my Dad and it sank'. Another child who reported that conkers floated on the pond in his garden challenged this. Of course, both children were correct and this proved a good opportunity to introduce the concept of density, with a 'fresher' conker containing more water and less air being denser and more liable to sink.

Rocks and CASE

Hawley (2002) argues that the teaching of rock identification to KS2 children has relied upon descriptive–inductive approaches characterised by children comparing a series of rock samples to secondary sources such as photographs. Such an approach results in children having a fixed image of a particular rock so that for example, those children who could identify a white granite were frequently unable to identify a sample of pink granite. Also this approach does little to develop children's understanding of a conceptual framework against which they can compare and test an unfamiliar rock. Indeed we saw earlier that the SPACE team found that children have no clear conceptual framework with which to investigate and classify rocks and rock groups (Russell *et al.* 1993).

Without this conceptual framework children will struggle to make meaningful interpretations of rocks, but by using it to identify and classify rocks into generic groups, children will begin to understand the geological processes that led to the rocks' formation.

In developing an approach that teaches primary school children how to identify rocks, the Earth Science Education Unit (ESEU) drew on the work of Hawley and the work of the CASE team at Kings College London. CASE, or Cognitive Acceleration through Science Education, was first developed in secondary schools in the 1980s, but more recently the CASE team has looked at the impact of cognitively stimulating activities on primary school children, and published two intervention programmes for Year 1 and Year 3 children (Adey *et al.* 2001, and Adey *et al.* 2003). Each activity is based around the 'five pillars of cognitive acceleration':

- Concrete Preparation: setting the scene for the problem
- Cognitive Conflict: the learner is presented with an activity which challenges their current understanding
- Social Construction: children are actively encouraged to work together to solve the problem
- Metacognition: learners are asked to reflect on the thinking they employed to overcome a problem
- Bridging: identifying where else similar thinking could be used and applied.

Moreover, the CASE team describe general ways of thinking that can be applied in many different contexts. These schemata are referred to in Table 2.3. So, the thought process that goes into putting a series of pictures in chronological order can also be applied to ranking a series of rocks in order of hardness.

Drawing together the work of Hawley, ESEU and the CASE team, along with that of the authors of this book, an approach to teaching about rocks in the primary classroom that enables children

TABLE 2.3 General ways of thinking suitable for primary school children (after Adey *et al.* 2003)

Schema	Characteristic features
Classification	Putting into groups that have some common characteristic.
Causality	Understanding the relationship between variables so that what is the cause is distinguished from what is the effect.
Combinatorial thinking	Thinking of as many different combinations as possible from a limited number of variables, and doing so in a systematic way.
Seriation	Developing the general ability to put things in order.
Concrete modelling	Building simple models to explain observations.
Relationship between variables	Deciding if there is a relationship between one variable and another.
Conservation	Developing the understanding that the amount of many materials stays the same even though their shape or location may change.

to develop a sound conceptual framework about rocks has been developed and is summarised in Table 2.4. Note that a number of schemata are developed through this approach including, most obviously, skills in classifying objects, and concrete modelling of different rock types.

TABLE 2.4 An approach to teaching rocks in the primary classroom (based on the work of ESEU and Hawley 2002)

Stage description and aim	Concrete preparation	Social construction and cognitive conflict	Metacognition	Bridging	Teaching points
1 What is a rock? Clarify ideas of what constitutes a rock and focus on the idea of grains	Activity focuses on finding a way to sort a collection of rocks	Find a working system to sort rocks, considering those rocks that don't easily fit into it.	How well do the rocks fit the system?	Is it okay for our class to have several different rock identification systems?	7–11 year olds most frequently sort using colour, shininess, speckliness and roughness.
As a follow up to 1 above	An observer needs to be nominated.	To move thinking on, one member of the group listens and the remaining members discuss their approach. What is it that makes a rock shiny/ colourful/ etc.? What can you see? Observer identifies commonly used words.	Which words were most commonly used? Is it apparent now what element of a rock is most important when classifying rocks?	Geologist uses the bits of a rock, their relationships and arrangement, to classify them. We can take this further with other activities.	Often word 'bits' is used although the correct scientific term is grains.
2 Are there differences between grains? Focus attention on just two very different rocks, such as sandstone and granite.	This activity studies in more detail the differences between the grains in each rock. Model the use of magnifying aids (hand lenses).	Begin by encouraging close observation of the grains of the two rocks. Invent a name for each to forestall the need to name each. Observe and describe the grains of each sample. What differences do you note?		Why do you think there are differences between the rocks?	Children most commonly describe the samples as having sharp edges and rounded grains. Responses may include ones about the differences being due to the way the rocks were formed.

Stage description and aim	Concrete preparation	Social construction and cognitive conflict	Metacognition	Bridging	Teaching points
3 Predictions and explanations Give children a concrete experience to reason about differences in textures.	Model how to use scales. Predict what will happen to the mass of each sample when it is immersed in water. This prediction should be based on experience gained in the workshop so far.	Carrying on with only the sandstone and granite, measure the mass of each before and after immersing in water. Note masses on the board. How closely did the changes noted match the predictions? How did the water penetrate the sandstone?	What process did you go through when predicting what you thought would happen?	Which other rocks in the collection do you think water would be able to penetrate?	
4 Modelling Help understand about grain relationships		Complete a tessellation activity to answer questions: 1. How do grains fit together with no space between them? 2. How do they fit together with spaces? Children are provided with two sets of paper shapes (circles/ovoids, and angular shapes) and are challenged to stick each set together to minimise space between the pieces. Next children model the structure in 3D using either marble or lego. Why don't the grains fall out of rocks like sandstone?	How has this activity refined your earlier understanding of grains in rocks?	Can knowledge of interlocking and glued together grains be applied to other rocks? Look at a conglomerate. Is it most like an interlocking or non-interlocking rock?	Grains are stuck together by 'rock glue' in rocks such as sandstones and conglomerates. This precipitates naturally between the grains during rock-forming processes. Although grains don't readily fragment, the conglomerate is most similar to the non-interlocking group of rocks.

TABLE 2.4 (Continued)

Stage description and aim	Concrete preparation	Social construction and cognitive conflict	Metacognition	Bridging	Teaching points
5. Classifying rocks Consolidate new understanding; introduce concept of grain arrangement	Provide a selection of rocks. Show how to use a frame to focus observation on a small area.	Grain relationships (how grains fit together) are reviewed. Does grain shape help us decide if a rock is interlocking or non-interlocking? Can a selection of rocks be sorted into crystalline and fragmental? Grain arrangement – introduce two forms of arrangement: i random, and ii aligned, using samples of schist and granite, drawing a sketch of each through a frame. Can children now classify a selection of rocks?	What approach did you adopt when confronted with a new rock?	Can the new approach be applied to any rock sample?	Some rocks such as gritstone have angular grains but with pore spaces filled or partially filled with rock glue. Frequently the fine-grained rocks cause confusion. Slate and mudstone are often put to one side and returned to later. Children could be asked to scrape these and use knowledge about crumbliness to draw conclusions. Most students sort the rocks into three categories based on textural relationships. The names igneous, metamorphic and sedimentary can be introduced at this stage.
6. Names	Now it is time to name the rocks by pairing each with a prepared description.	Which rocks continue to present difficulties and why?	Did using only the way grains are joined together provide enough information? What other criteria did you use?	Use your new understanding to set up a building stone trail.	

Using ICT to teach about materials and their properties

Information technology can play a role in supporting the development of questioning skills and decision-making. Software such as *FlexiTREE* (Flexible Software Ltd) can help create a binary tree or branching database that can then be used by other children. Using a branching database is rather like playing 'Twenty Questions'. The programme stores a series of questions, each of which must be answered yes or no, in relation to an object or material under consideration. Finally, only one of the items in the database matches your answers and the object is identified. If the item is not in the database, it can be added along with further questions and answers. Playing such a game will encourage children to generate questions such as Is it flexible? Is it transparent? Does it conduct electricity? Of course, similar games can be played without using IT although having the opportunity to input questions for others to use at a later date, and displaying them on an interactive white board, can be motivating factors.

Information Technology can also be used to support our teaching of rocks. After children have gained a basic understanding of some of the differences between rocks formed by sedimentary, metamorphic and igneous processes, it is illuminating for them to look at these rocks in thin section. An alternative to buying expensive microscopes and thin sections is to visit one of the many websites which display stunning images of sandstones, granites and the like. For example, images at http://www.microscopy-uk.org.uk/mag/artfeb04/iwouslides.html and http://www.cas.usf.edu/~jryan/rocks.html show mineral sections looking like very much like wonderful modern art paintings. Can children speculate from the images the processes that led to the rock's formation? Many of the sandstones show very clearly in cross-section grains that have been rounded by erosion as they were moved about by wind or water. By contrast the grains making up granite are tightly interlocking and are a result of minerals crystallising from molten rock.

Classroom management

Children can learn much about the compostion of materials and about their classification by handling them. To ensure they carry out their investigations safely, the ASE guide *Be Safe!* (ASE 2001) should be referred to for a comprehensive list of 'chemicals' that are suitable and unsuitable for primary school investigations.

Teaching with collections lends itself well to peer evaluation. Children can review each other's work and provide, hopefully, constructive feedback. For example, children could reflect on another group's branching database asking themselves how well did it sort the collection of objects? After trying out another group's database, children, as they feedback to classmates, may need reminding to focus on the positive features of the work as well as those areas which could be improved.

Summary

In this chapter we have examined ways in which teachers can help children become more informed about the materials – natural and manufactured – that make up their world. We have emphasised the role of scientific enquiry and the skills and the processes of science in developing conceptual understanding. With growing understanding of the variety of materials, the uses to which they are put and, particularly, the finite nature of the Earth's resources, it is hoped that they will, as adults, retain some of the curiosity and 'awe and wonder' demonstrated by very young children. If this results in adults prepared to take action to ensure a sustainable future for our world we will have achieved a great deal.

Discussion points

1. To which other topics in science could the CASE approach to teaching thinking skills be meaningfully linked?
2. In what ways can a teacher make the topic of materials relevant to children's experiences?

Further reading

Adey *et al.* (2003), ***Let's Think through Science: Developing Thinking with seven- and eight-year-olds***: this teachers' guide comes as part of an intervention programme to accelerate cognitive development in lower juniors. The theory underpinning cognitive acceleration is outlined along with a series of lesson plans that aim to develop children's thinking skills.

Howe (2004), ***Play Using Natural Materials***: a wealth of practical ideas to try with younger children.

CHAPTER

3

Changing materials

Purpose of this chapter

After reading this chapter you should have:

- an understanding of how the study of changing materials will progress from early childhood until the beginning of secondary education
- knowledge of key concepts and strategies for developing children's understanding of these concepts
- an appreciation of an approach to science education that begins with exploring children's existing ideas in order to develop or challenge their understanding.
- an awareness of the key role science plays in the teaching of issues of global significance

Introduction

STUDY THE NEWS on a given day for stories that are science-related, and it is likely the topic most often reported on is that of global climate change. We read about greenhouse gases, the need to find renewable energy sources, and how habitats are changing. Yet the scientific explanation for climate change may not be something we fully comprehend, and without this understanding we can wonder why there is a push to harvest wind energy with giant wind turbines, why driving our petrol car is affecting the climate but burning wood in a log burner is seen as green, why we should be doing something about our carbon footprint, and fundamentally we wonder why we are being asked to alter our lifestyle. How an understanding of the ways materials behave can lead to an appreciation of global warming is explored in this chapter.

In chapter 2 the big idea that all materials are made from tiny particles was briefly introduced. We will explore this further because, as well as helping us understand how properties of materials are determined, this idea also helps us to visualise what happens when materials change state, which in turn helps us to explain such processes as freezing, melting and condensing, and, indeed, changes which are reversible or irreversible. In this chapter we consider how to teach about these changes in a way that is matched to children's experiences.

Progression from the early years to the beginning of secondary school

In the Foundation Stage, through a wide and varied range of experiences with changing materials, children develop an awareness of change using all of their senses, and ask questions about why change has occurred. A balloon or rubber glove, as large as possible, filled with water and frozen to make an ice-balloon or ice-hand will immediately focus attention and give rise to questions: What will happen if we leave it in the classroom? How long will it take to melt? How can we make it melt more slowly? Work with food can provide further opportunities for finding out how materials change; baking biscuits, making jelly, porridge, ice lollies or chocolate cakes are guaranteed to motivate. Provided health and safety is kept in mind with the risk of allergic reactions assessed and controlled, such activities never fail to interest and allow for endless questions to be asked, answered and explored.

At Key Stage 1 (KS1) (Sc3, 1a–d, 2a–b) children should be taught to find out how the shapes of objects may be changed by processes such as squashing and bending, and should begin to explore more accurately the ways in which materials can be changed through the process of heating or cooling.

At Key Stage 2 (KS2) (Sc3, 1a–e, 2a–g, 3a–e) children are taught to describe the changes that occur when materials are heated or cooled, that temperature is a measure of how hot or cold things are, to distinguish changes that are reversible or non-reversible, and that burning results in the formation of new materials and is not usually reversible. They should also investigate ways to separate mixtures of materials through, for example, sieving, filtering or evaporating, and use their knowledge of solids, liquids and gases to decide how mixtures might be separated. Furthermore, when being taught the KS2 curriculum, children should begin to think about the negative effects of technological developments on the environment. The key concepts taught at KS1 and KS2 are identified in Table 3.1, along with some notes to inform the teacher's understanding.

In Key Stage 3 (KS3) (Sc3, 1a–h, 2a–i, 3a–g) children are introduced to the way in which the particle theory of matter can be used to explain changes of state, gas pressure and diffusion. They study physical, geological and chemical reactions in some detail and learn about the possible effects of burning fossil fuels on the environment (for example, by the production of acid rain, carbon dioxide and solid particles) and how these effects can be minimised.

Cross-curricular planning

The study of changes in materials provides an ideal opportunity for children to prepare and cook food. Take as an example the possible learning opportunities presented by something as simple as making bread. Initially, flour and dried yeast, both solids which seem to behave like liquids as they 'flow' into the bowl, are mixed with liquid water to form dough, a material that behaves like a liquid in that given time it will flow into the spaces of a bread tin. Too much water and the dough is too sticky to knead; too little and it resists our attempts to squash it. After kneading, the yeast will feed off the flour and produce carbon dioxide, a gas, which leads to the dough rising. During baking chemical changes will occur in the risen dough that result in bread being made, a change

TABLE 3.1 Changing materials: progression of key concepts

Key concepts	NC references	Teachers' background knowledge
In theory all substances can exist as solids, liquids or gases (kinetic theory).	KS2 Sc3 1e, 2b, c	For most substances it is not easy to demonstrate this fact but water provides an example that can be used relatively easily. An ice cube, as it is warmed up, changes from a solid to a liquid (water). If it is heated further, the liquid will turn into a gas (steam or water vapour). The temperature at which a solid melts to form a liquid is called its melting point. For pure water this is 0 degrees Celsius. This is the same as the freezing point; the temperature at which pure water turns to ice when it is cooled. Boiling point is the temperature at which a liquid turns to a gas. For pure water this is 100 degrees Celsius. If steam is cooled below 100 degrees Celsius it condenses back to a liquid again. Change of state can be explained by the particles from which they are made and the arrangement of these particles. In a solid the particles are: ■ closely packed ■ arranged in a regular pattern ■ able to vibrate about a fixed point but not move from place to place ■ strongly bonded by forces of attraction to neighbouring particles. The properties of a solid, ice for example, are: ■ not easily compressed ■ fixed shape ■ fixed volume. In a liquid the particles are: ■ fairly closely spaced ■ in a random arrangement ■ bonded to neighbouring particles by weaker forces, so able to move from place to place. The properties of a liquid, water for example, are: ■ not easily compressed ■ no fixed shape ■ fixed volume. In a gas the particles are: ■ widely spread out ■ in a random arrangement ■ moving about at high speeds ■ not bonded to neighbouring particles by forces of attraction.

TABLE 3.1 (Continued)

Key concepts	NC references	Teachers' background knowledge
		The properties of a gas, water vapour for example, are: ■ can be compressed ■ no fixed shape ■ variable volume. This simplified mental model of the structure of solids, liquids and gases helps to explain some of their properties. In the examples, the particles in the ice, water and steam are the same particles (water molecules). The arrangement of these particles is what makes for the different properties of the ice, water and gas.
Freezing, melting and boiling, condensation and evaporation, are reversible changes.	KS1 Sc3 2b KS2 Sc3 2d, e	When a solid is heated, the heat energy transferred causes the particles in the solid to vibrate more rapidly. In doing so they move apart, causing the solid to expand. If enough heat energy is transferred, the particles vibrate rapidly enough to break free from their fixed positions and they are able to move around each other. At this point the solid melts and becomes a liquid. If heat energy is transferred to a liquid, the particles move more and more rapidly until they are able to separate and move in all directions as a gas. The escape of gas particles from the surface of a liquid is known as evaporation. The temperature at which gas forms inside the body of a liquid (and escapes as bubbles) is known as the boiling point. In order to bring about the reverse changes of condensation and freezing, the movement of particles must be reduced, and this is done by cooling – removing energy from the particles. Evaporation, condensation, melting and solidification are examples of reversible change. Physical changes can be fairly easily reversed. This is because the particles that make up the materials are simply rearranged without fundamentally changing them. During physical change, the mass of the material remains the same before and after the change. Simple processes such as warming, cooling or mixing can reverse the change. Melted chocolate can be cooled until it sets as a solid once more. Water evaporated can be condensed to a liquid again, as when water vapour condenses on cold glass. Clay that has been shaped into a pot and left to harden can be reconstituted by adding the water that has evaporated.

Dissolving is a reversible change.	KS2 Sc3 2d	If a substance can totally mix with a liquid we call this dissolving. One liquid can dissolve in another liquid or a solid can dissolve in a liquid. A solution, a completely uniform mixture, is formed. The solvent is the liquid that does the dissolving. The solute is the solid that gets dissolved. The solution is the mixture of the two. Something that dissolves in a solvent is described as soluble. Those that do not dissolve are called insoluble. Salt and sugar are soluble in water. There is a limit to the amount of solute that can be dissolved in a given volume of solvent. The solution eventually reaches a point where no more solid can dissolve. This is called a saturated solution. The saturation limit depends on the solvent and solute concerned and also on the temperature. Usually, as the temperature is increased the mass of solute that can dissolve increases. Dissolving and melting are frequently confused. Dissolving: ■ can happen without heat, whereas heat is needed for melting to take place ■ requires two or more substances, melting only one ■ involves substances mixing; in melting the substance remains pure ■ cannot be reversed by cooling whereas melting can ■ involves two different kinds of particles mixing whereas melting involves the rearrangement of one kind of particle.
Chemical changes are non-reversible.	KS2 Sc3 2f	Chemical changes are usually permanent. A new substance is produced which is not easily returned to its original material. Chemical change can be accelerated or caused by heat. In baking, an egg once boiled cannot be made soft again by cooling, or dough baked into bread returned to the original flour and water. Once it has been fired in a kiln, clay cannot be returned to its original state. During chemical changes, a chemical reaction takes place in which the particles involved undergo significant changes. In the example of a candle burning, new chemical bonds are formed between carbon atoms and oxygen atoms to make carbon dioxide molecules. The carbon atoms are firmly bound to the oxygen atoms inside the carbon dioxide molecules and cannot easily be separated. A new compound has been created. During a chemical change no new matter is created or destroyed. The same number of atoms exists but they have been rearranged. Therefore the mass or amount of 'stuff' after the chemical change is the same as the mass before the change. The mass remains constant. Decay is another form of permanent change often brought about by the actions of micro-organisms. If a material decays in this way it is biodegradable.

TABLE 3.1 (Continued)

Key concepts	NC references	Teachers' background knowledge
Burning is a non-reversible change, resulting in the formation of new materials.	KS2 Sc3 2g	Burning, or combustion, is a familiar chemical reaction. It is a chemical reaction with oxygen from the air. When a candle burns, some of the wax (fuel), made from atoms of hydrogen combined with atoms of carbon, becomes a liquid and melts. Some is drawn up the wick, evaporates and becomes a gas. This gas combines (burns) with oxygen from the air to form carbon dioxide and water droplets. Heat and light is generated and a flame can be seen. Burning of fossil fuels from the time of the Industrial Revolution onwards is seen by many to be responsible for the rise in carbon dioxide in the Earth's atmosphere since the 18th century. Along with other greenhouse gases such as methane, carbon dioxide traps the sun's energy on the surface of the Earth and its lower atmosphere leading to global warming and climate change.
Mixtures and solutions can be separated.	KS2 Sc3 3a, c–e	When two or more substances are combined together without a chemical reaction taking place a mixture is formed. Instant coffee is a mixture of the chemicals in coffee granules and hot water. Mixtures can be made of elements – air is a mixture of gases – or of compounds: sea-water is a mixture of water and dissolved salts. Mixtures do not form new substances: they can have a variable composition and have similar properties to those of the original constituents. It is possible to separate a mixture using physical techniques. Sieving can separate a mixture of solids such as sand and rice. Insoluble solids can be separated from a liquid by filtration (e.g. soil from water). Soluble solids can be recovered by evaporation. In the case of instant coffee, you could boil away the water and get the coffee grains back. When a solvent is evaporated the solute (solid) remains behind. The solvent can be collected by allowing it to condense on a cold surface such as glass, a process known as distillation. Some mixtures of solutes can be separated into their components by paper chromatography. To separate inks into constituent colours, the solvent soaks through filter or blotting paper and the coloured inks separate out as they travel at different rates across the paper.

that cannot be reversed. Bake the bread for too long and it will be dry and burnt. Many other examples of chemical changes can be found in cookery. For an example from the kitchen of a change that can be reversed, making ice cream will prove to be a popular choice with children.

The study of changing materials also provides many opportunities to focus on citizenship and issues such as sustainability and interdependence. Burning a candle could lead to a discussion about the impact that burning fossil fuels is having on the Earth's atmosphere. Investigating a collection of packaging or 'clean' waste products might encompass the life cycle of manufactured objects from 'raw materials' and leads naturally to the environmental impact caused by 'waste' materials. Concepts of biodegradability and 'recycling' can be introduced through an investigation of paper, which does degrade, and plastic, which does not. Collecting the class or school waste for one week could lead to a discussion on landfill sites. Some sites welcome visitors, such as the Wood Lane Nature Reserve in North Shropshire or the Carymoor Environmental Trust in Somerset. At Carymoor, children consider some key questions about the huge volumes of waste that are buried at the site each month, such as:

> *Who creates waste?*
> *How is waste collected?*
> *How is waste treated at the landfill site?*
> *Why is production of waste increasing?*
> *What will be the effect of continued landfill?*
> *How can waste be minimised?*
> *How is compost made?*
> *What responsibilities do households have to the environment?*
>
> (www.carymoor.org.uk)

Assessment for learning

A formative assessment of children's current understanding can be made by noting what children say and the questions they ask. A particular material or object might be presented to the children, and their ideas elicited about how it might change. Such items could be an ice cube or ice balloon, a puddle of water, a burning candle, chocolate, perfume, clay, an egg, a rubber band, sugar, a rock or a coin. Key questions could include:

> *How could you change this material?*
> *Could you get the material to change back?*
> *Would any new materials be made?*
> *If we warmed the material, what would happen to it?*

Children's ideas about materials

The SPACE project (Russell and Watt 1990a) probed children's understanding of evaporation and condensation by getting them to monitor the change of water level in a large container over a five-week period. For many KS1 children the reason that the water level declined over that period was described through the use of non-techincal terms such as 'dried up'. At KS2 'evaporated' was used by children much more frequently as a way to explain their observations. When questioned further on the reason for the change, the great majority of children in both KS1 and KS2 did not discuss water as a substance having different states. Only a minority of children understood water could undergo a transformation from liquid to gas.

Research into children's ideas about global warming (Palmer and Suggate 2005) shows that at KS1 most children understand what effect warming would have on snow and ice. However, for some children, that this warming would transform ice to water was not clearly held as a view. Short-term effects on animals were described ('The penguin would have to go in the water'), and some children revealed a general understanding of the dependence of living things on their particular habitat. However, when questioned about the impact of deforestation, children believed that animals would simply move on somewhere else if their forest was destroyed. As to the reasons why the Earth is getting warmer, about one-third of children knew something about greenhouse gases or pollution by the end of KS2, but there was confusion between the greenhouse effect and the hole in the ozone layer. Other explanations for global warming given included the Sun getting nearer to the Earth and that it was simply as a consequence of seasonal change. (See 'further reading' at the end of the chapter for guidance on subject knowledge for teachers on this topic).

Summative assessment (assessment of learning)

The QCA (2003a) document *Assessing Progress in Science, Key Stage 1 and 2: Materials* describes how children's responses to elicitation actitivies about changing materials can be mapped on to National Curriculum level descriptors. At NC level 1 children might be expected to demonstrate or describe how the shape of some objects can be changed by squashing them between their hands but that other objects are too hard to be changed in this way. Describing the change observed in ice when heated as 'melting' and demonstrating how the shape of liquids can be changed by pouring into different containers is consistent with NC level 2. Recognising that some changes are reversible and others are irreversible is evidence of NC level 3. A child may demonstrate this by putting chocolate and ice in one group which can be changed by melting and then changed back again, and eggs and bread in another group which can't be changed back after heating. At NC level 4 children are expected to use their knowledge of reversible and irreversible changes to predict, for example, that a fruit drink will freeze because water freezes. Explaining that water vapour in the air changes to water on a cold glass because of condensation is further evidence of NC level 4. Recognising that dissolving is a reversible change and demonstrating how to recover solids from solutions both indicate NC level 5. Children at this level would also be expected to know how temperature affects the rate at which evaporation and condensation take place.

Scientific enquiry

We saw in the previous chapter that studying the properties of materials can develop the important scientific skill of raising questions for further investigation, and this equally well applies to investigations into the changes that materials undergo. Presented with an ice balloon, quizzical children can be encouraged to think: *What happens if powder paint is sprinkled on its surface? How can the ice be made to melt faster?* Children will note intuitively, even if they do not have a full conceptual grasp, that cornflour mixed with water acts like a liquid until it is hit, at which point it behaves like a solid: *What happens if it is poured, or scooped, or mixed in different proportions?* Questions may also be raised in response to concept cartoons (see chapter 1 on elicitation strategies for more details) on phenomena such as evaporation and dissolving. In response to a cartoon on where to hang the washing, investigations could examine the factors involved in drying laundry (air temperature, wind/air flow, type of material, etc.). A cartoon on getting sugar to dissolve in tea may lead to questions about the size of sugar granule, the temperature of tea, and the amount of tea/sugar. Encouraging children to ask questions is part of the planning strand of the National Curriculum (KS1 Sc1 2a and KS2 Sc1 2a).

As well as helping with the planning of investigations, talk also has a role to play in helping children review their work and reflect on their new understandings (KS1 Sc1 2, KS2 Sc1 2m). Children's thinking can be improved by encouraging them to reflect actively on their progress in solving a problem, on wrong turns taken and on how they were corrected (Adey *et al.* 2003). Thinking about one's own thinking, or metacognition, supports children as they evaluate their investigations into changing materials. For example, pouring water from one beaker to another and back again to confirm that the volume of water remains the same despite it 'changing shape' in vessels with different shapes, can be supported by children reflecting on the results of the investigation and explaining them. Going further they might be able to also explain what the decisive factor or factors were that helped them construct new meaning. Was it, for example, through discussion of their ideas with other people, or did someone say something that helped move their thinking forward? Explicitly knowing how a problem was solved provides a child with a 'learning tool' that can be employed on any similar problem s/he encounters in the future.

Developing children's understanding

Material transformations

Key questions include:

How do materials change?
Which materials change?
What makes materials change?
Could they be changed back to their original state?

At KS1, activities that address the key ideas above include:

- **Melting** Close observation of ice cubes, chocolate or cheese in plastic bags immersed in hot water encourages the development of vocabulary to describe what is happening. Teacher questions can help to focus on change of shape or colour and on what happens when the substance cools again. Keeping the sample in a bag throughout can show that no material is added or taken away. Another 'un-bagged' sample can be melted to allow children to feel and smell as well as see the changes.

- **Dissolving** Investigating what happens when sugar, jelly, paint or baking powder are dissolved in small amounts of water encourages prediction and hypothesis about what will happen: where the substance has gone, whether we could show it is still in the water (for example a taste test), how we could make it dissolve more quickly, whether it can be retrieved. Other insoluble powders or grains such as flour, sand or talc can also be tested to encourage further questioning and thinking.

At KS2, further investigations to develop understanding of the way in which materials can be changed chemically include:

- **Cooking** Making toast provides a simple example, with the advantage that the product can be eaten! There are lots of independent variables to explore: try making toast on different time settings, with different breads or with bread that is fresh or stale. Encourage children to observe the changes closely with a hand lens or microscope. Create a 'colour chart' that relates time to colour change. Investigate how long before the butter will not melt on the toast. Do different spreads have different melting points?
- **Burning** Ask the children to draw a lit candle placed in a dish of sand. Encourage close observation of the flame, wick and wax – ask them to identify what is seen, what changes and what 'disappears'. Encourage them to generate questions: Do different-coloured waxes burn in different colours? Do thick candles have thick flames? What happens when a saucer is held over the flame? What happens when a flame is 'blown out'? (A digital movie could be taken and reviewed frame by frame). Children can be asked if they think we could get the wax back again, which other materials they think will burn easily and which will not.
- **Decaying** Provides opportunities to observe over time the decay of substances such as milk, bread, cheese, yoghurt or apple, carefully sealed in dishes or bags. Looking at leaves in autumn or objects buried outside can be used to introduce the concept of biodegradability. Record the changes through drawing or photography, keeping careful note of time elapsed. What changes can be seen? Do different materials decay differently? Do all materials decay? Do things go rotten faster if they are wet, hot or buried? How can we keep things fresh longer? What is causing the decay? (See also chapters 9 and 11 for more discussion on micro-organisms.)
- **Rusting/corrosion** A walk around the school and playground or observation of a bicycle could be the starting point for identifying materials that rust or corrode. A collection of materials, some coated with paint or galvanised and clean and some rusty, can be used to find out what happens when metals are left in air or water or oil. The coins chosen by one trainee teacher for children to investigate rusting proved a poor choice since these are made from or coated with metals which do not rust! Investigations might determine which metals will rust, which conditions are necessary, how long it takes for iron or steel to rust and how we can stop things rusting.

Addressing global issues

Gaining an understanding of the Earth's climate can be developed effectively with younger children by studying the weather. However, to do this meaningfully teachers do need to be flexible in their planning so that spontaneous opportunities for learning are not lost. Equally and for the same reason it helps if resources are prepared in advance and are ready to use. Over the years the authors have developed a range of activities for different weather conditions, organising them into separate weather boxes, one for each weather type, with each box helpfully containing all the resources needed to carry out the activities and intervention cards.The ranges of activities for each weather type include:

- **Rain** Box contents: chalk, wipeable pens, rain catchers, powder paint, fabric squares, paper boats, paper towel strips. Activities: make different shaped rain catchers from plastic bottles, and use them to collect rain; form a shelter from the rain using a plastic sheet; create pictures using powder paint and investigate what happens to them in the rain; investigate what happens to a range of both waterproof and non-waterproof fabrics in the rain; make a range of boats to play with in the puddles; draw patterns on paper towels using felt-tip pens and investigate what happens to them in the puddles.
- **Wind** Box contents: pegs and washing line, streamers, plastic bag windsocks, windmills, paper kites, balloons and pump, bubble making, parachute. Activities: wash, wring out and peg out bits of cloth; play with the kites, windsocks and balloons, investigating what makes them fly, turn and move; stand in a group around the edge of the parachute feeling the force of the wind; play with bubble-making equipment, watching the bubbles move in the air.
- **Snow** Box contents: black card t-shapes, paper cups, gloves, magnifiers, scissors, white paper, track makers. Activities: fill up cups with snow and place around the school in the sun and shade; catch snowflakes on the black card and observe them using a magnifier; make different tracks in the snow; make or follow a trail around the school; investigate which glove is the best; investigate which movements keep you warm outdoors.
- **Sun** Box contents: chalk, collection of shapes, brushes and buckets, sand and trays, sunglasses, hat instructions, paper. Activities: trace chalk shadows of people and objects; observe the shadow created by a shape stuck to a sunny window over the course of the day; draw and write with water and brushes on walls and the playground, observing what happens to them after they are finished; feel the change in temperature of a sand tray placed in the Sun; evaluate the effectiveness of a range of sunglasses (but do not look directly at the Sun); make a range of paper hats and establish which is the best.

With older children an awareness of the greenhouse effect can be developed through a challenge activity with clear links to the Design and Technology curriculum. Children are set the challenge on a sunny day to raise the temperature of a beaker of water by as much as they can, using only the heat from the sun and a solar collector. What they use to create their solar collector is up to them, but typically children will be provided with a large plastic container such as an aquarium, tin foil and possibly cling film and mirrors. Turning over the container alone creates an effective solar collector which models the greenhouse effect by allowing solar energy to pass through it but only letting a limited amount of the energy escape. On a sunny day in the summer, expect temperatures in excess of 40 deg C to be reached.

For all ages, children need an opportunity to discuss the messages about global warming that they will inevitably hear through the media and friends, because, as was mentioned earlier, possibly two-thirds of 10-year-olds may still not fully understand the link between global warming and burning fossil fuels (Palmer and Suggate 2005). Children may hear arguments that question this link, which provides an opportunity to discuss how science works, and that science is about gathering evidence and establishing links between cause and effect (KS1 Sc1 1, KS2 Sc1 1a). Messages about thinking globally, acting locally can be supported in the classroom by children monitoring their use of energy, and interesting debates can be had around children changing their lifestyles. For example, would they be prepared to play on their games console for less time each day if it saved energy? The BBC website has a useful slide show about global warming that is pitched at about the right level for older primary school children (see http://www.bbc.co.uk/climate/evidence/greenhouse_effect_img.shtml).

Try to avoid 'doomsday' scenarios, which may cause undue anxiety. Instead focus on positive action children can take to reduce their carbon footprint; walking to school, learning to cycle safely, switching off unneeded electric lights and so on.

Solids, liquids and gases

During KS2 children are expected to begin to differentiate between solids, liquids and gases, particularly in terms of flow and maintenance of shape and volume. Exploring and sorting a collection of solids and liquids will stimulate thinking and raise a number of questions. Collections could include objects made from metal, plastic, wax, chalk, paper and wood, for example. More problematic solids that may raise questions include powders such as flour and dry sand, fabrics, wool and cotton wool, steel wool, Plasticine or Blu-Tack and jelly. Liquids could include water, washing-up liquid, honey, milk and cooking oil. Discussion about the viscosity, or ease of flow, of a liquid can be encouraged and apparent anomalies explored. Dry sand might be seen to 'flow' like a liquid, and children need help to recognise that the individual grains have the properties of a solid. In the DfEE/QCA (1998) unit of work for Year 5, children are required to learn about some important gases, including air, and that liquids evaporate to form gases. Providing examples of gases in the primary classroom is difficult but not impossible. Blowing up balloons, helium-filled balloons, cans of fizzy drink and air fresheners can be used to introduce the concept of gas and associated vocabulary: air, carbon dioxide, oxygen. Putting a small amount of water in a film canister and adding half an Alka-Seltzer tablet before replacing the lid can achieve a dramatic demonstration of the production of a gas. Stand well back, ensure children are out of range and wait for the lid to be 'blown off' as a result of the large volume of carbon-dioxide gas produced by the chemical reaction. The explosion occurs because the gas is compressed until the pressure is too much and the lid pops off. Another demonstration of gas production can be set up by putting a mixture of warm water, sugar and a teaspoon of yeast in a bottle with a balloon fixed tightly over the neck.

Left in a warm place the balloon should begin to inflate as a result of the carbon dioxide produced by the yeast. The aim of these activities is to help children to identify criteria that can be used to distinguish between solids, liquids and gases. For example, solids have a fixed shape and volume, liquids have no fixed shape but a fixed volume, and gases have no fixed shape and variable volume. (See Table 3.1 above.)

Changing state

From an early age, children meet examples of materials changing from solid to liquid, liquid to gas and vice versa. Helping to bake biscuits and cakes, making jelly, melting chocolate and ice cream, burning candles, and watching ice form, puddles evaporate, steam come from kettles and condensation form on car windows all provide everyday experience of materials changing state. At KS1 this is developed through observation, questioning, demonstration and investigation in order that children begin to understand the role of heating and cooling in bringing about these changes. An investigation into ways in which ice could be made to melt more slowly could involve a discussion of how to make the test fair, using ice cubes of the same size, drawing a table to record results and deciding what the results show.

In KS2 the activities in Table 3.2 could be used to develop the understanding that the same material can exist as both solid and liquid and the role of heat energy in this. IT sensors or spirit thermometers can be used to demonstrate the rise in temperature of water at intervals until it boils, or to plot the warming of ice and water over a period of several hours. Secondary sources such as video and CD-ROM pictures of molten metals and lava will be needed to extend children's understanding that different solids melt at different temperatures. Once evaporation and condensation are understood, children can be introduced to the water cycle.

TABLE 3.2 Activities for exploring particles (based on Johnston and Scott 1990)

Activity	Questions
Observation of an air freshener	*What do you notice when the cover of the air freshener is opened?*
Observation of ice cubes on a dish	*What will happen if these ice cubes are left on a work surface for several days?*
Put ice cubes into a screw-top jar. Dry the outside of the jar with a cloth and leave for 15 minutes. Observe the water vapour (condensation) that forms on the outside of the jar.	*Why do you think this has happened?*
Observe chocolate squares inside a sealed plastic bag placed in a dish of hot water.	*What is happening to the chocolate? What will happen if it is left to cool?*
Seal three plastic syringes, one containing air, the second water and the third sand.	*What happens when you press down the plunger of each syringe? What are your explanations for what happens?*

Particles

There is controversy amongst science educators about the teaching of the kinetic theory of matter at KS2 since in the NC this is placed in KS3. However, the QCA (2003a) makes specific mention of the usefulness of introducing children to the idea of particles, and many primary teachers believe that the concepts of solid, liquid and gas, change of state and reversible and irreversible reactions cannot be easily explained without reference to a theoretical model, albeit a much simplified one. We suggest that efforts should be made to help children appreciate the microscopic size of the particles which make up all matter, perhaps by imagining or trying to find out what would happen if we cut something in half, in half again, and again . . . What would we end up with? To appreciate the structure of solids, liquids and gases and the energy transfer needed to change from one state to another, drama might be used, with the children in the playground 'being' particles tightly packed (Figure 3.1) but 'vibrating' in a group with elbows linked, to represent a solid. When the teacher applies (imaginary) heat energy the 'particles' become a little excited and move slightly apart (Figure 3.2) – their bonds constantly break and reform so the particles of a once-ordered solid, for example boy–girl–boy–girl, mix and flow into the spaces of a container (for example a shape drawn on the ground) rather like a liquid. As more heat is applied, some particles have sufficient energy to break loose and run off (evaporate) as 'gas particles' (Figure 3.3) to distant parts

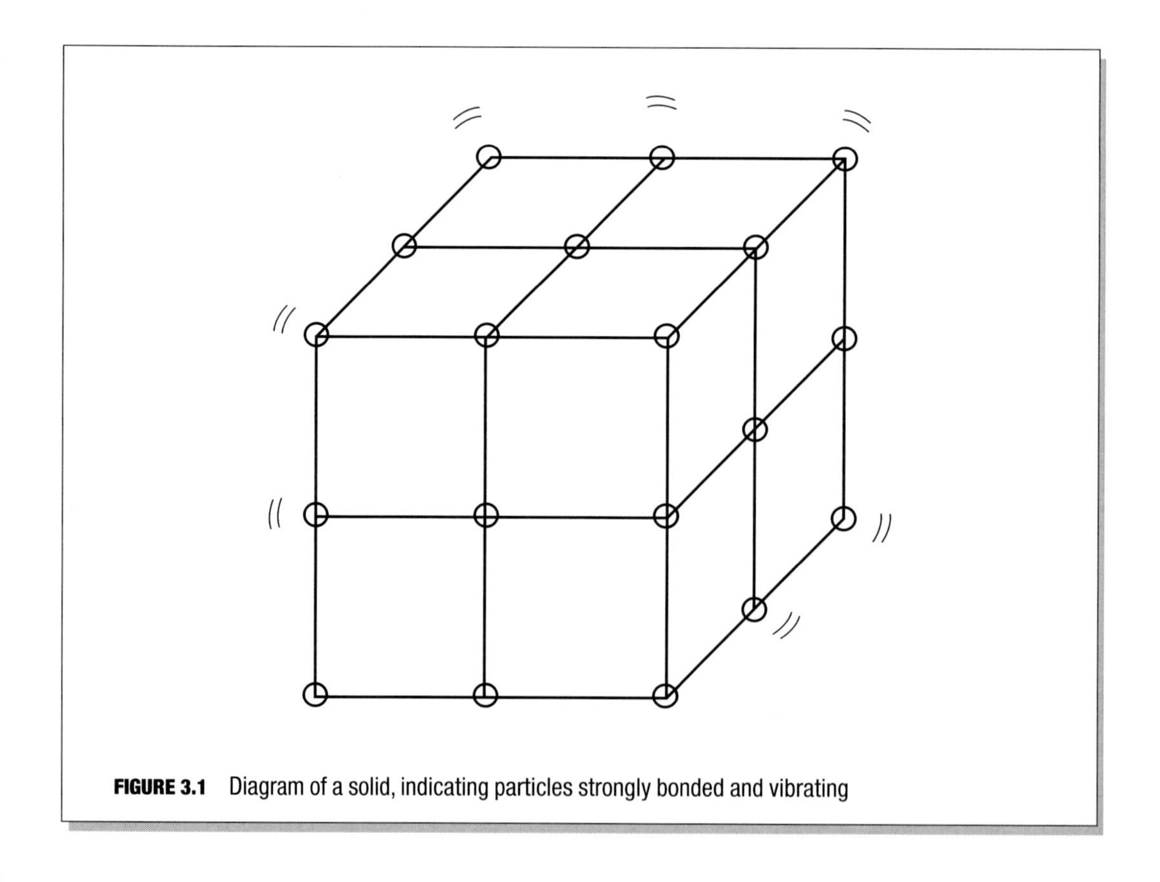

FIGURE 3.1 Diagram of a solid, indicating particles strongly bonded and vibrating

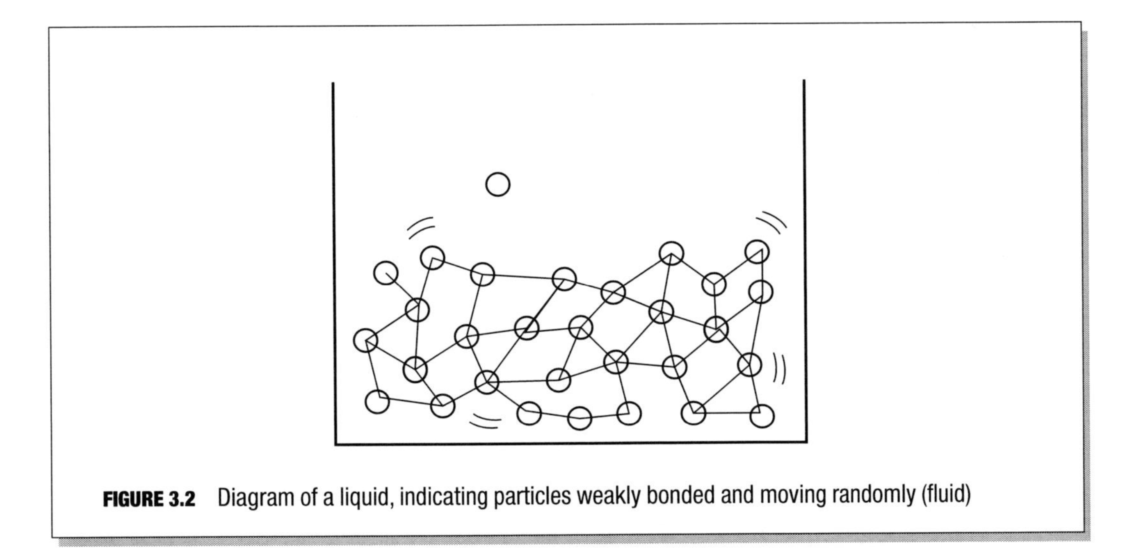

FIGURE 3.2 Diagram of a liquid, indicating particles weakly bonded and moving randomly (fluid)

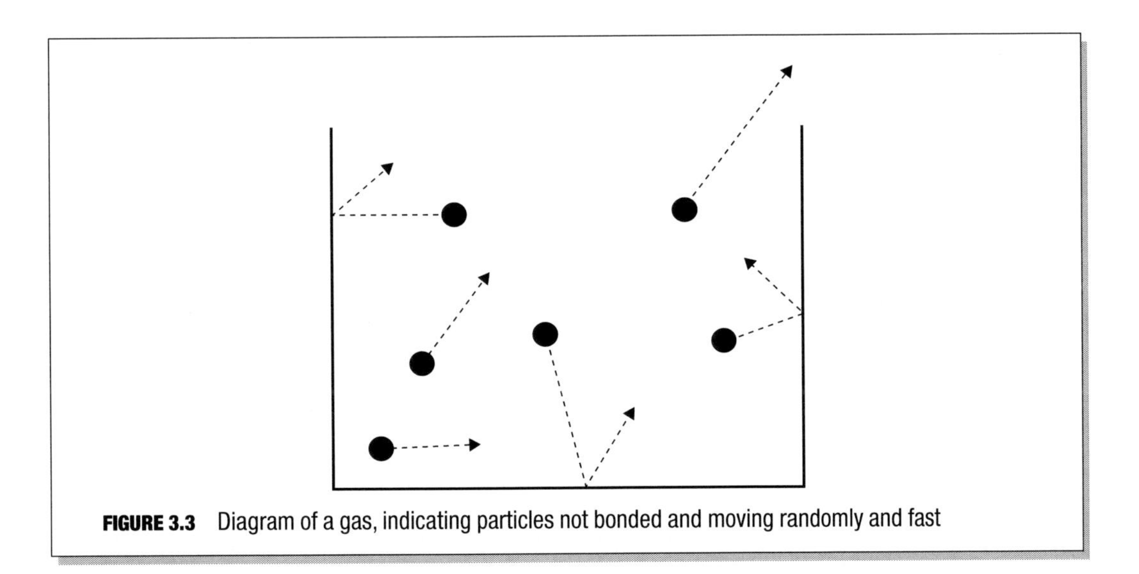

FIGURE 3.3 Diagram of a gas, indicating particles not bonded and moving randomly and fast

of the playground. Other ideas include making a 'mobile' for the classroom using polystyrene balls, glued together for the solid, connected with short lengths of dowel for the liquid and hung freely to represent the gas.

Understanding of this model of the nature and behaviour of matter might be developed by asking children to apply it in a series or circus of activities developed by the Children's Learning in Science Project (Johnston and Scott 1990). Children work in pairs or small groups and are asked to produce a poster or drama, with or without words, explaining their ideas about one of the activities. They then present their explanations to the whole class. Possible activities are outlined in Table 3.2.

Using ICT to teach about changing materials

Data loggers can be used to support a variety of investigations that promote awareness of global issues. We mentioned earlier how the greenhouse effect can be modelled using a large plastic container. Detailed measurements of temperature inside and outside the solar collector along with light measurements can be gathered using a data logger, and these readings can be displayed on a graphing package. The traces tell a story. For example if the temperature rose steadily but suddenly dropped at the same time as the light intensity fell, this could be interpreted as the sun was out warming up the 'greenhouse' but then went behind a cloud. Giving children an opportunity to tell these stories provides them with an opportunity to develop data interpretation and reasoning skills, so called 'data literacy'. Data loggers can also be used to monitor energy usage, for example by tracking classroom temperature over the course of a day. This in turn may lead on to a discussion about times during the day when the classroom thermostat could be turned down and energy saved.

Another way that Information Technology can support our teaching is to access time lapse images that capture changes in superb detail. For example, see http://www.fotosearch.com/photos-images/match-struck.html to reveal what happens when a match is struck, or http://www.fotosearch.co.uk/DVA004/033-0032/ for a speeded-up film of ice melting. Alternatively children could make their own videos by using the time-lapse option available with digital cameras and microscopes.

Classroom management

Children's health and safety are of particular concern when teaching about the way in which materials change since heat is often involved. A risk assessment will identify the need to ensure careful adult supervision of any activity involving the use of hot water or a naked flame. Teacher demonstration of the use of hot water for melting materials is probably safest. If children are to use water for melting it should be warm, not hot, and take place under strict supervision with a ratio of no more than six children to one adult. Lighted candles should always be placed in a container of sand and again require careful supervision. Children should know what to do if the candle is knocked over – do not try to stand it up but place a wet towel over it and allow it to cool. Children should also know how to deal with a burn or scald – run the affected part under cold water for five minutes. Burning other materials, such as fabric and paper, should be done by the teacher as a demonstration, and care should be taken to ensure that substances that produce unpleasant or dangerous fumes are not used. Decaying matter should be carefully sealed in small dishes or plastic bags. Refer to the Association for Science Education's *Be Safe!* booklet (ASE 2001) for definitive guidance.

Summary

In this chapter we have seen how an understanding of what happens to materials when they are changed can lead to an appreciation of issues of global significance. Ways of teaching about the

Earth's climate and the changes that are happening to it were discussed with meaningful links to ICT data monitoring made. Throughout we have emphasised the importance of ensuring science is seen as having relevance to everyday life, so that teaching about global issues begins with studying the weather and reversible and irreversible changes could be taught through cookery. It is our hope that children will make choices about their lifestyle now and in the future for the good of the planet. Our teaching should contribute to them making these choices in a more informed way.

Discussion points

1. How will teaching about materials contribute to education for sustainable development (ESD)?
2. What arguments are there for and against teaching children about the particulate nature of matter at KS2?

Further reading

Summers *et al.* (2000), *One Small Step: Understanding the Science of Environmental Issues*: a useful text for practising and trainee primary teachers who want to feel secure about their own subject knowledge of global warming, the carbon cycle, the ozone layer and other environmental issues.

http://www.bbc.co.uk/climate/evidence/extreme.shtml: clear factual information about global climate change.

CHAPTER

Sound

Purpose of this chapter

After reading this chapter you should have:

- gained an understanding of progression in the main concept areas of sound
- become aware of a variety of illustrative activities to develop children's understanding of the concept areas of sound
- appreciated ways of making cross-curricular links with music more explicit.

Introduction

SOUND CAN BE an enjoyable, hands-on (and 'ears-on'!) science topic to teach, particularly if you make the most of the extensive cross-curricular links with music. There are plenty of exciting and surprising illustrations of sound-related phenomena that can easily be set up in the primary classroom using everyday equipment. It is also possible to convert some of these into 'fair test' investigations to challenge children's enquiry skills. Classroom management can be challenging – a whole-class sound workshop can be rather noisy so you may need to warn your neighbouring teachers – but there is also potential for listening as well. Simply sitting in silence for a minute or two and recording the ambient sounds in the environment can be a revealing (and peaceful!) activity, which links in well with the National Primary Strategy focus on speaking and listening (DfES 2003).

In many ways, sound has much in common with light: both are forms of energy that travel from one place to another and are used for communication. Both travel in waves (although sound has *longitudinal* waves, whilst light is believed to have both *transverse* wave and particle properties). Both are received by our sensory organs (eyes and ears) giving rise to similar kinds of alternative ideas about how we see and hear, as well as offering teachers opportunities for linking these topics with each other and with 'our senses' in work on humans or other animals.

Progression from the early years to the beginning of secondary school

During the early years children will begin to notice similarities and differences between sounds and music and will learn to discern different sounds and their sources. They will enjoy making sounds and music with their own voices and bodies and with instruments. In the Early Years Foundation Stage the exploration of sound in a play context can be achieved through 'listening walks', identifying sounds with eyes closed, circle games such as 'keeper of the keys', and through using musical instruments such as drums, shakers and scrapers. The *Statutory Framework for the Early Years Foundation Stage* recommends that children should 'investigate objects and materials by using all of their senses as appropriate' (DCSF 2008: 14), so it is important to use opportunities to develop awareness of sounds when children are engaged in their play or in adult-initiated activities. The progression in key concepts about sound in KS1 and KS2 is described in Table 4.1.

At KS3 children learn more about the effects of sound on the inner ear and how sound causes the eardrum to vibrate. They learn about the speed of sound and the relationship between the loudness and pitch of a sound and the amplitude and frequency of the vibration causing it.

Cross-curricular planning

Musical instruments

There is so much potential in this cross-curricular context because it is possible to engage children of all ages and levels of attainment, returning to this theme often by focusing on a different aspect of sound or music each time. There is a wide variety of instruments from all over the world that make sounds in different ways – usually through either beating (includes plucking and strumming), blowing (e.g. recorder), shaking (e.g. maracas) or scraping (e.g. violin). Children can explore ways to make sounds with instruments, feel the vibrations when sounds are being made and explore pitch and loudness. They can examine how an instrument is made, noting which materials have been used, identifying the parts that vibrate and the parts which amplify the vibration. Later they could try to identify a range of instruments whilst blindfolded. Children usually enjoy making and decorating their own instruments such as shakers, drums and 'box guitars' – this provides a natural link with D&T.

Houses and homes

This theme provides a relevant context for developing awareness of sources of sound, the variety of sounds in our environment and sound travelling through different materials. Children enjoy identifying a range of 'mystery' household sounds from a tape, for example filling a kettle, shutting a door and cleaning teeth. The story *Peace at Last* by Jill Murphy (1995a) and the poem 'The Sound Collector' by Roger McGough are good starting points when working with young children. Children can explore how far the sound of a clock, a telephone or an alarm will travel. Where is the best place to put a smoke alarm or an intercom for a baby to make sure they can be heard? Which materials can be used to make a room soundproof? You could discuss with the children

TABLE 4.1 Sound: progression of key concepts

Key concepts	NC references	Teachers' background knowledge
There are many kinds of sound and sources of sound.	KS1 Sc4 3c	Sound is produced when an object vibrates; this causes vibrations in the air, which we call sound waves.
Sounds travel away from sources getting fainter as they do so.	KS1 Sc4 3d	Sounds travel in all directions, outwards from the source, like ripples when you drop a pebble in a pond. Sound waves can travel through the air at approximately 332 metres per second. Hard surfaces such as walls reflect sound waves. When you hear an echo, you are hearing a reflected sound a short time after the original sound.
Sounds are heard when they enter the ear.	KS1 Sc4 3d	Sounds are heard when vibrations from an object travel through the air and enter the ears, causing the eardrums to vibrate. There are three bones in the middle ear: the hammer, the anvil and the stirrup. The vibrations from the eardrum cause these bones to move, and the vibration then travels round the cochlea where thousands of hairs containing nerve endings carry impulses to the brain.
Sounds are made when objects vibrate but vibrations are not always directly visible.	KS2 Sc4 3e	Vibrations are (often minuscule) backwards and forwards movements of materials. Some hard materials are 'resonant' – vibrations are amplified, making them easier to hear (e.g. placing a tuning fork on a wooden table).
The pitch and loudness of some vibrating objects can be changed.	KS2 Sc4 3f	The number of waves per second is called the frequency (pitch) and is measured in hertz (Hz). Sound waves can differ in amplitude (size) and frequency and this leads to differences in loudness and pitch, respectively.
Vibrations from a sound source require a medium through which to travel to the ear.	KS2 Sc4 3g	Sound waves need materials to travel through: they can travel through air, liquids and solids but not through a vacuum.

Sources to develop further background subject knowledge
Wenham (2005)(2nd edn), *Understanding Primary Science: Ideas, Concepts and Explanations.*

when a sound becomes a 'noise' – is this just to do with whether we like the sound or not, or is it about loudness?

Sounds to communicate

The exploration of how sounds are used to communicate in our environment can give opportunities to learn about the variety of sounds, how sound travels and how to compare or classify sounds. There are sound signals that help to keep us safe, such as fire alarms, pelican crossings, police sirens and car hooters. Other sounds such as a whistle during break time or a sports match, alarm clocks and doorbells give us different messages. Communication between animals is an interesting area of enquiry. Children can use secondary sources to find out how different animals make sounds and hear (what shapes are their ears?), the range of frequencies they are able to produce/detect, and how far their sounds will travel. For example, dogs have a higher frequency range than humans (hence the 'silent' dog whistle), bats navigate by sending pulses of ultrasound (very high frequency) that reflect from surfaces giving them 'echo-location', and whales communicate across vast distances of ocean using low-frequency sounds that travel further in liquids.

Stories with sounds and music

There is a lot of scope for having fun with sounds when creating sound effects and background noises for a story or play. Children enjoy exploring the qualities of sound to create a certain atmosphere or to describe the movement of an animal or character. A good starting point for this might be to listen to a recording of Prokofiev's *Peter and the Wolf*, in which every character has a different theme tune, or to watch an episode of *Scooby Doo* in which sound effects are used to create atmospheres of fear or suspense. Children could discuss the choice of sounds for each effect – Why do we associate certain sounds (e.g. creaking) with particular emotions?

Assessment for learning

Class discussion, annotated drawings and asking children probing questions whilst they are engaged in practical activities are particularly useful elicitation strategies for finding out children's ideas about sound. For example, if we choose to start by listening for a minute or two as a whole class to the sounds we can hear around us, or by taking a 'sound walk' around the school, the following questions could explore children's ideas about types of sounds and the ways in which we hear them:

> *What sounds can you hear?*
> *How can you tell what it is that you are hearing?*
> *What things do you think affect how well you can hear a sound?*
> *Why do you think some sounds are heard more easily than others?*
> *How do you think you can hear these sounds?*

(Nuffield Primary Science 1993)

A further set of questions is offered by QCA (2003b):

> *What did you notice about the sounds you heard?*
> *Can you tell where the things are that make a sound? Or how far away they are? How can you tell?*
> *How many ways can you think of that animals use to make sounds?*

Asking children to draw how a sound travels from the source to our ears can reveal some interesting ideas, particularly if these drawings are annotated by them or a scribe. You could ask: *Can you draw the journey the sound makes from the sound maker all the way to the person who makes the sound?* or *What's a good way of drawing something such as sound, which we can't actually see?* (QCA 2003b).

Commonly, children tend to associate hearing with the active will of the hearer – 'I can hear the sound by listening hard' (Watt and Russell 1990) – which is similar to ideas about seeing (see chapter 5). It is actually our brain that 'listens'; it filters out all the sounds entering our ears that it is not interested in and 'homes in' on those which are of interest.

Other children may draw straight or wiggly lines connecting the source with the ear (possibly indicating an awareness of waves). When questioned, they may not be aware that the sound travels in every direction, or may say 'the wind blew it to my ear' (SPE 1995), indicating a lack of awareness of how vibrations get 'passed on' through the air in a wave. Even children who say 'the sound goes in my ear' may not be aware of the effect vibrations in the air have on the eardrum (making it vibrate). Making sounds with a drum, 'elastic-band guitar' or by 'twanging' a ruler on the edge of a table can offer further opportunities for probing understanding:

> *How do you think the drum makes a sound?*
> *What do you think happens to the skin of the drum?*
> *Does it matter where you hit the drum?*
> *Can you make a sound with the drum in a different way?*
>
> (Nuffield Primary Science 1993)

> *What word could you use to describe the moving up and down of the elastic band?*
> *How can you change the volume of the sound made by the drum?*
> *How can you change the pitch of the sound made by the ruler?*
>
> (QCA 2003b)

Some children may observe the vibration of the drum skin or elastic band, but not make a connection between this and the sound they hear. Others may suggest that the sound 'causes' the vibration or vice versa, implying that sound and vibration are separate phenomena, and thus lack the scientific understanding that equates one with the other (Nuffield Primary Science 1993). Many children confuse volume with pitch, describing a loud sound as 'high' and a quiet sound as 'low'.

Children's ideas about the materials through which sound can travel could be further probed using the following questions:

> *What materials do you think sound can travel through?*
> *Do you think you could hear sounds if you were under water in a swimming pool? On the Moon? At the bottom of the ocean? In a deep cellar?*
>
> (QCA 2003b)

Some children, whilst acknowledging that sound travels through air, may not see air as a 'material' and may therefore deny that sound can travel through liquids or solids. Others may suggest that sound travels only if there is nothing to get in the way: 'Tunes are very small and they can get through gaps in the doors.' This child may be saying that sound does not need any substance for travelling in (Nuffield Primary Science 1993: 46). Listening to sounds through open and shut doors could further explore this idea: *How does shutting the door change the sound? How can some sound still get through?* Another useful elicitation activity is to walk away from a very quiet sound (e.g. a ticking clock) and describe the way the sound changes. *Why does it get fainter? When you can't hear it any more does that mean the sound can't get that far?*

Summative assessment (assessment of learning)

QCA (2003b) provide some helpful advice on interpreting children's statements and annotated drawings in this area. If a child is able to name some sound-makers (e.g. people, animals, machines), this provides evidence of NC level 1, whilst if he or she mentions that the sound comes to our ears, this is consistent with an NC level 2 understanding. Drawing sound travelling through the air to our ears, or making the observation that sounds get quieter as we move away both indicate level 3, whilst drawing sound travelling in all directions and using the term vibrations to describe how sounds are made can provide us with evidence for NC level 4. Relating the loudness of the drum to the 'size' (amplitude) of vibrations or describing how shortening the ruler changes the pitch of the 'twang' is consistent with NC level 5 in conceptual understanding (Sc4), whilst we may also wish to assess their enquiry skills in relation to sound (Sc1) as suggested in the following section.

Scientific enquiry

As suggested in the introduction to this chapter, this topic lends itself particularly to 'illustrative activities' – carefully planned practical experiences that demonstrate particular concepts, many of which will be described in the 'developing ideas' section below. However, another of the AKSIS project's categories of enquiry, 'investigating models' (Goldsworthy *et al.* 2000a), can also be used to help develop children's understanding. For example, by using a 'slinky' spring stretched over a flat surface, we can show how longitudinal waves can travel through a material by giving one end of the spring short pushes (Figure 4.1).

A compression can then be seen to pass along the slinky and bounce back from the other end (an 'echo'). Be careful not to shake the spring from side to side – this is a *transverse* wave more characteristic of light or water ripples. Using several slinkies all radiating from a cluster of children facing outwards and giving them short 'pulses' together can model sound waves travelling outwards from the source in all directions.

Children enjoy exploring different ways of making sounds: with their bodies, with instruments and with objects around them. They can sort them into different types of sound such as banging sounds or tinkly sounds, or sort them according to how the sound is made, for example by shaking, plucking, scraping or blowing. They can explore ways of changing sounds by using instruments to make quiet or loud sounds.

There are also some 'fair test' type investigations of sound suitable for developing particular enquiry skills. For example, when using a 'string telephone' (two tins or plastic cups fastened together with a long piece of string that needs to be kept taut), children could investigate how changing the length, thickness, type of string or material of the cup affects the sound they can hear. The 'measurements' for this investigation will inevitably be rather subjective, although it is possible

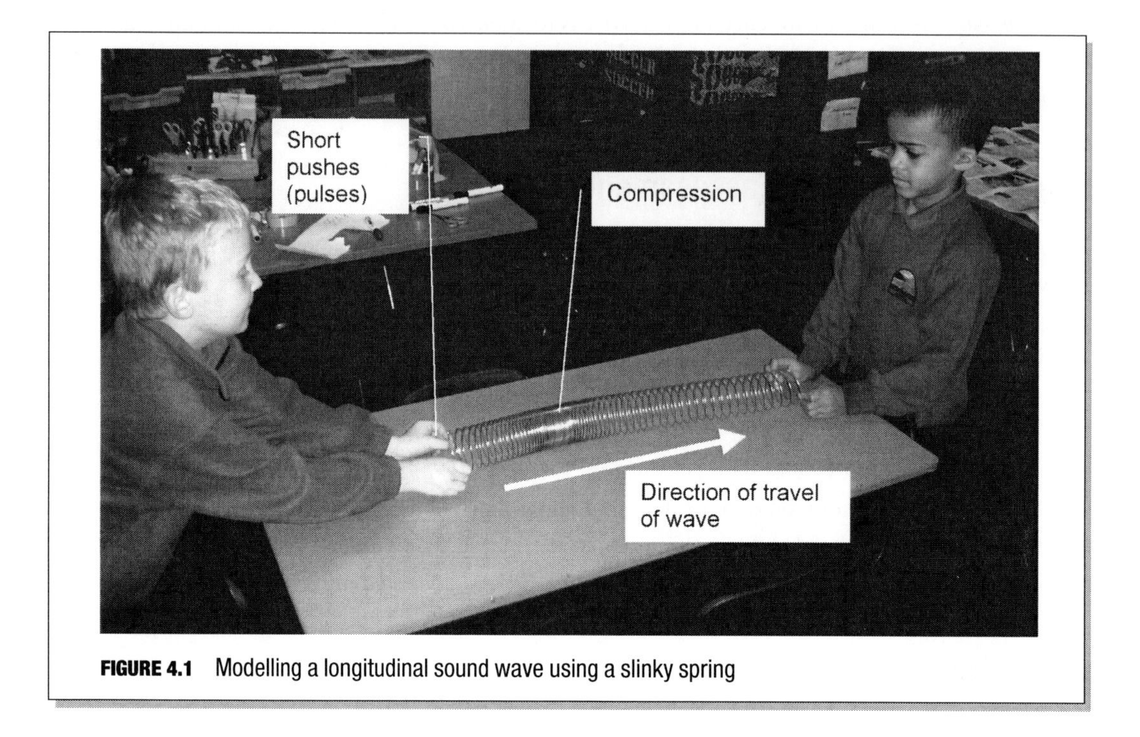

FIGURE 4.1 Modelling a longitudinal sound wave using a slinky spring

to record them with some degree of precision by using a sound sensor connected to data-logging equipment (see 'using ICT' section below).

Developing children's understanding

There are many kinds of sound and sources of sound

To develop their awareness of sound, children need to listen to and identify a range of sounds, to experience different ways to make sound, to differentiate between types of sound and to explore ways in which they can change sound.

Listening walks, discussing sounds in the environment, listening to tapes and using musical instruments can provide children with lots of experience that will extend their awareness of sounds. Playing a version of 'Kim's game' (where a set of objects is displayed to be memorised, then one removed and the question asked 'Which object is now missing?') with sounds encourages listening skills and helps children to learn to identify sound when they cannot see the source.

Sounds travel away from sources, getting fainter as they do so

Exploring the quality and volume of sounds at various distances, walking away from a sound source until it can no longer be heard, walking around a sound source to find out about the direction of sound are all experiences that can help to develop this concept. One child could ring a bell in the middle of the playground, whilst the rest of the class walk away in different directions. The resulting discussion can be used to challenge the idea that sound only travels in one direction. The idea of sound travelling through air can be demonstrated dramatically by using an 'air cannon' (a large-diameter plastic cylinder with a flexible diaphragm that can be pulled back and released). This sends a pulse of high pressure through the air, enough to 'blow you away' at several metres' distance! In effect, the air cannon is working like a very-low-frequency loudspeaker, with the compression wave felt as well as heard (see Figure 4.2).

Although not directly related to this concept, children will probably have noticed echoes in the school hall or when walking through a pedestrian underpass, so the idea of sound travelling until it is absorbed or 'bounces off' (reflects from) hard surfaces may be worth exploring here. An adaptation of the activity to investigate angles of reflection using two cardboard tubes and a mirror (see chapter 5) can be used to explore the way in which sounds reflect from a surface, by putting a ticking clock at the far end of one tube whilst the other is moved until the optimum angle for hearing the clock is achieved (see Figure 4.3).

Sounds are heard when they enter the ear

It is not until KS3 that the NC requires children to learn formally that sound causes the eardrum to vibrate and that people have different audible ranges. However, children are usually interested in how their bodies work and often ask questions about how their ears can hear things. They may be aware

FIGURE 4.2 The 'air cannon' sends a compression wave that can be felt and heard

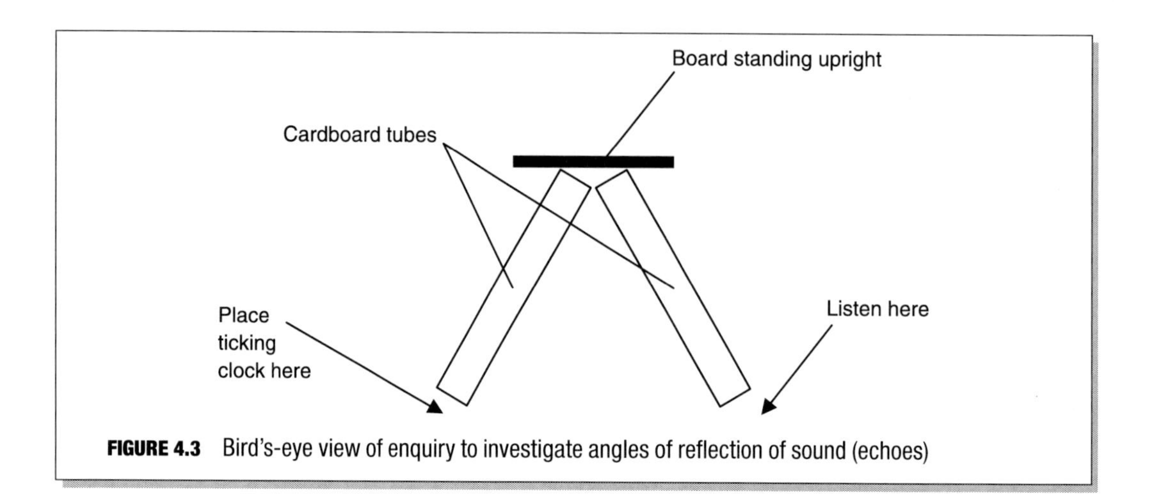

FIGURE 4.3 Bird's-eye view of enquiry to investigate angles of reflection of sound (echoes)

that a grandparent finds it difficult to hear, there may be someone in the class who wears a hearing aid, and most children will have experienced having their hearing tested by the health visitor or by the audiometrician visiting schools. A significant number of children suffer from hearing loss at some time during their years at primary school, so it is important to deal with this area with sensitivity.

Extending awareness in this area involves exploring how the outer ear collects sound and the idea of sound travelling to our ears. It is interesting to note that when playing circle games that involve passing a message by whispering to the next person some young children do not realise that they need to speak into the next child's ear. They move their face nearer but do not attempt to direct the sound towards the ear.

Make an ear trumpet from a cone of card to explore how this amplifies the sound we hear (it collects sound over a wider area). Children can investigate how changing the size, shape or material of the ear trumpet affects its performance – another opportunity for data-logging. Exploring how different animals detect sound can extend awareness of hearing and sound travelling. Use reference books or ICT sources to find animals with ears that can prick up and turn towards the direction of a sound. The reason we have two ears can be investigated by asking a child to stand in the middle of a circle of friends, who take it in turns to call their name from different positions. They can be asked to point to the direction of each call, and then try again with one hand over an ear. Their sense of the direction of sounds should be considerably better with both ears (stereophonic) than with one ear.

The idea of the eardrum picking up sound can be demonstrated by placing a sheet of tissue paper or a piece of burst balloon across one end of a cardboard tube with a rubber band. By placing two fingers gently against the tissue paper and shouting or singing down the tube, the children should be able to feel the vibrations in the 'eardrum' caused by sound travelling down the tube ('outer ear').

Sounds are made when objects vibrate, but vibrations are not always directly visible

We hear sound when an object vibrates at a frequency that our ears can detect. When we hear a sound there will be a vibrating object, which is the source of the sound. Activities to illustrate vibrations demonstrate the frequent need in science to 'make the invisible visible' (Harlen 2000).

Children can explore vibrations producing sound by:

- plucking guitar strings (the vibrations are easily visible)
- 'twanging' a metal ruler or steel knitting needle on the edge of a table
- watching rice on a drum move when the drum is hit
- touching a ping-pong ball on a string with a tuning fork (this is a spectacular way to show the energy in vibrations – the ball bounces a long way!)
- putting a tuning fork in water (another favourite producing quite a big splash)
- feeling their throats as they hum or sing.

It is possible to demonstrate how vibrations move through the air by banging a cymbal or beating a drum close to another drum that has small pieces of paper or rice on its skin. The vibrations created by banging the cymbal will travel through the air causing the drum skin to vibrate and the paper to move.

The pitch and loudness of some vibrating objects can be changed

As emphasised in the assessment for learning section above, it is very common for children to be confused between the pitch (frequency) and the loudness (volume) of sounds. The size of a vibration, that is, how far the object moves from its starting point, is called its amplitude. A large vibration will need a larger force to get started and will produce a loud sound. Children can observe this by using different amounts of force on a guitar string or elastic band, to see how this changes the loudness (volume) of the sound. This can be recorded using data-logging equipment that measures loudness in decibels (dB).

Pitch, or the frequency of sounds, measured in hertz (Hz) or vibrations per second, can be explored in many different ways. Generally, the smaller or shorter the object or material vibrating, the higher will be its pitch. For example, if children 'twang' a ruler or steel knitting needle on the edge of a table as suggested above, but move it towards the centre of the table during the vibration, they can hear and see how the vibrations become more frequent as the length free to vibrate shortens. A lovely and simple way of showing this is to make a paper straw 'oboe' by cutting one end into a 'v', flattening it and blowing through. It takes a bit of practice to get the lip position and force of breath right, but children should soon be able to produce a 'toot', a little like the sound some people can make by blowing over a blade of grass held between thumbs. Making 'oboes' of various lengths, or cutting pieces off the other end of the straw as they blow, very clearly demonstrates pitch rising as the length shortens.

Another simple demonstration is to stretch an elastic band whilst a child plucks it near their ear. However, this can be confusing, as the pitch rises as the elastic band is stretched (i.e. gets longer!), so might be better as an 'extension' activity to challenge higher attainers. Similarly, the familiar row of glass bottles with differing amounts of water can be a tricky example. Blow across the top of each one and the pitch gets higher as the amount of water increases. However, hit each gently (bearing in mind health and safety precautions) and the pitch *decreases*. The explanation, which some children may come up with, is that when you are blowing, the column of *air* in each bottle vibrates, whereas when you strike the bottles it is the column of water that vibrates – as one increases, the other decreases! A variation on this activity is to blow across a steel tube as you move it up and down in a bottle of water. This creates the same effect as a Sewanee whistle or trombone, where the pitch increases as you shorten the amount of air in the tube.

Vibrations from a sound source require a medium through which to travel to the ear

Children are often surprised to find that sound can travel through liquids or solids. Activities to illustrate this concept include the following:

- Tap a table with a pencil and ask a child to listen, then ask the child to put their ear on one end of the table: is the sound different? Children can explore this in pairs.
- Listen to sounds underwater, perhaps during swimming lessons.
- Can you hear a ticking clock through a water-filled balloon or through the wood of a metre rule?

These experiences can provide useful starting points for dialogic discussion in the classroom. Children could listen to a CD of whale calls and offer ideas for how whales can hear each other over thousands of kilometres underwater. Is it because whale 'voices' are very low-pitched? How can astronauts communicate in space? Can they talk to each other without radios? If children have waited on a station platform some might have noticed that they hear a sound in the rails before they hear the train approaching. What does this tell us about the speed of sound along the solid rails? Children should realise that in some circumstances they actually hear sounds *more clearly* through solids or liquids – sound actually travels faster the more dense the material. This can be modelled kinaesthetically for older KS2 children by arranging them in a line, initially standing close together (like the particles in a solid). A small 'nudge' at one end of the line is rapidly transmitted to the other, whilst if the children stand a few centimetres apart (a 'liquid') the 'wave' travels more slowly. If they stand a metre or so apart and are asked to move until they touch the next 'particle' the wave is slower still, showing the relatively slow speed of sound in air (about 330 m/s). Shipman (2007) suggests turning this 'longitudinal' wave into the sort of undulating 'transverse' wave you would see on an oscilloscope by asking the children to raise and lower their arms as they feel the nudge. Why then, if sound travels so much better in solids than in gases, does closing a door reduce noise? This is because sound, being a wave, reflects off hard surfaces. Children can model this using a 'slinky' spring (see Figure 4.1 above): if you give the end of the spring a sharp push when the other end is loose, the pulse you see travelling down the spring does not return to you. However, if someone holds the other end still (simulating a hard surface such as a door) this longitudinal wave will be reflected back towards you. Only sounds which are produced in the solid itself or in direct contact with it can travel easily through it – sounds in the air hitting the solid tend to be reflected.

Making a loud sound that is also very visual (for example clashing two cymbals together) at one end of the playground whilst the class watch and listen from the other end can demonstrate the different speeds travelled by sound and light, which can be extended to a discussion of the time delay between lightning and thunder and estimating the distance from a storm by counting between the two.

Using ICT to teach about sound

Some of the above hands-on experiences can be reinforced – though not replaced – by simulated activities. For example, Collins' *Virtual Experiments* contains an activity to classify different types of musical instrument by the way they produce the sound, together with a simulated investigation to measure the volume of sounds at different distances. Taking real volume measurements is more tricky, though children can use datalogging equipment such as EasySense Q, LogIT Explorer or Philip Harris First Sense to monitor noise levels around the classroom and school. How loud is the traffic on nearby roads? How do the noise levels in the school hall vary over the day? This kind of environmental mapping can be used to develop children's interpretation and presentation of data, particularly if it is being used as part of a bid for 'Eco-school' status (see www.eco-schools.org.uk). Another useful investigation using data-logging equipment starts from the question: Which material would be the best sound insulator for a pair of ear defenders? Children can think of a good way to make a 'standard' sound (perhaps a simple circuit including a buzzer, though this can become rather irritating!) and can set up the sensor and material being tested in the same place each time to make the test 'fair' (see Figure 4.4). Unfortunately, because sound sensors tend to be rather sensitive to extraneous noises, it is rather difficult to obtain reliable results, although this can be a useful point for discussion during the plenary!

Classroom management

Given the potential for noise in much of the practical work in this topic, it may be best to focus the noise within a few sessions, perhaps by organising a circus of activities, around which groups of children move in the course of a lesson. Below is a useful set of equipment for the activities suggested above:

- sources of sound: different types of musical instruments, demonstrating four different ways of making sounds: bang, scrape, shake, blow
- sound travels: slinky spring, string telephones, water-filled balloon, ticking stopclock, metal metre rule
- hearing: sheets of card to make ear trumpets, blindfold, cotton wool, sound sources, cardboard tube with piece of burst balloon stretched over one end (model ear drum)
- vibrations: drum, rice, balloon, paper and comb, tuning fork, bowl of water, ping-pong ball on thread
- volume (amplitude, loudness): guitar, slinky, sound-insulating materials to make ear muffs, data-logging equipment set up to measure sound level, buzzer and circuit

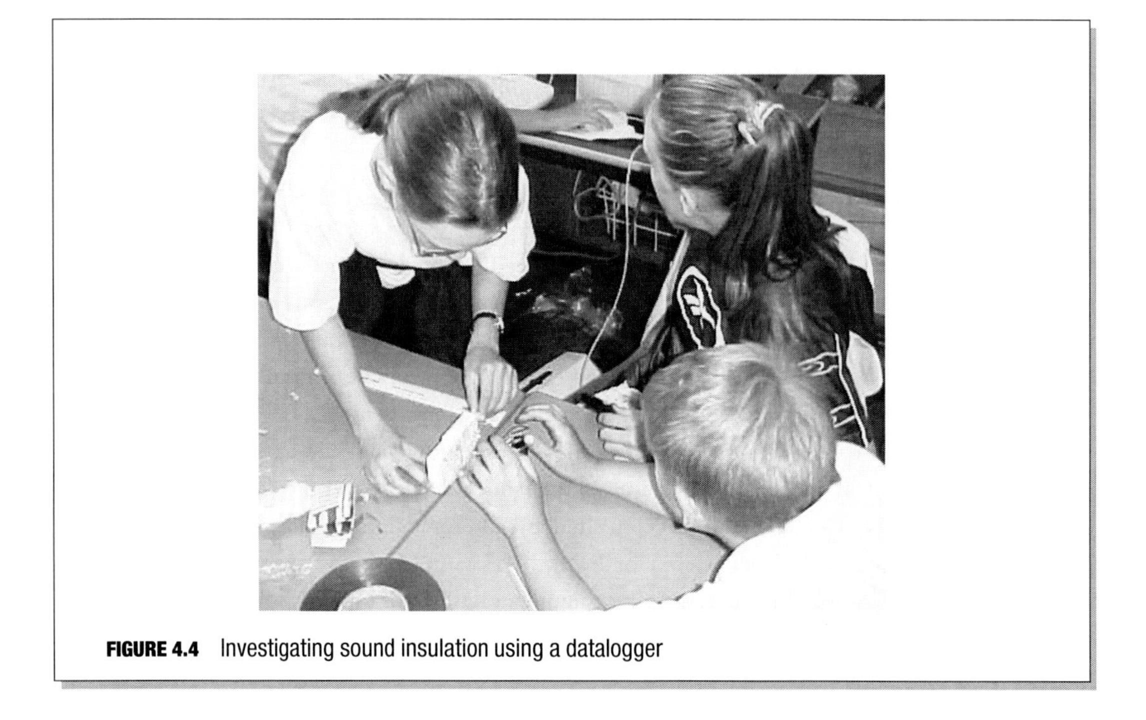

FIGURE 4.4 Investigating sound insulation using a datalogger

- pitch (frequency): ruler, knitting needle, metal tube in water-filled beaker, elastic band, milk bottle xylophone, artstraws, scissors.

Health and safety

If children are holding listening devices up to their ear such as 'ear trumpets' or 'string telephones', others must be warned not to shout into the device no matter how tempting it seems as this could damage the ear drum. Children should be informed about the dangers of putting things in their ears and of damaging them by listening to loud music on headphones. They should also exercise care when 'hitting' the bottle xylophone.

Summary

In this chapter we have explored some of the many practical opportunities there are for children to develop their awareness and understanding of the sounds around them. We have looked at various ways of making sounds, finding out children's ideas about how these sounds travel through air and enter our ears. The potential for investigating ear trumpets, string telephones and sound insulation using data-logging equipment has been explored, together with kinaesthetic ways to help children model how sound travels through different media. Children's awareness of vibrations and confusion between volume and pitch has been addressed with a range of illustrative activities.

Discussion points

1. In what ways are sound and light similar, and in what ways are they different?
2. In what ways do we risk confusing children with the language we use to describe volume and pitch of sounds? What words would help them distinguish between these concepts?

Further reading

Qualifications and Curriculum Authority (QCA) (2003b), ***Assessing Progress in Science, Key Stages 1 and 2: Unit 6, Sound and Light***: this booklet provides useful guidance on assessing pupils' understanding of sound and their enquiry skills when investigating aspects of sound.

Watt and Russell (1990) Primary Science Processes and Concept Exploration Project Research Report: Sound: this seminal research document lists the most common 'alternative frameworks' children hold about concepts related to sound, to enable teachers to plan suitable interventions.

CHAPTER

Light

Purpose of this chapter

After reading this chapter you should have:

- an understanding of the key concepts in the topic of light
- encountered examples of how annotated drawing can be used as an elicitation strategy
- knowledge of a range of contexts and activities that can support children's learning about light.

Introduction

EACH DAY, from the moment we open our eyes, we make use of light. When we read a book, look at a screen and enjoy works of art, the beauty of flowers or a view from the mountains we are sensing light that has reached our eyes. Light travels through space across distances that are unimaginable and so we can see stars that may not exist any more. Light from the Sun is the energy source that keeps our planet alive – plants photosynthesise and provide the basis for all other life on Earth.

So what *is* light? It is a phenomenon that is not entirely understood, and although scientists have various models of what it might be, in primary schools we focus instead on how light behaves, on what it does, and on how we use it in our everyday lives. Our experience of light is largely determined by how we detect it – by our sense of sight. To begin to understand the relationship between light and how we perceive it, it is important to understand what it means to 'see' something and how our brains affect our perceptions of the world. 'We are – or at least we seem to be – linked by light to objects. What is this link? How does it allow us to perceive, to know, objects beyond the reach of touch?' (Gregory 1981: 183).

Another 'big idea' about light, that it travels at a great but finite speed, has been highly significant in understanding the nature of the universe. In Einstein's famous formula $E = mc^2$, c refers to the speed of light. In the time taken for one flap of a hummingbird's wing a beam of light would cross the Atlantic Ocean (Clegg 2007).

The science of light continues to develop. In the biggest British investment in a science project for 40 years, 370 million pounds is developing the Diamond Light source – a beam of light synchronised to generate X-rays 100 billion times brighter than conventional machines. One of its applications will be to read documents too ancient and precious to be unwrapped safely – like the Dead Sea Scrolls and original Mozart scores.

Progression from the early years to the beginning of secondary school

Lights that twinkle, sparkle, glitter and flicker will have intrigued children from an early age. Young children will know that lights can brighten a room, decorate a cake or light up the sky. They will have sung songs about colours, stars and rainbows and played games that involve hiding in the dark or covering their eyes and shutting out the light. The Foundation Stage builds on children's natural curiosity to explore the world around them by offering them more structured experiences and by helping them develop observational skills and awareness of their senses. Young children will have been given opportunities for play that develops their experience of light through exploration of collections of shiny, transparent and translucent objects, mirrors, kaleidoscopes and torches, making shadows on a sunny day, making dark dens and looking at the world through different colour filters. They will have been encouraged to communicate what they see and will begin to learn the vocabulary to enable them to describe their observations: light, dark, shiny, dull, smooth, rough, mirror, shadow, reflection.

During KS1 children will begin to consider darkness as an absence of light and identify various light sources. KS2 sees the introduction of the concept of light travelling, and children learn how shadows and reflections are formed. Although *colour* is not featured in the NC it is an interesting topic and one that lends itself to some intriguing primary science activities through which concepts such as 'white light is a "mix" of different colours' can be introduced. The key concepts of light and colour are explained in Table 5.1.

At KS3 children build on their experiences of light in primary schools, developing the idea that light travels in a straight line at a finite speed and that non-luminous objects are seen because light scattered from them enters the eye. They explore in more depth what happens when light meets different objects or a material, investigating how light is reflected at plane surfaces and how light is refracted at the boundary between two different materials. They also learn about colour, that white light can be dispersed to give a range of colours, about the effect of colour filters on white light and about how coloured objects appear in white light and in other colours of light.

Cross-curricular planning

Dark, dark caves

Creating a dark area such as a cave can give children first-hand experience of darkness and of how the introduction of light enables them to see objects. Stories such as *Can't You Sleep Little Bear?* by Martin Waddell (2001) or *Dark, Dark Tale* by Ruth Brown (1992) can be used to set the context for

TABLE 5.1 Light: progression in key concepts

Key concepts	NC references	Teachers' background knowledge
There are many different light sources, including the Sun.	KS1 Sc4 3a	Light is a form of energy; it is the energy source that keeps our planet alive. Only objects that emit light are sources, and these include the filament of a bulb, a TV screen, a fire and the Sun.
Darkness is the absence of light.	KS1 Sc4 3b	Light illuminates objects; in the absence of light nothing is visible to our eyes.
Light travels from a source.	KS2 Sc4 3a	Light travels in straight lines from its source. Light travels at 300,000,000 metres per second. Nothing can travel more quickly. Light is the visible part of the electromagnetic spectrum. This spectrum contains radio waves, microwaves, infrared light, ultraviolet light, X-rays and gamma rays. Scientists describe light as having wave–particle duality – it can behave as both a particle and a wave.
Light cannot pass through some materials; this leads to the formation of shadows.	KS2 Sc4 3b	Light can travel through transparent materials. Some light passes through translucent materials, which may cast grey or coloured shadows. Light cannot travel through opaque materials and shadows are formed because they block the path of light.
Light is reflected from surfaces.	KS2 Sc4 3c	When light hits an object it can be absorbed, reflected or scattered. If the surface (in a microscopic sense) is uneven, the light will be scattered (reflected off in all directions). If the surface is smooth like glass, the light will be reflected off evenly in the same direction giving the image we know as 'a reflection'. When light meets many materials it is partly scattered and partly absorbed.
We see things when light reflected from them enters our eyes.	KS2 Sc4 3d	Our eyes can be likened to a camera: light passes through our pupil (aperture), and is focused by a lens onto our light-sensitive retina (film) that sends electrical messages to our brain.
Visible light consists of different wavelengths which we see as different colours.		White light can be split into a spectrum or 'rainbow' by using a prism that refracts (redirects) different wavelengths by different amounts. The colours that are visible are (according to Newton) red, orange, yellow, green, blue, indigo and violet. The process can be reversed by adding coloured lights together to create white light. Mixing paint is a different (subtractive) process: each time a paint colour is added to a mix, fewer wavelengths of light are reflected by the pigment.
We see objects as coloured because they reflect different wavelengths of light.		When we see an object as red it is because only red wavelengths from the object have reached our eyes. White objects reflect all visible wavelengths. Objects that appear matt black absorb most of the light that hits them.

young children. The cave could have curtains to open and let in the light from the classroom, or children could use torches to help them find objects in the cave. Topics on 'The Victorians' or trips to mines and caves also give opportunities to explore various sources of light and to demonstrate how we need to shine light onto objects to be able to see them.

Celebrations

Celebrations such as birthdays, Christmas, Divali and Hanukkah are often used as topics in which to explore aspects of light. There are opportunities to explore reflective materials, shiny papers, stained-glass windows and various sources of light, for example candles and Christmas-tree lights. The spiritual and symbolic meanings of light can be explored through religious education (RE) and PSHE links.

Shadow puppets

Through devising and performing shows using shadow puppets, children can explore transparent, translucent and opaque materials and can learn that light travels through some materials but not others. Stretching white fabric over a rectangular frame can make a simple screen. Children can learn how light is blocked by some objects, how shadows are formed and how to make coloured shadows. They will notice that the position, shape and size of a shadow depend upon where the object is in relation to the position of the light source.

How can we make the monster look really big?
Can we made the shadows coloured?

There are good opportunities here for cross-curricular work, for example with storytelling in Literacy: children can either dramatise their own stories or retell stories from around the world. There are also possible links with D&T: making their own shadow puppets and putting on a show for others, making posters, selling tickets, selling popcorn at the show and evaluating the event.

Road safety

Road safety is a familiar theme in schools and provides a relevant context in which to develop awareness of how our senses of sight and hearing help to keep us safe. There are many starting points for exploring aspects of light, including bicycle reflectors, reflective jackets, warning lights and traffic lights.

Ask the children questions such as:

How do drivers use the mirrors to help them keep safe?
How do cat's eyes help drivers on the road?
How are drivers and pedestrians able to see on the road at night?

Schools often hold a road-safety week where a visiting speaker will talk to the children about safety and distribute leaflets and reflectors. Ask them to include something about light and dark in their presentation.

A global dimension

Showing the children posters or satellite images of the world at night is a good start point for raising questions about the impact and effects of how light is used by different people.

> *Where is the most light?*
> *Why is this?*
> *How would we manage without electric light?*
> *Is it a good thing to make so much light?*

Internet access to webcams will allow children to see live pictures of day and night across the world.

Issues of global inequality in the use of energy could be discussed. Children could speculate on the effects of light pollution on people and animals. They could research the various sources of light that people use, perhaps linking this to geography topics, and find out about day length around the world.

> After school in the afternoon I go to the well again with my friends, to fetch water . . . after that I light a fire in the house so that I can see to read my book. The reading I do isn't homework; I choose to do it.
>
> (Fati, Mali – www.oxfam.org.uk)

As always when discussing global inequalities, it is important that negative stereotypes of countries and people as 'underdeveloped' are not reinforced. Looking at images of the Earth at night is a graphic way to initiate discussions about why some parts of the world have access to more resources than others and whether we use them as wisely as we might.

Assessment for learning

When eliciting children's understanding about light or sound, the use of annotated drawings can be particularly useful for helping them to communicate what they know and can become a focus for the discussion of ideas with the teacher or with peers. The children can label their drawings and write explanations of what is happening, or discuss their drawing with the teacher, who can scribe their explanation. As always, teacher questioning is important – key questions are identified below.

Light sources

Questioning children while they are engaged in an exploratory activity will extend their ideas, reveal their level of understanding and give opportunities for assessment. For example, when looking for light sources in the classroom or in the school, teachers could ask:

> *Can you find any areas that are very light?*
> *Where is the light coming from?*
> *What about the dark places, why are they dark?*
> *What happens to bright-coloured things when we put them in a dark place?*
> *What is getting in the way of the light?*

Sorting and classifying objects or pictures can be another starting point for discussion or for questioning about existing ideas. *Assessing Progress in Science* (QCA 2003b) suggests questions for eliciting children's ideas about light sources. After looking at a range of objects or pictures, including some light sources, some very good reflectors and some light-coloured objects, ask the children if they can sort them in some way.

What made you decide that these objects gave off their own light?
How could you check whether it gives off its own light?
Would you be able to see this in a dark room with no light?
Do you think a really shiny trophy could be a light source?

Some children may say that shiny objects or reflectors are sources of light; it is worth noting that some children in KS2 still draw the Moon as a source of light (Osborne *et al.* 1990).

Reflections

Sorting a collection of shiny and dull objects is a good way to get started and to help children develop their ideas on reflections. The collection could include curved and flat surfaces such as spoons and mirrors, smooth and crumpled foils and different papers.

What happens when you shine the torch on the shiny objects?
Why can you see your reflection in some things and not in others?

The SPACE project research (Osborne *et al.* 1990) showed that some children confuse reflections and shadows. For some children there seems to be an alternative idea behind this about light going around objects and for others the idea of a shadow as a tangible entity rather than an absence of light is quite strong. Some children will draw shadows with details such as clothing and faces. Helping them to observe shadows carefully can begin to challenge these ideas.

Shadows

After some practical experience and exploratory activities, such as going for a 'shadow hunt' around the school grounds, ask children to make annotated drawings. They can draw their own shadows (Figure 5.1) and shadows formed by other objects such as football posts or fences, and record their ideas about what shadows are and how they are made.

Children can be encouraged to make careful observations:

Are the shadows the same shape as the objects?
Are they the same size?
Are the shadows joined onto the objects?
Do people always have shadows?

Summative Assessment (assessment of learning)

The example of shadows illustrates how judgements about children's understanding can be made against the NC level descriptors (DfEE/QCA 1999) and informed by the QCA *Assessing Progress in Science* materials (QCA 2003b).

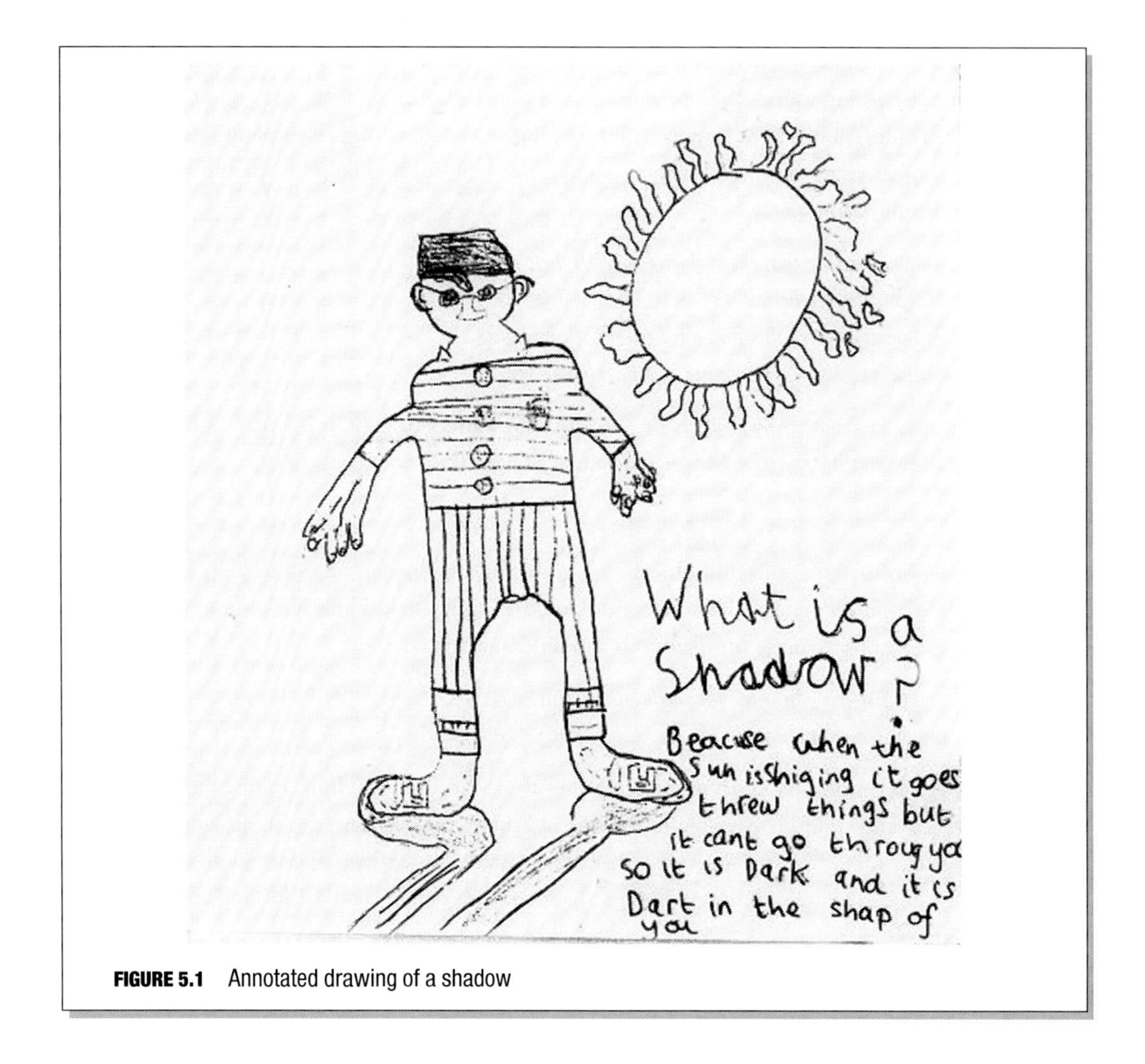

FIGURE 5.1 Annotated drawing of a shadow

A response typical of NC level 2 would be a dark area on a drawing that shows some understanding that the shadow is distinct from other areas around it. In Figure 5.2 there is not yet a clear understanding about how shadows are formed by blocking light, but the Sun is included in the drawing so there is evidence that a source of light is needed.

To indicate NC level 3 there would be evidence of some understanding that light does not pass through the object and that it is blocked, but this may not yet be clearly articulated. If the drawing shows a shadow on the other side of the object in relation to the position of the light source, and if the child can give a clear explanation of how the light is blocked and the shadow is the absence of light, then this would indicate NC level 4. The annotated drawing in Figure 5.1 would suggest that this child is working at this level. If the child can go a step further and begin to explain the relationship between the position, and possibly size of the shadow and the light source, they would have achieved NC level 5.

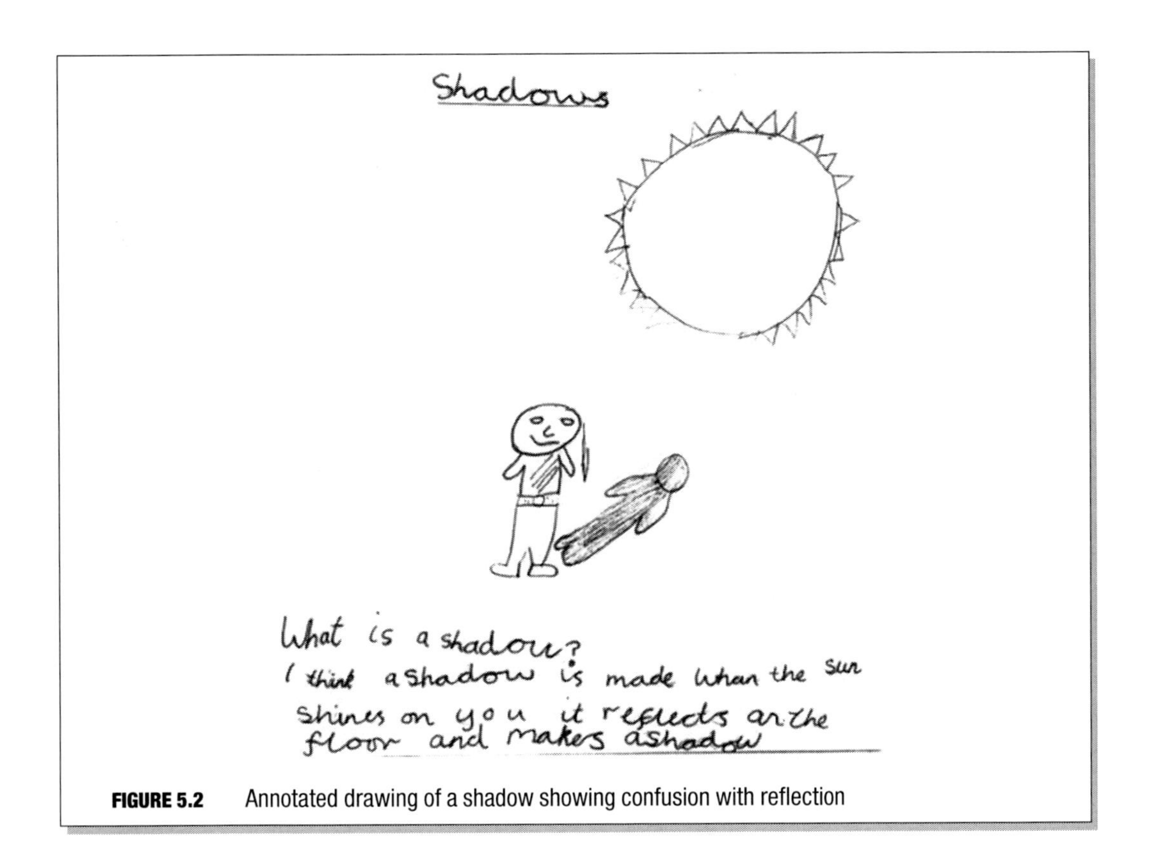

FIGURE 5.2 Annotated drawing of a shadow showing confusion with reflection

Scientific enquiry

Light is an area of science in which it is often appropriate for children to carry out practical tasks that have been set up by the teacher in order to illustrate a particular phenomenon, such as the use of a light box to demonstrate that light travels in straight lines. This type of practical work is often known as an 'illustrative activity' and was introduced in chapter 1.

During an illustrative activity the children can be involved in hands-on practical tasks, and can be developing important skills such as using equipment appropriately, recording observations, making measurements, drawing conclusions and communicating their findings. Their findings can then be used as starting points for child-initiated investigations.

This example of a teacher-directed activity leads to opportunities for children to test an explanation. During an exploration of a collection of shiny objects, the teacher can ask a specific question such as *Why can we see reflections in shiny objects?* Children's responses might include statements such as:

- because they are shiny
- because they are different shapes and sizes

- because you can see through some things
- because some are the right colour for reflection.

It is important to give children the opportunity to test out their own ideas in order to make sense of what they are investigating and to find evidence to challenge their existing ideas. These responses could be followed up by carrying out systematic tests, for example by looking at different reflections in different sized and shaped jars or bottles, of the same kind and colour of glass.

A problem solving approach to enquiry may also be productive:

How can you use these mirrors to see round the corner?
Can you write your name by looking at what you are doing in a mirror?
Which sun glasses are the best?

Children could be given a collection of candles as a stimulus for question raising and may come up with start points for enquiry such as:

Does the size of a candle affect the size of the flame?
Which candle is the brightest?
How far away can you see a burning candle?

They could be asked to discuss in small groups how they might go about finding out the answers to a question and present their ideas orally to the rest of the class for feedback. Plans do not always have to be written down.

The awe and wonder of counting the images when you look at an object in a hinged mirror, opening and closing it slowly is a pattern seeking enquiry. It may lead to further questions: *What happens when you close the mirror?*

Older children can explore their ideas about what affects the size and position of a shadow, developing their use of measurement and looking for patterns in their results as shown in the case study in Box 5.1.

Assessment of scientific enquiry

To achieve NC level 1 children need to show that they have responded to their experiences of light and communicate this, either through talking or drawing. An example of this would be a child giving some examples of different sources of light that they had used or explaining how switching off the bedroom light at night makes it hard to see.

BOX 5.1 An investigation into shadows

Eliciting Yasser's ideas about shadows (Figure 5.3) showed that he already had a good understanding of how shadows were formed and was ready to explore in more depth how their position and size could be changed. He worked collaboratively with three other children to raise questions (Figure 5.4) and to plan and carry out an investigation into how the area of a shadow was affected by moving the light source further away (Figure 5.5).

Yasser then went on to draw a graph of these results (Figure 5.6). A close look at the y-axis reveals that choosing a scale was the next skill that needed to be developed. Also, although he clearly was identifying patterns and relating them to his predictions, the process skills of making generalisations and trying to link them to scientific explanations were not yet developed.

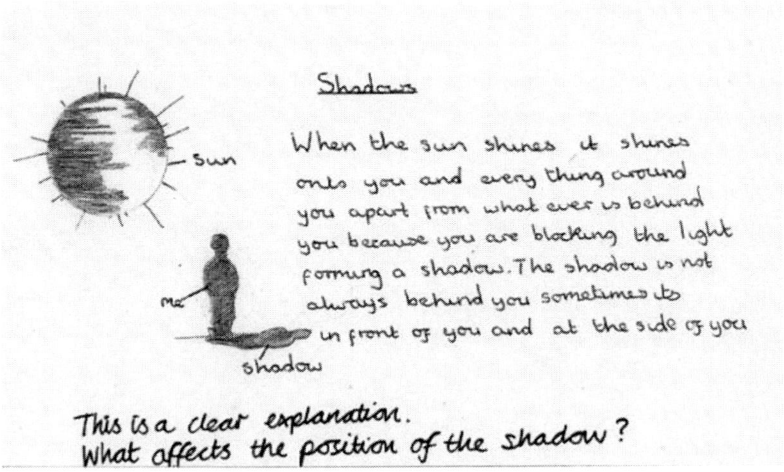

Shadows
Sun
When the sun shines it shines
onto you and every thing around
you apart from what ever is behind
you because you are blocking the light
forming a shadow. The shadow is not
always behind you sometimes its
in front of you and at the side of you
me
shadow
This is a clear explanation.
What affects the position of the shadow?

FIGURE 5.3 Yasser's explanation

Shadow investigation
1. Exploring
1
Does the shadow change when you move the light?
2.
If so why?
3.
How does the shadow appear?
Shadows
5.
I think that that shadows take a lot of investigati
4.
What is a shadow?

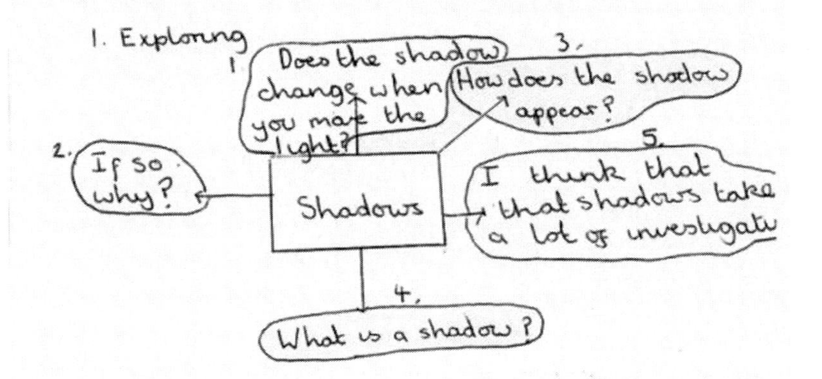

FIGURE 5.4 Questions about shadows

BOX 5.1 (Continued)

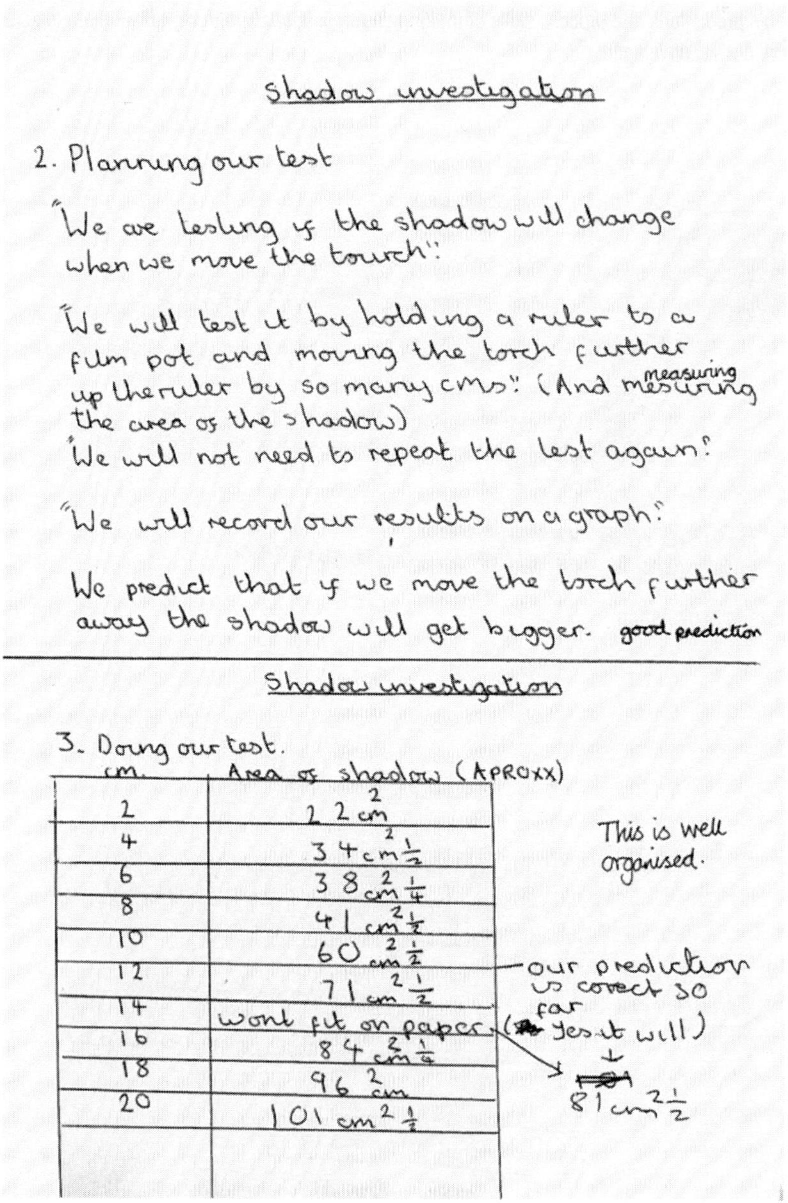

Shadow investigation

2. Planning our test

"We are testing if the shadow will change when we move the tourch".

"We will test it by holding a ruler to a film pot and moving the torch further up the ruler by so many cms". (And measuring the area of the shadow)

"We will not need to repeat the test again."

"We will record our results on a graph."

We predict that if we move the torch further away the shadow will get bigger. good prediction

Shadow investigation

3. Doing our test.

cm.	Area of shadow (APROXX)
2	22 cm^2
4	34 cm^2 ½
6	38 cm^2 ¼
8	41 cm^2 ½
10	60 cm^2 ½
12	71 cm^2 ½
14	wont fit on paper (Yes it will) → 81 cm^2 ½
16	84 cm^2 ¼
18	96 cm^2
20	101 cm^2 ½

This is well organised.

our prediction is correct so far

FIGURE 5.5 Planning a shadow investigation

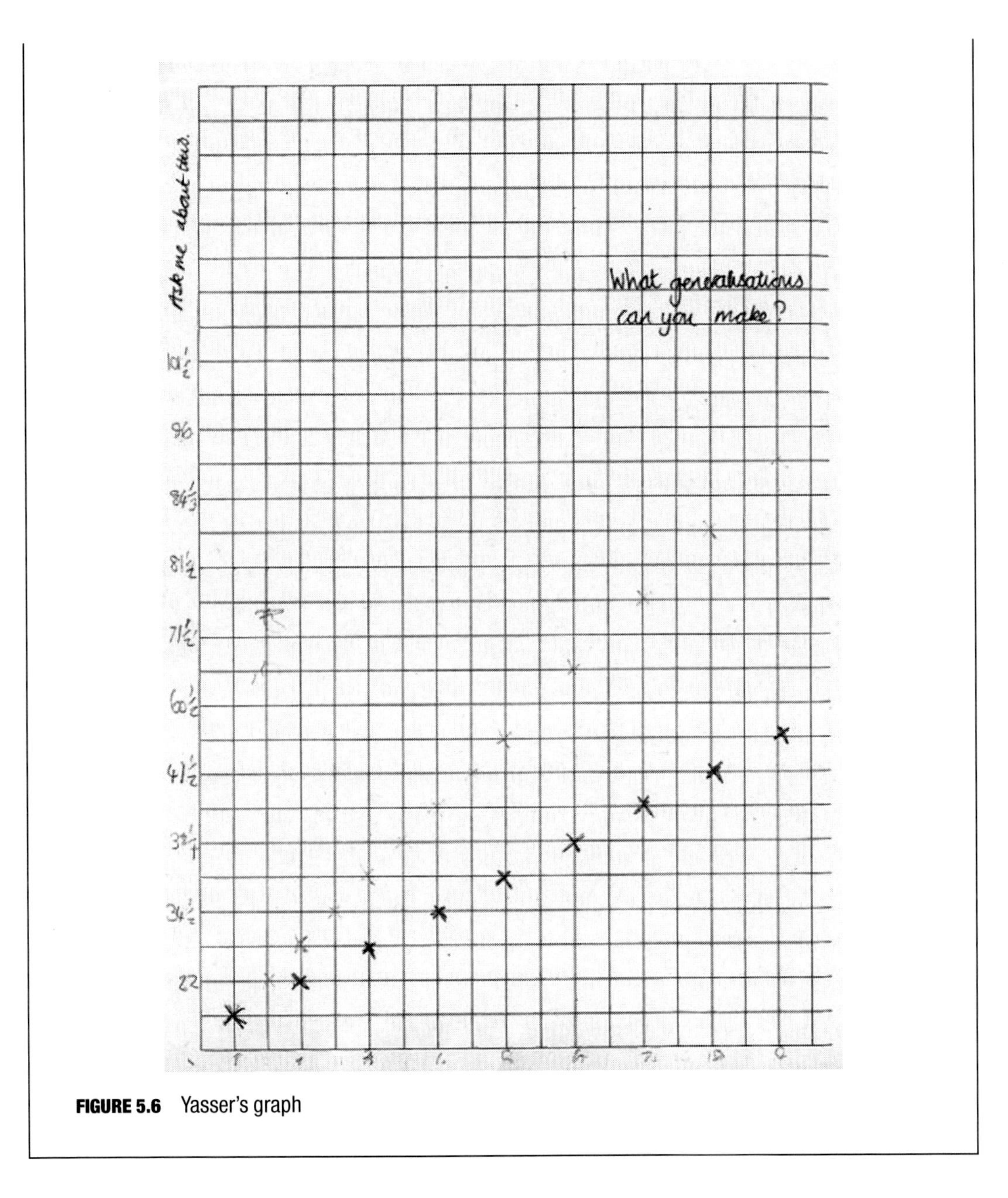

FIGURE 5.6 Yasser's graph

Evidence of NC level 2 might be a child making some suggestions about how they could find out if you can see shiny things in the dark, perhaps by drawing the curtains or by putting various shiny objects in a dark box and investigating whether you can see them. Making comparisons, such as 'I could see the mirror bit, but I couldn't see the red cube at all' is characteristic of level 2. You would also expect children to be able to say whether or not it was as they expected.

NC level 3 would be characterised by children planning systematic investigations with some help, perhaps testing out what shadows are made by various materials and grouping them accordingly. The investigation shown in Box 5.1 demonstrates many aspects of attainment at NC level 4: the child has decided on an appropriate approach to answer a question with very little support, making a series of relevant measurements and recording these in a table. Simple patterns have been identified and related to the prediction. To extend this to NC level 5 there would have needed to be an accurately drawn line graph and attempts to link the findings back to scientific knowledge and understanding, in this example, to explain why the shadow became bigger as the light source was moved further away.

Developing children's understanding

We need light to see objects; darkness is the absence of light

Young children rarely experience complete darkness and sometimes say that they can see in the dark because they are accustomed to streetlights and night-lights in their bedrooms. During the day their environment is flooded with light, so children are often unaware of the need for a light source because the light is 'just there'. Children may also think that it is possible to see a bright or shiny object in the dark.

If the classroom can be darkened, it can be demonstrated that it is more difficult to see any object unless it emits its own light. Gradually increasing the light in the room can illustrate how we need light to see. Alternatively, objects can be placed in a box with a lid and a peephole on the side. Looking through the hole reveals darkness until the lid is lifted. It can be helpful to ask children to think about their other senses, the importance of hearing and touch when they cannot see.

A visit to a mine or a cave can also be a powerful experience of darkness. For example, during a trip to the former coal mine 'Big Pit' in South Wales, children carry battery packs and wear miners' lamps as the only sources of light, and there is a very exciting moment when everyone is invited to switch their lights off!

Sources of light

The next step is to develop awareness of different sources of light. Children can think about where light comes from in the classroom or at home. We often ask children to draw different sources of light. It can be helpful to see how sources of light are depicted in picture books or works of art, and this can also encourage discussion when comparing the colour or brightness of lights. Asking children to bring in a toy that they can see in the dark is a useful starting point for discussions: some will glow in the dark, some will light with battery power and some may be reflectors that are not light sources.

Teaching visually impaired children about light can be a challenge for teachers. The RNIB suggests that feeling the warmth of light is one way of making it more accessible as a concept.

Are all things that give out light warm?
What about: luminous stickers, festival light sticks, and glow worms?

Invite children to work in groups to come up with examples of light that travels a long way and discuss them as a class. *What do the sources have in common?*. Chldren could talk in pairs to think of a very dim light and a very bright light and share their ideas with a larger group. The teacher could build on this by asking children to comment on what each other have said – *Why do you think that the TV is brighter than the torch? How could we be sure?*

Shadows

To gain a good understanding of how shadows are formed, children need to develop the concept that light travels and that it can pass through some materials but not others. A variety of experiences with making shadows is needed to understand that a shadow is created when an object stops the light from travelling and that the position of the light source affects the size and shape of the shadow. Children are usually aware of their own shadows: in school they can draw round them with chalk on the playground and can explore making different shadow shapes. Ask children about what they are seeing:

What can you tell me about your shadow?
Where does the shadow begin?
How can you change the shape of your shadow?
How do you think it is made?

To develop an understanding of the relationship between the position of the Sun, the object and the shadow, ask the children to point to their shadow with one hand and to the Sun with their other hand and to try this in various positions. This work can link with the topic of Earth and beyond (see chapter 8). It is useful to follow this up indoors, by making shadows from a light source that they can control, such as a torch, lamp or projector light. They can place two- and three-dimensional objects in front of the light and explore how to change the size and shape of the shadows. It is also a good idea to look at shadows in photographs and in pictures: *Where is the light source to create this kind of shadow?* Children can use the digital camera to take pictures of their own shadows and other shadows in the playground and to photograph shadows on various surfaces, for example the sandpit, playground or a wall.

Further exploration of shadows can be carried out with various types of material to illustrate how light can pass through some materials. Experimenting with a torch or projector light will show how light travels through transparent materials and casts a very slight shadow (because some of the light is reflected from the surface). Translucent materials form a lighter shadow and opaque materials form a darker shadow. Ask the children to present their findings to the rest of the class and try to explain what is happening. Ask them if they can think of any other examples of how light goes through different materials in different ways. Giving children time to discuss their ideas in pairs can be more fruitful than expecting a response 'cold'.

Reflections

The key concepts being developed here are that light travels and that when it hits an object it can pass through or is bounced back. When we see an object, such as a book, it is because light from the Sun or another light source is reflected from the book into our eyes. We can see light reflected on smooth flat surfaces as an image, but light from an uneven surface is scattered – reflected in all directions – and therefore no distinct image is visible. Most of the objects that we see around us scatter light from the light source.

A range of experiences of shiny objects and mirrors will help children to develop an understanding of how light can be reflected. Explore collections of shiny objects, papers, spoons, saucepans, boxes, etc. The use of torches with mirrors can demonstrate how light can 'bounce off' a mirror: children enjoy using mirrors to send light round a corner or under a table. Ask children to talk about what is happening from the point of view of the beam of light – can they tell the story of its journey?

Other illustrative activities include making kaleidoscopes and periscopes. There are obvious links with mathematical work on symmetry: some computer art programmes such as Fresco have the facility to draw pictures with a simultaneous mirror image. Kinaesthetic approaches such as mirroring a partner's movements in dance or drama are also useful.

We see things when light enters our eyes

Our eyes are the sense organs that detect the light around us, sending signals to the brain, which then interprets what we are seeing. Light enters our eyes through the pupil, which is opened or closed by the iris to control the amount of light entering, and travels through the lens to the retina at the back of the eye. The retina is made up of cells that are sensitive to light: these cells send signals along the optic nerve to the brain. In this way our eyes detect light and our brain makes sense of what we are seeing.

Primary-aged children are not required to learn about the internal structure of the eye, and drawing cross-sections of the eye is not a helpful activity as it is rather meaningless for most children. But children are often interested in how their eyes work, why some people wear glasses and why some people are blind. This is an area that needs to be discussed with sensitivity, as some of the children will wear glasses, and there may be children in the school who wear an eye patch. These children may be happy to talk about the subject as 'experts'. Most of the children will have experienced having their eyes tested by the school nurse and many will have visited an optician at some time. Ask the children to discuss the statement in groups:

> *It is easier to see something when it is close up.*

Do they agree or disagree? Invite different children to justify their ideas.

Careful observation in a mirror will reveal that the pupil of the eye gets smaller when the observer moves towards a sunny window. Children may not realise the pupil is in fact an opening that allows light into the eyeball. They might measure the amount of time it takes for the pupil to widen as the iris dilates when the classroom lights are dimmed and notice it is more difficult to see clearly until the pupil has adjusted. These experiences can be used as starting points to develop understanding of how our eyes respond to light. Children enjoy looking at optical illusions and these are a good way of demonstrating how the brain decodes what we see.

We are able to see the objects in our environment when light is reflected from them into our eyes. Children often understand the idea that light enters their eyes from an object that emits its own light such as a candle. But it can be difficult for them to conceive that light is scattered from all the objects around them.

The SPACE project research found that many children believe that we see actively with our eyes, that we just have to look carefully, and they draw pictures showing arrows coming from eyes to the object being seen (Osborne *et al.* 1990). This idea parallels that of the Greek philosopher Euclid who thought of vision as being due to some invisible 'rays' that come out of our eyes. Plato developed this idea imagining three forms of 'light': 'fire' from the eye, from the Sun, and streaming off objects; this interaction led to seeing. It was the Arab scientist Alhazen (born in Basrah, Iraq as Abu Ali Hasan Ibn al-Haithamwho, ca. 965–1039, when Europe was in the 'Dark Ages') who realised that somehow the objects must interact with light from the Sun and that this altered light would enter the eye and form images (Gregory 1981). This is not an idea that children will 'discover' and teachers will need to introduce it, judging when children have sufficient other experiences of light to make sense of the explanation.

Light can make images

A pinhole camera works in a similar way to the eyeball and can be made using a cereal box. Make a pinhole in the front, cut a window in the back and cover with a tracing paper 'screen'. Shield the screen with a 'visor' of black paper. With some experimentation, an upside-down image will be visible. Simple 'Sun prints' can be made using sugar paper. Place objects with strong shapes onto the paper and leave on a surface in strong light for up to a week. The exposed paper will fade leaving a silhouette of the object. Children could experiment with different papers and discuss how this idea is used in photography and to bleach clothes in some countries.

Colour

The science of colour is not part of the primary curriculum but as a theme can enhance children's awareness of light and colour in the environment and can provide a useful foundation for later work. Spectra or rainbows can be created in the classroom using a strong light source and a prism – a glass bowl of water can work, as can water mist and some plastics. The playing surface of a CD makes a particularly effective spectrum. Light can be 'mixed' by making colour wheels divided into the six primary and secondary colours and spinning them quickly, by mounting them on a motor, for example. If you have access to coloured lights such as stage lights, discoveries to be made include the fact that shadows will be the complementary colour to the light source (for example red light creates a green shadow) and some objects lit with coloured light will appear to change colour. Colour is a fascinating area for exploration, and has strong links with art. Activities such as colour mixing, mixing dark and light colours, and using paint colour charts to stimulate colour hunts outside are examples of cross-curricular activities. Teachers need to be aware that mixing paint colour is a different phenomenon to mixing light (see Table 5.1). Light can also be mixed 'in the eye' – artists such as Seurat made use of this phenomenon by painting coloured dots (pointillism) that merge together when viewed from a distance, so an orange hat is in fact created by a juxtaposition of red and yellow dots. A similar effect can be created using 'spray' functions in Microsoft Paint. If a computer screen is viewed with a magnifying lens images can clearly be seen to be made from dots of colours. The white page of a Word document is actually made from dots of light and the words are created by an absence of light. There are also links to be made with other areas of science, such as camouflage, the use of colours for warnings and signals in the animal kingdom.

Using ICT to teach about light

There are many opportunities for exciting uses of ICT to learn more about light. Comparing how reflective different materials are is greatly enhanced for older children if they use a data-logger to measure the amount of light that is being reflected (Figure 5.7). Children can apply their ideas about light in topics on ecosytems, using light meters to measure the amounts of light in different habitats and linking this to the plants that live there.

Hillfields Primary School in Bristol used ICT in a whole school topic on light. Children used digital cameras to capture images of different textures around the school and projected these onto a huge screen made from sheets hung up across the hall. They also experimented with shining different colour stage lights at the screen and making silhouettes with their bodies in dance (Figure 5.8) This whole body kinasthestic approach enabled children who were developing English as an additional langauge to access the topic alongside their classmates.

Perhaps you have tried making hand shadow 'rabbits', or maybe even a swan? Professional performers on YouTube videoclips might inspire you and your class to develop your ideas further!

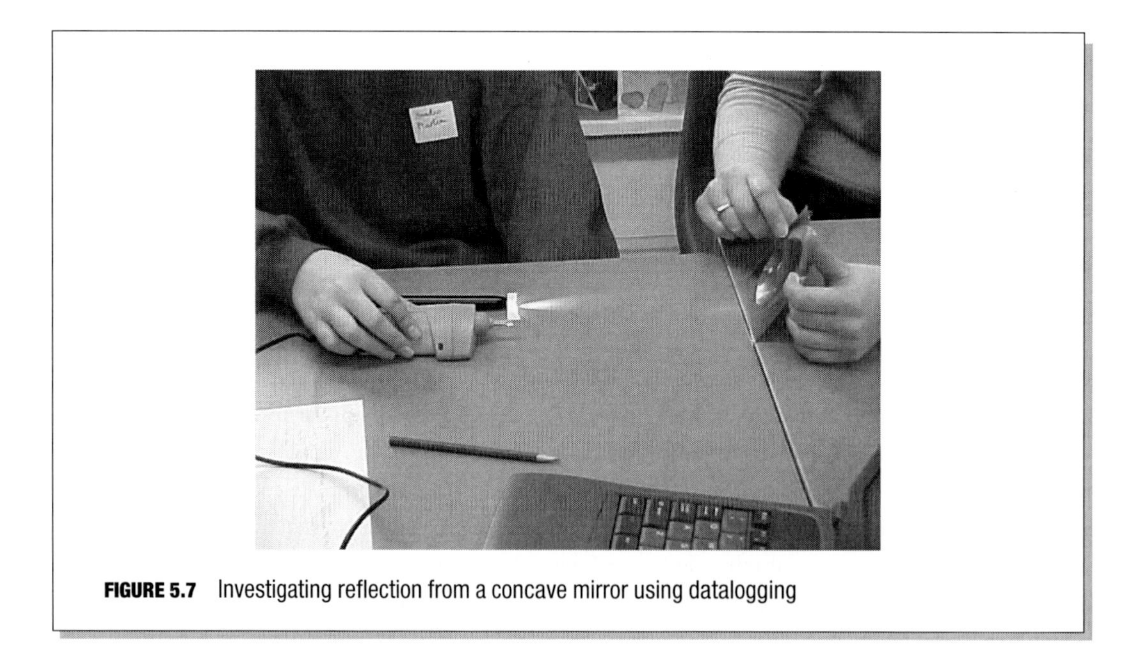

FIGURE 5.7 Investigating reflection from a concave mirror using datalogging

FIGURE 5.8 Children at Hillfields Primary School explore light through dance

Classroom management

Health and safety issues should be brought to children's attention at an early stage in any work on light. It is essential for them to know that they should never look directly at the Sun, even through coloured filters. When using magnifying glasses outside, children should be reminded not to look up at the sky. Teachers need to be alert to the possibilty that magnifying glasses could become 'burning glasses' if they focus the Sun's rays. If observing each other's eyes, children should not point or have a pencil in their hand during the activity.

It can sometimes be a problem creating sufficient darkness in the classroom for working with light. If there are no blackout curtains or blinds then spaces such as stock cupboards could be used, under careful supervision, or mini darkrooms can be created by using cardboard boxes with holes cut in them and curtains or 'flaps' to look through or shine torches through.

To collect resources cheaply, encourage parents to donate old decorations from festivals and celebrations. Mirrors can be made from bathroom mirror tiles, but need to be backed by sticking them onto cardboard, so that if they break the glass stays in place.

Summary

In this chapter we have explored different contexts for work on light, including some with a multicultural or global dimension. Analysing children's annotated drawings has shown how they provide useful insights into children's thinking, such as eliciting the common confusion between shadows and reflections, and can be used to inform summative assessments too. A range of possibilities for explorations and illustrative activities to develop children's understanding of light has been suggested.

Discussion points

1 What stories and books do you know that would provide interesting starting points for a topic on light?
2 What happens to shadows when there is more than one source of light?

Further reading

Clegg (2007), ***Getting Science:The teacher's guide to exciting and painless primary school science***: this readable book sets scientitifc knowledge about light within a discussion of cutting edge science research. It has useful sections that set out to answer specific questions such as 'Why is the sky blue?'

Farrow (1999), ***The Really Useful Science Book***: this book provides good coverage of the subject knowledge, taking it beyond what children will be taught to support teachers' background knowledge.

CHAPTER

6

Forces

Purpose of this chapter

After reading this chapter you should have:

- an understanding of how children's knowledge and understanding of forces will develop from early childhood until the beginning of secondary education
- knowledge of research into children's ideas about forces and strategies for eliciting children's understanding
- knowledge of a range of appropriate activities to teach about forces through an enquiry-based approach and whole-class interactive teaching.

Introduction

EINSTEIN, GALILEO AND NEWTON would probably feature in most people's 'top ten' scientists. They all made their name, in part, by offering explanations of how and why things move as they do; what we might call 'mechanics', or the primary curriculum topic of forces. This can be a difficult area of science to teach for two reasons. The first is that forces seem a bit abstract – we cannot see, hear, smell or touch them. The second is that some ideas associated with forces can be tricky because they seem not to fit with 'common sense'; teachers may be concerned about their own knowledge and understanding. This chapter alerts you to some of these counter-intuitive bits of science and discusses the importance of *contexts* in making forces interesting and understandable. These contexts include water-play, toys and PE. It goes on to show how children can develop an understanding of forces appropriate to various stages of primary schooling through explorations and investigations. The chapter concludes with a discussion of how whole-class interactive (and dialogic) teaching can support children's learning in this area.

Progression from the early years to the beginning of secondary school

Children will have lots of experiences of forces during their early years through playing in the bath or the play park; in fact in any situation where they are making themselves or objects move, float or fall. They may have developed some language to describe forces – push, pull, twist, turn – and the effects of forces: go, stop, start, faster, slower. Foundation Stage activities such as construction play with vehicles, water-play and play with mouldable materials will have given them appropriate first-hand knowledge of forces and their effects.

At KS1 it is time to formalise some of this understanding and for children to begin to develop the big idea of 'forces' that brings all the earlier experiences together. It is not the time, however, to set aside those contexts in which children have learned about forces. It is much better to use experiences that children have found 'naturally' relevant and motivating. This bridging between the informal learning of the Foundation Stage and the more formal learning of primary school needs to be done skilfully so children continue to see relevance and enjoyment in what they are asked to learn. We need to ensure that our teaching allows children to incorporate new ideas into their existing conceptual understanding, such as the realisation that when things speed up, slow down or change direction there is always a cause. Children should begin to distinguish between a push and a pull and recognise that forces can change the shape of some materials such as modelling clay. Always this conceptual understanding must be developed through enquiries in appropriate contexts: investigations into their own bodies and movements, vehicles moving and rolling, objects floating and sinking, toys flying and falling.

At KS2 further key concepts are introduced, and this is usually where teachers will need to ensure their own subject knowledge is secure. During this Key Stage, children may be able to understand science in new ways; they move from being rooted in the world of objects to the world of pictures and diagrams that can 'stand for' a real event. Some children will be able to think about forces as represented by numbers and measured in standard units (newtons). Some develop the capacity to understand forces on a more abstract level, posing a challenge for differentiation. The key concepts children will learn during KS1 and KS2 are summarised in Table 6.1.

TABLE 6.1 Forces: progression in key concepts

Key concepts	NC references	Teachers' background knowledge
All movement begins and ends with a force.	KS1 Sc4 2a	Whenever something starts moving, speeds up, slows down, stops or changes direction, a force is involved. Forces can also change the shape of an object – this can be seen when a pull stretches an elastic band or a push squashes some clay.
Forces are pushes and pulls.	KS1 Sc4 2b	A push, a shove, a twist, a jerk, a nudge – all these are words to describe a force – a push or a pull.
When things speed up, slow down or change direction, there is a cause.	KS1 Sc4 2c	Forces are invisible, although the causes and effects of forces can be seen.
Gravity is a force.	KS2 Sc4 2b	We experience gravity as a pull towards Earth. Gravity is a somewhat mysterious force of attraction (a pull) between all objects. Its strength depends on the masses of the objects and their distance apart. Since the Earth is a very massive object very close to us, in practice this is the only

		gravitational pull we experience. The size of the force of gravity on an object depends on its mass (the amount of 'stuff' in the object, measured in grams). A more massive object is pulled towards the Earth with a greater force. We call the size of this pull towards the Earth the object's weight (measured in newtons) – so a more massive object weighs more in Earth's gravity. If gravity changes, weight changes. Imagine you could turn a knob and turn up gravity. If you did this, you would get heavier. If you could turn down gravity you would get lighter. If you stood on the Moon, which has only one sixth of the Earth's mass and therefore one sixth of its gravitational pull, you would only weigh one sixth of your weight on Earth. However, your mass would not have changed!
Friction is a force.	KS2 Sc4 2c	Friction in solids is caused by an interaction between two surfaces. It is a force that slows objects and can also prevent them from moving. Friction increases with the speed of movement between the objects e.g. the faster a car engine runs, the greater the friction between the moving parts.
Air resistance is a special name for friction between an object and air.	KS2 Sc4 2c	Air resistance is caused by air 'rubbing' on an object moving through it. There is no air resistance on still objects in still air. Faster moving objects will experience greater air resistance (observe a dog with floppy ears with its head out of a car window – the faster the car goes, the more its ears will be pushed back). Children will begin to learn about the effects of air resistance and identify it in different contexts such as when running or cycling, and when dropping light objects such as spinners, parachutes and dandelion and sycamore seeds. Air resistance should be distinguished from wind – we can still experience air resistance cycling on a perfectly still day, although a headwind will tend to increase its effect. As objects fall they gather speed (accelerate) and the air resistance on them increases. In some situations, the air resistance (push) will come to balance their weight (pull) and the object will not fall any faster. This happens with parachutists. It does not mean parachutists float – it means that they will not accelerate past the point of balanced forces. This point is called terminal velocity.
When objects are pushed or pulled an opposing force can be felt.	KS2 Sc4 2d	When you sit in a chair, your body exerts a downward force on the chair and the chair exerts an upward force on your body in order to support you – otherwise you would fall through! These two forces are called action and reaction forces.
When objects float, forces are balanced.	KS2 Sc4 2d	Water is displaced when an object is placed in it. Water then 'pushes up' objects in it (upthrust). If the weight of the water displaced is equal to the weight of the object, it will float. In other words, the upthrust is equal to the weight of the object. Some light objects that are denser than water (e.g. a needle) can be made to float because they rest on the 'skin' of the water (surface tension).
Force is measured in newtons.	KS2 Sc4 2e	Weight is expressed in newtons (N). The weight of an object is calculated by the formula:

TABLE 6.1 (Continued)

Key concepts	NC references	Teachers' background knowledge
		(mass) × (acceleration caused by gravity). This tells us that an object will not have any weight if it is not experiencing a pull of gravity. For most people, mass and weight will mean the same thing, as we are not likely to be in situations where a distinction is necessary. It is therefore unlikely a primary-aged child will grasp the distinction between mass and weight, but a teacher should be aware that mass is a measure of the amount of matter in an object. We express this in grams and kilograms.
Forces are represented by straight arrows.	KS2 Sc4 2e	An arrow can be used to describe the size and direction of a force.
Magnetism is a force.	KS2 Sc4 2a	You may find magnetism teamed with electricity in many textbooks as they are linked by the concept of 'electromagnetic' fields. In NC science, magnets (permanent magnets, to be precise) can be found in 'Forces' at KS2 because the most visible property of such a magnet is that it can exert a push or a pull on another magnet, or can pull on anything containing iron, steel, nickel and some other rare metals. When a magnet pulls on such an object it is said to be a force of 'attraction'. Magnets have two ends or poles: north and south (strictly speaking, north-seeking and south-seeking). These are so named because the Earth is a huge magnet (it contains a spinning iron core) and all permanent magnets tend to align with its magnetic poles. The only true test of a magnet is that it will push away or repel another magnet if the two like poles are aligned: like poles repel and opposites attract.

Sources to further develop subject knowledge
Carlton and Parkinson (1994), *Physical Sciences; A Primary Teacher's Guide.*
Wenham (2005) (2nd edn), *Understanding Primary Science: Ideas, Concepts and Explanations.*

At KS3 children will move on to learn more about the relationships between speed, distance and time for moving objects, together with the idea of pressure as a force over a given surface area.

Cross-curricular planning

We have noted that it is particularly important to put any work on an abstract topic such as forces into a meaningful context that helps the teacher to teach with enthusiasm. Six contexts are identified below which might be adapted for different age groups. Suggestions for links with other curriculum subjects are made at the end of each section.

Swings and roundabouts: a visit to the play park

Children can experience different types of forces in a kinaesthetic 'whole-body' way. Many schools have on-site play equipment, or are likely to be located near a play park with access to a slide, swings, a roundabout, seesaw and climbing frame (see the classroom-management section below for guidance on risk assessment). A pre-visit discussion will help children to think in terms of pushes, pulls, starting, stopping, speeding up, slowing down and changing direction when they are on the equipment. Perhaps organise one group to play, while another group watches and get the children to describe what is happening: 'Karla is pushing the roundabout', 'Drew is sliding down', 'Nathan will fall down when he lets go'. Take some digital photographs or movies of the children and discuss these afterwards. Ask questions such as: *Can we see anyone pushing? Why did the seesaw go up and down? What did it feel like on the swing?* The topic provides opportunities for work in Design and Technology – designing and making play equipment as models or 'lifesize' with large scale construction kits (e.g 'Quadro'.) The redesign of a playspace can lead to work relating to citizenship and PSHE objectives.

Busy bodies: dance and gymnastics

This starting point also involves kinaesthetic learning. Following a similar pattern to the last example – a short preliminary talk and a follow up – children can again be involved in learning about pushes and pulls on their own bodies. Digital cameras can again be used to record the action. Working in pairs, children can cooperate to balance pushes or pulls – by leaning into each other or pulling away from each other to create body shapes and dance movements. When jumping and landing, the children can experience large and small pushes and their effects. There is even potential for talking about gripping (more friction) and slipping (less friction) in relation to appropriate shoes for gym, or when trying to hold on to a smooth bar. There is clearly potential to link this topic with PE objectives. Children could also compose and perform music to accompany dance or gym routines.

Toys

This starting point involves gathering a collection of toys that can be pushed or pulled in some way. The best way to make such a collection is to ask children to bring in toys from home – simple toys such as those for toddlers, or wind-up toys given away by burger bars in 'kids' meals' are ideal. Avoid complex or battery-operated toys as these may confuse. The toys can be displayed and played with in the class and added to over a few days. Questions such as: *How do we make the toy move? How do we make the toy stop?* can begin to elicit children's understanding. The collection can be sorted into toys that are pushed, pulled or both. Other categories might be toys that can move fast, toys that can only go slowly, toys that float, toys that fly. Designing and making toys provides a motivating context for learning across the curriculum. The project could begin with some research, e.g. KS2 children observing and interviewing KS1 children. It could then proceed with some idea-generation and trialling and conclude with manufacture of toys, marketing and evaluation.

Floating and sinking

Be prepared to get wet with this starting point, and be sure you know how to deal with slippery floors, as water will not necessarily stay in the water tray. As with the previous context, make a collection of objects on a theme – this time it could be toys that float, or things that float and sink. You could ask children to bring in groups of three items – one that will float, one that will sink and one that can float or sink. Initially, allow children to play and explore: can they make 'floaters' sink or vice versa? Introduce some challenging items such as very light objects that sink (for example paper clips); objects that are heavy but float (for example a large off-cut or log of wood); objects that are obviously very light for their size (for example a balloon); and objects that can be made to float or sink (for example, a foil tray or a lump of Plasticine that can be made into a boat). There are opportunities here to link with mathematical understanding – measurements of capacity.

Stopping and starting

Bicycles are ideal props to stimulate thinking about forces. With due care and appropriate permission from parents and the head teacher, ask some of the class to bring in bicycles to elicit a discussion about how a rider starts, stops and stays at a steady speed. You might extend this to other wheeled vehicles, perhaps by observing the reception class at play or a teacher's car as it starts and stops. This topic may be developed alongside a road-safety theme, asking *Why do we wear seatbelts? Why do we wear cycle helmets? Why does a car skid in the rain?* Another angle could be to look at air resistance on moving objects (aerodynamics). Running along with an open umbrella is a good way to demonstrate the forces involved, but may be hazardous – perhaps it is better to run with a large sheet of corrugated card or plastic. Cycling is seen as a 'green' way to get around. This assertion could form the basis of an investigation into the environmental effects of travel – carbon 'footprints', CO_2 emissions and atmospheric pollution. Children might be motivated to develop a campaign to encourage more pupils (and teachers) to cycle to school. They could also investigate the reasons why many people prefer to get in their cars.

Whose trainers are best?

This is not a suggestion that children compare designer labels, but a starting point for an investigation into friction. The work could begin with a look at a collection of shoes from a number of perspectives – their uses, materials, ways of fastening, construction – similar to a D&T 'investigative and evaluative activity' (IEA). The focus could then move to asking questions (Sc1 : 2a) about the collection, for example *What sports could they be used for? What differences are there between the design of the sole?* After the class has generated a list of questions, those that could be answered scientifically could be identified. Finally those questions that would involve investigating friction are identified and refined – perhaps rephrasing them as *Which trainers grip best on the school hall floor?* or *Will a shoe grip more if the sole is dry or wet?* Such questions would lead to the planning and carrying out of a fair-test type of scientific enquiry (see below).

Assessment for learning

Some of the above starting points – a visit to the play park, play with toys, a look at bicycles – could be considered as orientation and elicitation activities for a unit of work on forces. Elicitation can be achieved by using some appropriate techniques, which could include discussions of events suggested above, drawing and writing (plus the use of arrows to represent forces at KS2), discussion of concept cartoons (Naylor and Keogh 2000) and concept maps.

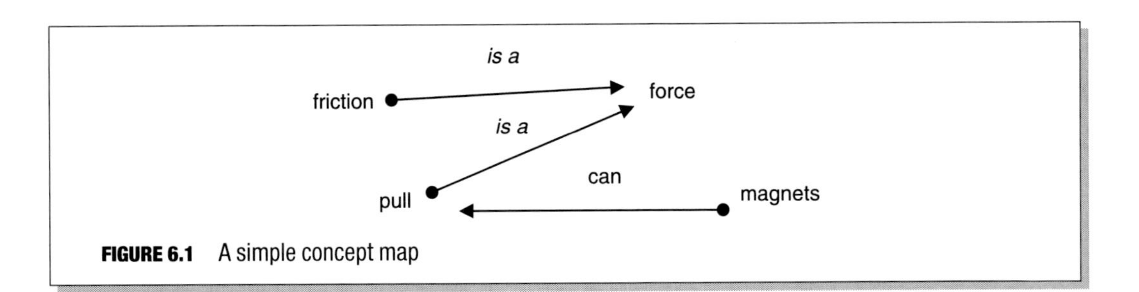

FIGURE 6.1 A simple concept map

Concept-mapping is a technique for representing knowledge diagrammatically and is a useful way for a learner to 'sort out' their ideas and record them on paper. It can therefore be used as a formative assessment tool. A concept map shows propositions: two or more concept labels linked by words that describe their relationship. The proposition 'friction is a force' would, for example, appear on a concept map as two words, friction and force, and linked by the words 'is a' (see Figure 6.1).

The map is then extended to represent the extent of understanding of an individual or group and so may contain a number of concepts linked together. In the case of forces, the words that form the basis of the map for children in KS2 might include force, *push, pull, friction, gravity, magnetism, air resistance, the Earth, slow down, speed up, change direction, change shape.* At the start of the unit of work the children's maps may be limited, but would, one hopes, show that conceptual development had occurred if the map were revisited towards the end of the topic.

Children's ideas about forces are a very well researched area of science education. Key research reports have been published by Driver *et al.* (1985), Kruger *et al.* (1991) and Russell *et al.* (1998) – the Science Processes and Concept Exploration (SPACE) project report. This body of research throws fascinating light on teachers' and children's 'alternative ideas' or 'intermediate thinking' (as the SPACE authors prefer), and some of these are outlined below.

The first alternative idea to be aware of is that 'force' can have other meanings, and it is more likely that children know these meanings than the scientific one: for example 'he forced me to do it', 'I want to join the air force', 'may the Force be with you'. Driver *et al.* (1985) identified the main types of alternative ideas a teacher is likely to encounter:

- Forces are to do with living things, for example, the object is 'fighting against' gravity.
- Constant motion requires constant force, rather than recognising an object will continue moving unless other forces (e.g. friction) slow or stop it.
- If an object is not moving there are no forces acting on it, rather than seeing balanced forces keeping something static.

Kruger *et al.* (1991) added other groups of ideas, including:

- A force is contained within a moving object, for example 'the force is in the ball' (a confusion between force and kinetic energy).

The research of Russell *et al.* (1998) added further insights into children's thinking. They found, for example, that children believed that when an object is falling there is no visible cause so children will apply their prior knowledge to develop an alternative explanation: 'the air pushed it down' or 'the wind made it fall'.

Children may not recognise cause and effect – saying for example 'it stopped because it slowed down' – or they may confuse effect with cause – 'the car made a push', 'the pedals made the bike move'. There seems to be a particular problem in recognising that a force is the cause of an object's slowing down; the push to start movement may be far more obvious than the forces causing the object to stop.

The teacher will then need to make judgements about the rest of the planned work in the light of what is found out about children's interests and understanding of the topic. The intended contexts and key concepts will need to be reviewed. The next phase of teaching is likely to involve children in investigating forces through scientific enquiry. Guidance on summative assessment is offered in the next section.

Scientific enquiry

The suggestions in this section follow on from the starting points outlined above. Again, this is merely a suggested set of enquiries that may be adapted to suit the context, ages and experience of children, together with your own teaching style and children's learning styles.

Swings and roundabouts

At the start of KS1 teachers will need to support children in developing a systematic approach to scientific enquiry, recognising that many children will not have moved on from informal exploratory play during Year R. Children working towards NC level 1 will need to be given the opportunity to describe simple features of objects and events, communicating their findings in simple ways. Within the context of the playground, this may involve identifying apparatus that can be pushed or pulled, and that goes up and down, round and round, or back and forth, through talk and drawing. Children could be encouraged to make models of such apparatus with construction kits such as Brio or Georello which reflect these types of movement. Photographs taken during the visit to the park could be sorted by the children using similar criteria and labelled accordingly. Children working towards NC level 2 might make a comparison between, say, a swing and a slide, and identify how each is used differently and what happens: 'I climbed up the slide and went down fast but on the swing I needed a push.' This kind of statement would show an understanding that a force (push) is needed to make something move, although the child does not recognise that gravity (pull) is acting on them in the case of the slide. If the children are asked to make some record of their findings, such as a drawing of how they made the apparatus move, and to report on their findings to others then they will be addressing the Sc1 2g requirement to 'communicate what happened' and the Sc1 2j requirement 'review their work and explain what they did to others'.

Busy bodies: dance and gymnastics

Begin with an open-ended question such as *How can our bodies push and pull?* A theme where children are using their own bodies can lend itself to a performance as the mode of communication for their findings. They might develop a dance or sequence that involves 'two pushes', 'a push and a pull', 'everything balanced', 'twists and rolls' or 'hard and soft pushes' (see NC physical education programme of study). Some children will be able to record their observations; for example, everyone's 'personal best' at standing long jump or the difference between a jump off one leg or two can be noted. Simple predicted correlations could be discussed, for example *Will the oldest person jump the furthest?* These kinds of enquiry would address the NC programme of study at KS1 for both Sc1 (scientific enquiry) and Sc4 (physical processes). Sc1 skills being developed here include 2b: 'using first-hand experience to answer questions', and 2d: 'recognising when a test is fair or unfair'. Sc4 statements addressed might include 2a: 'that children are able to describe the movement of familiar things', and 2c: 'they recognise that when things speed up, slow down or change direction, a force is involved'. This type of enquiry would allow children to work at NC level 1 and 2 in Sc1 by, for example, 'describing or responding appropriately to events they observe' (level 1) or 'observing and comparing events . . . describing observations using scientific vocabulary (push, pull, balance)' (level 2).

Toys

It requires a good deal of planning – ideally by the children, supported by the teacher – to carry out a scientific 'fair test' type investigation of toys rolling down a slope. The orientation phase suggested above will have given the children the opportunity to explore a collection of toys. The next stage is to raise a question to investigate. Children might initially ask *Which toy is the best?* which could become *Which toy goes the furthest?* With further guidance an *investigable* question such as *Does the size of wheels (or weight of vehicle, or shape of vehicle) affect the distance that a toy rolls?* can be developed. Rolling two or three different toy cars down a slope seems a straightforward way to answer the question but is fraught with problems as the cars may differ in all sorts of ways – weight, diameter of wheel, width of wheel, length, shape, etc. To help children control variables a construction kit can be used, such as Lego, where test vehicles can be constructed that are nearly identical, apart from the factor under investigation. Keeping the slope fairly short will ensure more manageable measurements either in centimetres or non-standard units, although very short or shallow ramps will not give enough variation in the data to compare and contrast. This is another area where the teacher will need to help children in their investigation design. Such an investigation would give children the opportunity to operate at NC levels 3 to 5. If operating at NC level 3, children would carry out the investigation with some help and would be able to see a simple pattern in their findings, for example by lining up three cars in order of distance travelled and noting that the cars are also in order from lightest to heaviest. At NC level 4, children should be able to conclude the investigation with clear statements such as 'The larger the wheel, the further the vehicle travelled.' At NC level 5, they should be relating their findings to ideas about friction and gravity through statements such as 'There is less friction on larger wheels – that is why they went further.' (Although a larger wheel has a larger arc in contact with the floor, it will rotate slower, which in turn means lower friction between the wheel and the axle. Friction between surfaces increases with speed.) The investigation could be developed through different groups investigating different factors and reporting back to each other during a plenary session.

Floating and sinking

To understand the reason why objects float or sink a number of subsidiary concepts need to be in place:

- Some light objects sink and some heavy objects float
- Water 'pushes up' objects in it (upthrust)
- Objects 'light for their size' (with a density less than water) float and objects heavy for their size (with a density greater than water) will sink in water
- Water is displaced when an object is placed in it
- If the weight of the water displaced is equal to the weight of the object it will float.

This suggests a sequence of guided investigations or illustrative activities to help children develop their thinking rather than a 'fair test' type enquiry. The teacher will need to decide on activities which best address children's level of understanding. Such activities include:

- hanging objects from elastic bands or force meters, then lowering the object in water to demonstrate that objects weigh less in water
- measuring displacement by observing levels rise on a graduated tank or measuring jug
- using 'push-meters' to investigate how much force is needed to make floating things sink – a trip to the swimming pool to conduct some investigations with inflatable toys could be much more fun!

Further suggestions for activities based on children's common ideas are made in Table 6.2.

Stopping and starting

It is sometimes good practice to link investigations to D&T activities as this will provide an opportunity for children to apply their scientific knowledge through a 'design and make assignment' (DMA) and so gain maximum benefits in learning in both subjects (Howe *et al.* 2001). Setting children a task or challenge can promote, with guidance, purposeful investigations to research a solution. Such challenges could include those described in Table 6.3.

Differentiation

One way to differentiate a task is to give children more or less independence. If children are allowed to make their own decisions about how they go about tasks, to select suitable equipment themselves, to record observations accurately and to evaluate their work, they will have the opportunity to attain a number of features of scientific enquiry at level 4. Increasing the demand in respect of 'obtaining and presenting evidence' (KS2 Sc1 2h) is another way to differentiate. In the parachute investigation described in Table 6.3(a), plotting the time taken for the parachute to fall against type of material (discrete variable) will result in a bar chart. If children are asked to investigate the area of the parachute canopy (continuous variable), however, the resulting data can be plotted in a line graph, which is an element of level 5 science. Of course children will need a

TABLE 6.2 Suggestions for questions and activities based on children's common ideas (adapted from Davies and Howe 2003)

Children's common ideas	Suggested questions and interventions
'It sinks because it's heavy/big.'	*Do all heavy things sink?* *Can you find any big things that float?*
'It floats because it's small/light.'	*Do all small/light things float?* *Can you find any small/light things that don't float?*
'It sinks because it's made of metal.'	*Do all metal things sink? (e.g. a cake tin)*
'It floats because it's made of wood.'	*Do all wooden things float?* (liquorice root *and lignum vitae* don't) *Can you find things that float that are not made of wood?*
'It floats because it's spread out.'	*What happens if we spread this Plasticine out?* (it sinks) *What can you do to make this Plasticine float?* (make it into a boat shape with sides)
'It floats because it's got air inside.'	*Will a sponge float if you squeeze it in the water?* *Do boats have air inside?* Try using a long Perspex tube filled with water to watch objects sink at different rates.

TABLE 6.3 Design and make assignments leading to learning in science

Design and make assignment (DMA)	Type of science enquiry	NC reference and learning outcome
(a) Design a parachute that will bring an egg safely to Earth.	**Fair testing:** *Which shape or material provides greatest air resistance?*	Sc4 2c Air resistance is a force that slows moving objects.
(b) Make a device that will prevent Barbie and Ken hurting themselves in a road-traffic accident.	**Identification and classification:** *What are the forces involved when a vehicle hits another object?*	Sc4 2e How to measure forces and identify the direction in which they act.
(c) Research stopping distances for cars and make full-size illustrations in the playground for wet and dry conditions.	**Reference:** *What are the forces and factors involved when a car stops suddenly, in wet and dry conditions?*	Sc4 2c Friction is a force that slows moving objects and may prevent objects from starting to move.
(d) Make a game for the school fair that uses the force of magnet attraction.	**Pattern-seeking:** *Is there a connection between the size of magnet and the distance over which it will act?*	Sc4 2a There are forces of attraction and repulsion between magnets.

number of such opportunities to perform at an appropriate level, and teacher assessment will draw on evidence from more than one investigation.

Whose trainers are best?

How do we go about answering the question *Which trainer provides most grip on the school hall floor?* The challenge arising with this investigation is that each shoe tested will vary in a number of ways. This will give children the opportunity to think creatively about how to control factors such as the size of the shoe, its mass and how a push or pull is applied and measured. Newton meters (which come in both pull and push varieties) will be required if children are to make measurements using standard units. If children have little experience of using newton meters, time will need to be spent on teaching them how to take accurate measurements (KS2 Sc1 2e–g). Goldsworthy and Holmes (1999) discuss a number of activities intended to help with this teaching. For example, they suggest asking the children to pull down on the meters to 'give me a 6 newton-pull', 'give me a little 1-newton pull'. Once the children have had practice using the meters then they will be more likely to make accurate measurements and understand what the numbers mean. Teaching points would include ensuring the scale and divisions are understood, and recognising inaccuracies can be minimised by taking a number of readings and being consistent about the point at which readings are made (for example, as the shoe begins to move). The data gained could be represented in graphical form. Such an investigation would allow children to attain NC level 4, by plotting simple graphs and by using these graphs to point out patterns in the data, for example 'The bumpier the sole of the trainer, the harder it was to pull.' They should also be able to relate this to scientific knowledge and understanding by statements such as 'There was more friction between the bumpier sole and the ground, which stopped the shoe from moving', and to suggest improvements in their investigation.

Developing children's understanding

Friction

Young children can begin to understand the concept, though they do not need to name it, for example, a Year 1 child described friction as a 'naughty force'. Children will also come to realise that there can be a 'grip' between two surfaces, such as shoes and a floor. They will notice that different surfaces might be 'grippy' or slippery. Bumpy soles may be grippy, but water will make a floor slippery.

Friction between solids is caused by an interaction of two surfaces. Imagine pushing a heavy box across the floor. A force will oppose this movement: this is friction. It is the same force that opposes the movement of a computer mouse across a mouse mat or a child along a slide. In some cases, friction will prevent movement from starting. A child may get stuck on a slide because the interaction between their coat and the dirty slide produces a frictional force equal to their weight due to gravity, so the child stays still. A clear demonstration of friction as a force between surfaces can be given by pulling the bristles of two hairbrushes against each other. The interlocking bristles *model* the microscopic unevenness of any two surfaces acting against each other.

You might let children put sand, water, talc, hand cream or cooking oil on their hands to experience the reduction of friction by lubricants. Lubricants act by filling in those uneven surfaces so small particles which do not soak in or evaporate as the surfaces get hotter tend to work better, though even large objects such as marbles, rollers and wheels can be effective since they reduce the area of contact between the surfaces.

A common idea held by children is that friction does not act on still objects. One experience that will help to challenge this is to set up a slope that can be slowly raised at one end. An object such as a coin is placed on the slope. As the slope is raised the coin will eventually slide down. Changing the material on the slope will help to show that friction can be changed to prevent or allow movement: higher angles can be reached with 'rougher' or 'stickier' surfaces. The key question is *What stops the coin from moving?* This experience can be used to make effective links with the properties of materials. (Purpose-made equipment can be purchased from suppliers such as Technology Teaching Systems, www.tts-group.co.uk.)

Arrows and their meanings

The use of arrows to represent forces is a scientific convention that needs to be understood and used by children in KS2 Statutory Assessment Tests (SATs) but is often a cause of confusion. More generally, the *representation of ideas* plays an important part in developing scientific understanding. It was Bruner (1966) who first described the three *modes of representation* with which learners need to engage before full understanding is reached. The first mode is 'enactive' where representation, and thus learning, occurs through interactions with physical objects, the second is 'iconic' (for example, the use of pictures and diagrams) and the third is 'symbolic' where representation occurs in the abstract (e.g. that forces can be described mathematically.) During KS2, when many children will be learning to represent the world iconically, we can support them in doing this by focusing their attention on the 'iconic' conventions in science. Furthermore, we have already discussed how the teacher can use children's drawings to gain insights into pupils' thinking and understanding. Consequently, teachers should help pupils to make their drawings and diagrams more scientifically accurate and complete. It is therefore interesting to note that Russell *et al.* (1998: 133) found 'very little evidence of [children] having been exposed to teaching and learning about the conventions of using arrows to represent forces'.

Arrows can actually mean many things in science, for example:

- direction of movement
- size or magnitude
- energy transfer in a food chain
- position or location of a feature.

When forces are being described, however, an arrow represents the size and direction of a push or pull (Figure 6.2).

It is very important to note at this stage that the arrow is describing the direction of the force, not necessarily the direction of movement of the object. In Figure 6.3 the dashed arrow has been used

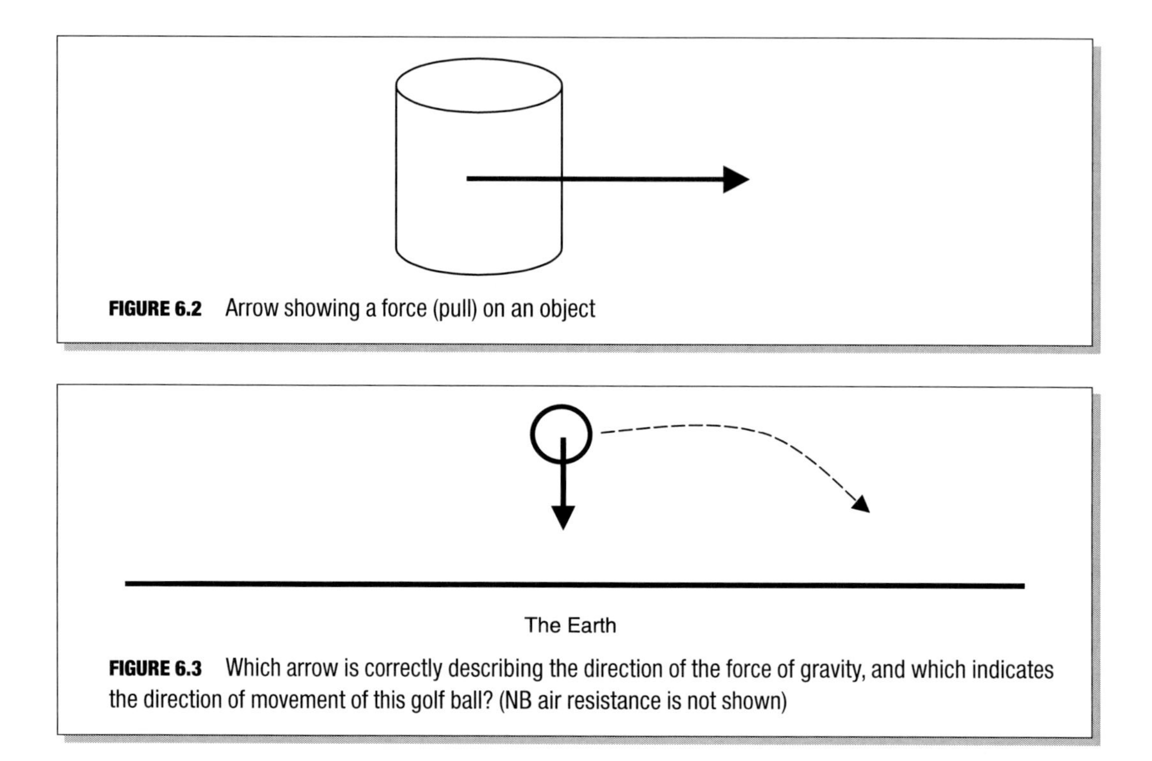

FIGURE 6.2 Arrow showing a force (pull) on an object

FIGURE 6.3 Which arrow is correctly describing the direction of the force of gravity, and which indicates the direction of movement of this golf ball? (NB air resistance is not shown)

to describe the trajectory of the fine golf shot that has just been played. It is the solid arrow that correctly describes the force of gravity acting upon the ball. (Note that the force of air resistance opposing the motion of the ball has been omitted in this example.)

Other key points to note about force arrows are these:

- Forces act in straight lines and therefore arrows need to be straight. Problems arise because forces are confused with trajectory (Figure 6.3). When England's football captain Faye White takes a free kick, she applies a push in a straight line at the moment of contact with the ball. The trajectory of the ball as it curves through the air is determined by a number of complex factors, including air resistance and spin.
- The lengths of the arrow can represent the strength of the forces. So one arrow can describe both direction and magnitude at the same time. The longer arrow represents the larger force (Figure 6.4). At primary level this will generally be a relative indication (x is bigger than y), not an absolute measure.

Using ICT to teach about forces

We have discussed above how taking photos can be a useful record of children's experiences of forces in action. If an interactive whiteboard is available the pictures can be projected and used to

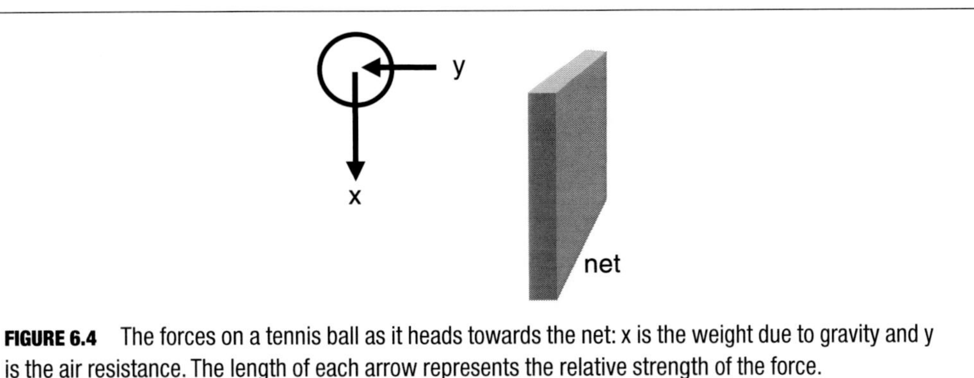

FIGURE 6.4 The forces on a tennis ball as it heads towards the net: x is the weight due to gravity and y is the air resistance. The length of each arrow represents the relative strength of the force.

promote a dialogue about the classes' understanding of pushes and pulls; annotating the photos with arrows can provide a focus for these discussions.

Video clips are a good way to capture events that happen too quickly to see with the naked eye. By using the freeze-frame and rewind functions, the behaviour of parachutes, spinners and other falling objects can observed and measured more accurately. Children could take video of sporting action – a ball being kicked, hit or thrown – and then make an accurate measurement of the trajectory of projectiles as they travel. This could lead to a pattern-seeking investigation to explore the relationship between angle of release and distance travelled.

Datalogging equipment can be used to measure the speed of a trolley rolling down a track (see 'toys' above) by connecting a 'light gate' sensor which times how long an infra-red beam is interrupted by the trolley passing through it. Data Harvest produce a digital timer which consists of a data-logger configured for using with one or two light-gates, so older children may be able to deal with the concept of acceleration as the trolley picks up speed down a slope. Children can try changing the mass of the trolley or the distance up the ramp it is let go from, and can measure stopping distances on different surfaces or the force of impact using a 'push newton meter' as part of an investigation into road safety.

Classroom management – 'whole-class interactive teaching'

There will be occasions during the teaching of a topic of forces when the teacher wishes to teach the whole class through questioning, discussion or demonstration. Whole-class interactive teaching (Muijs and Reynolds 2001) has become recognised as one effective way of teaching science, particularly when it actively involves the class and is used alongside group and individual work. It is closely linked to the idea of 'dialogic' teaching discussed in other chapters in that the teacher is seeking to value as wide a range of children's ideas as possible, helping them to reason with and test their ideas rather than favouring the 'authoritative' version at the outset, which would close down the discussion.

Interactive whole-class teaching is not a return to 'chalk and talk', where the teacher transmits information to the learner from the front of the class, nor is it a 'question and answer' session, where the teacher quizzes the children on their understanding nor even a demonstration session where the children are passive onlookers. We should see whole-class interactive teaching as an opportunity to use a range of strategies for involving every child in the social learning of the whole group. It may take place during any part of the lesson, but any decision on how much to use this strategy is likely to be based partly on the age of the children – it should not be seen as a substitute for the hands-on, experiential learning so vital to younger children. Perhaps the most important reason to use some of the strategies outlined below is that they will help to establish a culture of dialogue about scientific thinking in the classroom.

1 Provide children with a scenario to consider or a concept cartoon (Naylor and Keogh 2000) and three alternative points of view. For example, three children are watching a friend come down a playground slide. Child A says, 'I think our friend will stop at the bottom because the slide levels out.' Child B says 'I think she will stop because of the rubbing between her coat and the slide,' whilst Child C comments 'I think she will stop because the air stops her.' Ask the children to discuss with a partner the merits of each comment and what they think the explanation might be, then to share their choices and reasons with the whole group, perhaps by means of mini-whiteboards.

2 As part of a demonstration, ask children to make a prediction, for example *Will this object float or sink?* Ask them to discuss with a partner, then make a prediction by holding up their mini-whiteboard with 'float' or 'sink' written on it. Older children could make a prediction in graph form to a question such as *If we plotted 'surface area of parachute' against 'time taken to fall', what would the graph look like?*

3 Plan part of an investigation with the class using Science Investigator software (Goldsworthy *et al.* 2000a), or a similar planning format in which children have to decide on:
- a question that can be investigated (e.g. *Whose trainers are best?*, see above)
- variables to change (the independent variable) and keep the same (control)
- a prediction
- an explanation (hypothesis).

At each stage, ask the children to discuss their ideas with a partner and to record them as notes on a small white board. Then ask all groups to share their ideas by holding up the white board. The ideas are quickly collated and recorded by the teacher.

4 Ask the class to comment on data from an investigation similar to one they have conducted (see Goldsworthy *et al.* 2000b). Key questions might be:
- *What measurements have been taken?* (for example, surface type from very smooth to very rough or the distance a car rolls in centimetres)
- *What sort of graph could be made using this data?* (bar chart)
- *Can you see a pattern in the data?* (The rougher the surface . . .)

A plenary, where the whole class comes together to discuss an aspect of their work, is also an opportunity for interactive whole-class teaching and need not happen at the end of a lesson. Ofsted suggests that in successful lessons:

> Some of the most effective lessons now include a starter activity that is designed to find out what pupils already know or have learnt from previous lessons. In these lessons, the teacher also maintains a flow of questions throughout the main activity, including:
>
> *Why do you think that . . .?*
> *How do you know that . . .?*
> *What does that tell us about . . .?*
> *Can you be sure about that . . .?*
> *How can you explain that . . .?*
>
> Many of these effective lessons also include a plenary, not always at the end, when children discuss what they have done; teachers use probing questions to find out what the children have learnt and encourage them to articulate this.
>
> (Ofsted 2004: 8)

Health and safety

There are few dangers associated with forces in the primary classroom. A number of the activities suggested in this chapter involve dropping things, with obvious risk to toes. Ensure children keep away from the drop zone, perhaps by cordoning off the area with a table, or by arranging a drop into a large cardboard box, which might also protect the floor. Floating and sinking activities will inevitably lead to a wet floor; the children need to know where to find the mop and how to clear up spillages. A risk assessment should be completed by the teacher when a trip to the playground is planned. Model forms are available from teachernet.gov.uk and many local education authorities which highlight the procedures that teachers need to follow when planning a trip out. Most forms will ask five fundamental questions:

- What are the hazards to health and safety?
- What risks do they pose, and to whom?
- What is the level of risk? (What is the likelihood of an accident happening?)
- What precautions have been taken to reduce the risk?
- What will you do in the event of an accident?

To prepare answers for such questions it is usual for teachers to vist the site of the trip. A playground is likely to present some obvious hazards (tripping, falling, being hit by a swing), as is the trip there and back. Most importantly the teacher will need to be clear, when they brief other adults and children, how those risks are to be minimised by appropriate behaviour.

Summary

In this chapter we have argued that the conceptual difficulties in the topic of forces can more easily be overcome if the topic is taught through contexts that are familiar and motivating for children. A range of contextualised activities has been suggested. There is a wealth of research into children's learning of forces, from which we have identified some clear teaching sequences. Concepts that prove more difficult to grasp and the alternative ideas held by learners are well known. Some of the 'trickier' forces concepts can safely be left for specialist teachers at KS3, although primary teachers will need to have a secure understanding of these ideas in order to avoid reinforcing children's misconceptions. Perhaps the best way to ensure learning is through genuine opportunities for children to discuss their ideas during dialogue with peers and teachers.

Discussion points

1. Can you identify key concepts about forces in the following example?

   When a child learns to swim they learn to push themselves forward by pulling and pushing the water back. The more they pull the more they move, but it is hard work as the water seems to push back. They notice this too when they try to push an inflatable below the water surface and it bends in the middle but will not sink. They learn to float by using the water's upthrust, even though gravity is pulling them down. They find that a strong current or wave will push them in a different direction. If they swim with a current, they can swim faster.

2. It has been suggested that 'forces' be dropped from the primary curriculum. Do you think they should be?

Further reading

McGuigan and Hughes (1998), ***Primary Science Processes and Concept Exploration (SPACE) Project Research Report: Forces***: this is the original research report still available from Cripsat.org.uk. These reports led to the excellent Nuffield Primary Science books, which can still be found lurking in staffrooms and in university libraries.

www.fearofphysics.com: If you are a visual learner you may find *Fear of Physics* a good way to develop an understanding of forces. Children will also appreciate being able to crash vehicles together or drop elephants from great heights without hurting anyone.

CHAPTER

7

Electricity

Purpose of this chapter

After reading this chapter you should have:

- an understanding of children's development in electrical concepts from early childhood until the beginning of secondary education
- an awareness of a range of strategies for eliciting children's understanding of electricity, and for building on their ideas using illustrative activities, models and analogies
- an appreciation of a problem-based approach to teaching electricity, involving a series of progressive challenges to engage children's enquiry skills.

Introduction

ELECTRICITY IS, IN SOME SENSES, 'easy to do, hard to understand'. Children in nursery classes can join electrical components together to make a complete circuit, yet to explain what is going on within that circuit requires understanding of some very abstract concepts. This creates a problem for primary teachers: how can we help children to develop in their electrical understanding so that an electricity lesson at the end of KS2 looks qualitatively different from one in Foundation Stage, when we may be rather hazy about the concepts involved ourselves?

The answer, as in so many aspects of science teaching, lies in assessment for learning. If we can come to appreciate how children make sense of what is going on inside a circuit, whilst at the same time coming face to face with our own 'alternative frameworks', we can plan activities that challenge those understandings: do they really accord with evidence? It helps, of course, to have some neat 'tricks' – ways of making the abstract concrete, the invisible 'visible'. This is where models and analogies come in; they can help us relate phenomena we are familiar with (e.g. a bicycle chain) to those we find difficult to conceptualise (e.g. the flow of current in a circuit). Electricity is also, of course, one of the most overtly 'dangerous' science topics; children need to become aware of the hazards and know how to avoid them as part of their personal, social and health education (PSHE), citizenship or life skills education.

Progression from the early years to the beginning of secondary school

Table 7.1 summarises the progression in key electrical concepts for children in the primary age-range. However, such sequences need to be approached cautiously. Many studies (for example those undertaken by researchers in the Science Processes and Concept Exploration (SPACE) project 1989–1998) suggest that children's scientific development is non-linear: they do not always learn the same steps in the same sequence and may appear to 'regress' between periods of 'steep' learning, rendering many such prescribed lists obsolete.

Some of the things for children to 'do' (for example, make a bulb light up) could be achieved earlier, while the understanding to underpin it may develop much later. Hence this sequence could apply to children from Foundation Stage (some of the 'doing', for example, identifying things which use electricity) to KS3 (understanding of the relationship between current, voltage and resistance). A detailed understanding of series and parallel circuits does not appear until the KS3 programme of study – together with exploration of electromagnetism – but there is nothing to stop teachers in Upper KS2 approaching these topics with children.

TABLE 7.1 Progression in learning about electricity

Key concepts	NC references	Teachers' background knowledge
Electricity is a form of energy which has a wide variety of everyday uses.	KS1 Sc4 1a	Electricity (current) involves the flow of billions of tiny particles (electrons) through conducting materials (e.g. metals). This movement can be generated by converting another form of energy (e.g. chemical energy in batteries, heat energy in power stations).
We need a complete circuit to make a bulb (lamp) light up.	KS1 Sc4 1b	There needs to be a complete circuit for the electrons (electricity) that are already in the battery, wires and bulb to start moving – like a bicycle chain. The bulb has two connections (base and side) so electrons can flow through the filament, heating it until it glows.
Switches can control the flow of electricity in a circuit.	KS1 Sc4 1c KS2 Sc4 1a	A switch acts like a gate, interrupting the flow of electrons by introducing a gap in the circuit of conducting material. At low voltage, electrons do not usually flow through air, though they can 'jump' a very small gap, making a spark.
Changes to the resistance of a circuit (e.g. by altering the number or type of components or the circuit layout) will alter the flow of current.	KS2 Sc4 2b	Adding more bulbs to a series circuit increases the resistance ('difficulty of electron flow' measured in ohms) and hence reduces the current. Adding cells (batteries) increases the voltage ('push') and thus increases the current. Making a parallel circuit in which each bulb has its own supply from the battery increases the overall current, since there are more pathways through which electrons can flow.
Circuits can be represented using circuit diagrams, which can be used as a plan to construct new circuits.	KS2 Sc4 2c	Circuit diagrams are a standard way of representing circuits, using a standard set of symbols and conventions to indicate connections. They have evolved to enable people all over the world to communicate electrical information precisely.

Cross-curricular planning

It is generally a good idea in science teaching to start with a context that is familiar to children. This both provides a 'hook' upon which to hang more abstract ideas and reinforces the message that science is relevant to children's everyday lives. It also enables the teacher to make cross-curricular links that support children's learning; the most obvious of these for the topic of electricity is with D&T. Ofsted (2004) reported that 'few schools take the opportunities that exist in the NC to establish fertile links between science and design and technology', and although a more recent report (Ofsted 2008) cites 'effective cross-curricular links to literacy, numeracy, ICT and subjects such as geography', the potential for D&T links is yet to be fully realised. Using concrete examples of everyday appliances (e.g. a torch), either through disassembly or designing and making, the 'reality' of D&T can assist scientific concept formation. Most young children will have seen, and may have played with, a torch – the ability to shine a light where you want it is fascinating and seems like magic. Manufacturers have cashed in on this sense of wonder with a range of different torch styles, some based on cartoon characters and featuring various battery configurations and switch mechanisms. A collection of torches, while offering rich evaluation potential for D&T, can also be used to focus children's attention on the electrical concepts they embody:

How do you make the torch switch on?
What do you think it's got inside to make the light come out?
Can you open the torch and tell me (or draw) what it's like inside?
What are the batteries (cells) for? Why do you think some torches have more than one?
Can you make the bulb (lamp) light outside the case?
Can you use wires to make the bulb (lamp) light?
What do you think the torch has inside instead of wires to complete the circuit?
How do you think the switch works?
What does the switch do to the circuit when you press it?

See Figure 7.1 for a simple schematic drawing of the inside of a torch. Children could also sort and classify the torches, for example in order of brightness (an opportunity for data-logging in KS2). A design and make assignment (DMA) is another way of contextualising the study of electricity – why not design lighting for the bears' cave in Martin Waddell's *Can't You Sleep Little Bear?* (2001). Of course, torches and other lights are not the only electrical appliances with which children are familiar, though they are probably the simplest. A display of battery toys and other small mains appliances (not to be plugged in!) can be used for sorting activities; perhaps leading towards a Venn diagram using overlapping hoops for mains, battery and 'both' (for example a radio that can be plugged into the wall or used unplugged). You could even challenge children's categories using a 'wind-up' radio!

Many of the gadgets children use during their leisure time (computers, electronic toys, mobile phones, etc.) rely on electrical energy, so any of these could be used as a motivating starting point, but why not embed the study of electricity within education for sustainable development (ESD)? Thinking about how electricity is generated, distributed and transformed into storable sources of

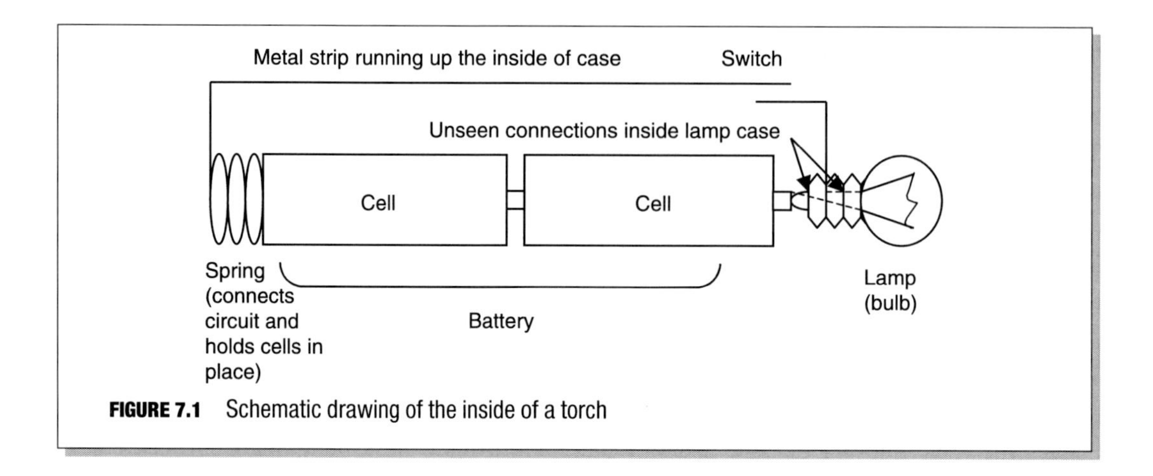

FIGURE 7.1 Schematic drawing of the inside of a torch

energy (e.g. chemical energy within batteries) could lead to a link with global warming – the burning of fossil fuels to generate electricity contributing to carbon-dioxide emissions and hence the 'greenhouse effect'. Older children could explore alternative methods of generation (wind turbines, wave and tidal harnessing, solar panels, hydroelectric and geothermal sources), evaluating the environmental impact of each. The Centre for Alternative Technology in Wales (www.cat.org.uk) has some excellent pupil resources to support this process. The disposal of batteries is also an environmental issue. Household batteries contain a variety of chemicals including heavy metals (nickel, cadmium, mercury), which can pose serious environmental health hazards. At the time of writing, 98 per cent of batteries from homes end up in landfill sites. The other 2 per cent are recycled abroad. There is currently no facility for processing them in the UK. Local campaigns to change this situation are beginning to be set up across the UK – perhaps there is one starting in your area.

Assessment for learning

For young children, talking to them and observing what they do with components whilst they 'play' with a torch or with wires, battery and bulb, is probably the most direct form of assessment for learning. Questions that could be asked in this context are suggested in the *Assessing Progress in Science* unit for KS1 (QCA 2003c):

What electrical things do you need to plug in to a socket?
What things use a battery?
What are the smallest/biggest electrical things you can think of?
What is electricity like?
Where does it come from?
Can you name and describe some of the things in front of you?
What materials are used to make the wire?
Why are there metal pieces on the bulb holder, battery and wire?
What would happen if you took out the battery/loosened the wire?

The SPACE research into children's ideas about electricity (Osborne *et al.* 1991) revealed the following common ideas about the nature of electricity:

- Children linked their ideas about electricity to the (domestic) purposes it serves ('electricity comes out of the plug').
- Electricity is seen as a semi-concrete 'substance', for example, 'Electricity comes from shops' – there was a recent television advertisement showing people buying boxes of electricity!
- It is strongly associated in children's minds with gas, heat or burning.
- Electricity is thought of as moving very fast.
- Children are generally aware of the uses and dangers of mains electricity but do not always associate it with batteries, which are seen as 'safe, because all the electricity is inside them'.

Older children can be asked to draw the circuits they have made. The QCA (2003c) suggests the following aspects to look for in KS2 children's circuits and drawings:

> Look for those children who can complete the circuit independently. Check their understanding and use of the vocabulary of 'open' and 'closed' circuits. Is each component understood to have two terminals? Can children identify the terminals on the bulb when it is not in the bulb holder . . .? Wires may be attached ambiguously, or to the wrong parts of batteries or bulbs. Do those using symbols show the correct symbols? Do they have problems fitting symbols into circuits?
>
> (QCA 2003c: 6)

Children's drawings of the circuits they have made, if analysed carefully and discussed with them afterwards, can be used to diagnose common alternative frameworks about the flow of electrical current in circuits, identified by Osborne *et al.* (1991). These are as follows.

The 'source–sink' model

In this common idea, the battery is seen as the 'source' of the electricity for the circuit, literally a store of electricity that is released down a wire and used up in the bulb (the 'sink' – think of electricity flowing down a plughole). It is easy to see where this misconception comes from: we commonly plug one flex into the wall (though it is actually composed of two or three strands of wire) and think of the electricity coming out of the socket and down into our appliance. We have electricity bills that invite us to pay for the electricity we have 'used' – surely the electricity in the battery must get used up in the same way, so they go 'flat'? The usual indicator for this concept is a drawing showing one wire connecting the battery to the bulb (a 'circuit', which clearly does not work if you try it, even though the child may have had to use two wires to make their bulb light up). Because in the source–sink model there is no need for a second wire to carry electricity back to the battery, children do not include it, introducing an inconsistency between their actions and the way they record them.

The 'clashing currents' model

Children holding this idea generally draw two wires connecting the battery and bulb, though the positioning of these on the correct terminals may be rather vague. If, however, we ask them

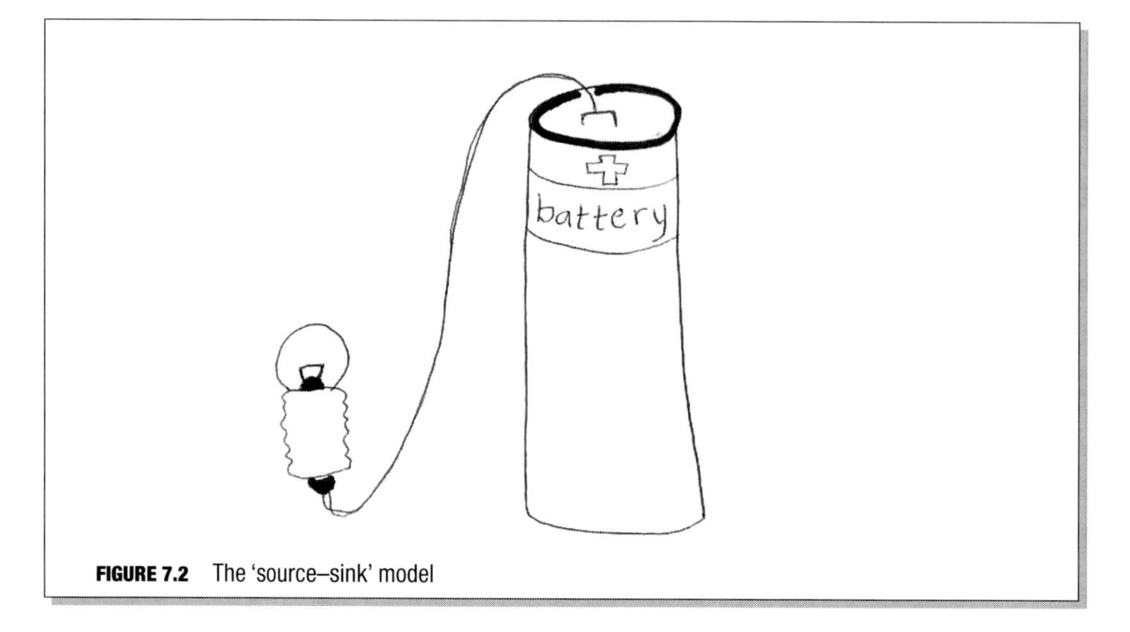

FIGURE 7.2 The 'source–sink' model

to draw arrows to show the direction of flow of electricity in the wires, they tend to draw it flowing away from the battery towards the bulb in both cases. If asked about what makes the bulb light, children with this model commonly refer to the two flows 'crashing together', likening it to the crashing together of clouds to make lightning and thunder (another alternative framework!). The clashing-currents model is really another version of the source–sink idea; children have often only added another wire because they've observed that the circuit would not work without one!

The 'consumption' model

The consumption model contains a key feature common to scientific explanations of simple circuits – that the electricity flows in the same direction all the way round the circuit. However, when asked to indicate using the size of arrows how much electricity is flowing in different parts of the circuit, children holding this model tend to draw a bigger arrow 'upstream' of the bulb – the idea underlying this is that some of the electricity is 'consumed' by the bulb. If this is your idea too, do not worry; it's an alternative framework widely held by adults as well as children (see 'Developing children's understanding' below).

Summative assessment (assessment of learning)

Many of the activities recommended by the QCA (2003c) can also be used to indicate the 'level' (in NC terms) of children's understanding. This is a different function of assessment from the elicitation discussed above, and the two should not be confused. Assigning a level to a child will never help them to improve, yet it can be a valuable indicator to a teacher for target-setting. For example, in the KS1 activity from *Assessing Progress in Science*, the following indicators are provided for making level judgements through observation and discussion:

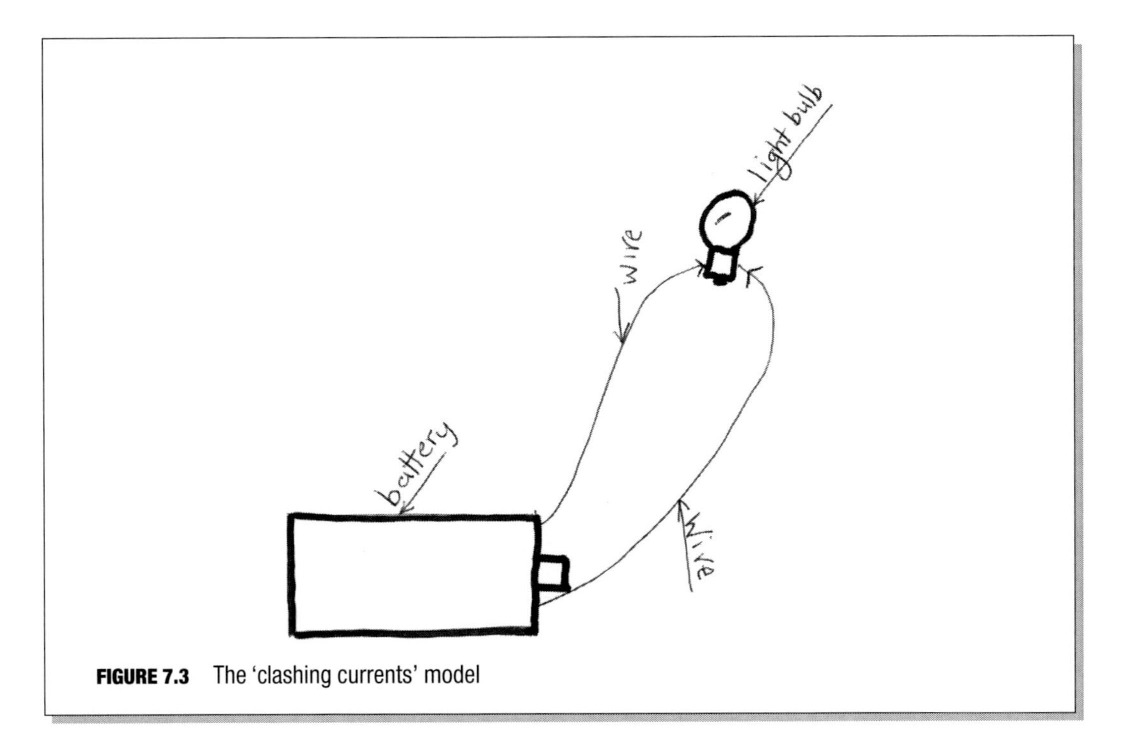

FIGURE 7.3 The 'clashing currents' model

> Level 1: Names the battery, bulb and wire. Describes what happens to the bulb when one of the wires is disconnected.
> Level 2: Makes the bulb light by connecting wires to battery. Knows that the battery makes the bulb light. Draws components in a circuit (connections not clearly shown).
> Level 3: Draws a picture of the circuit that shows a battery and knows that the circuit must be complete.

The accompanying guidance suggests probing children's understanding by exploring any differences between the drawn and 'made' circuits. This may well diagnose a source–sink or clashing-currents idea as well as help to refine the level of judgement. However, beware of 'levelling' a child on only one source of evidence: you will probably need to observe them making circuits in at least one other context (for example in disassembling a torch) to make a 'best fit' judgement using the scale above.

Similarly, in the KS2 unit 7.2 'How a switch works' (QCA 2003c), the guidance suggests the following probes of understanding before making a level judgement:

> Do children appreciate that the switch has both electrical conductors and insulators in it?
> Do they appreciate that only metal parts of the switch are attached to the wire?

The following indicators of 'levelness' are provided, which again need to be treated with caution, with judgements made on more than a single source of evidence:

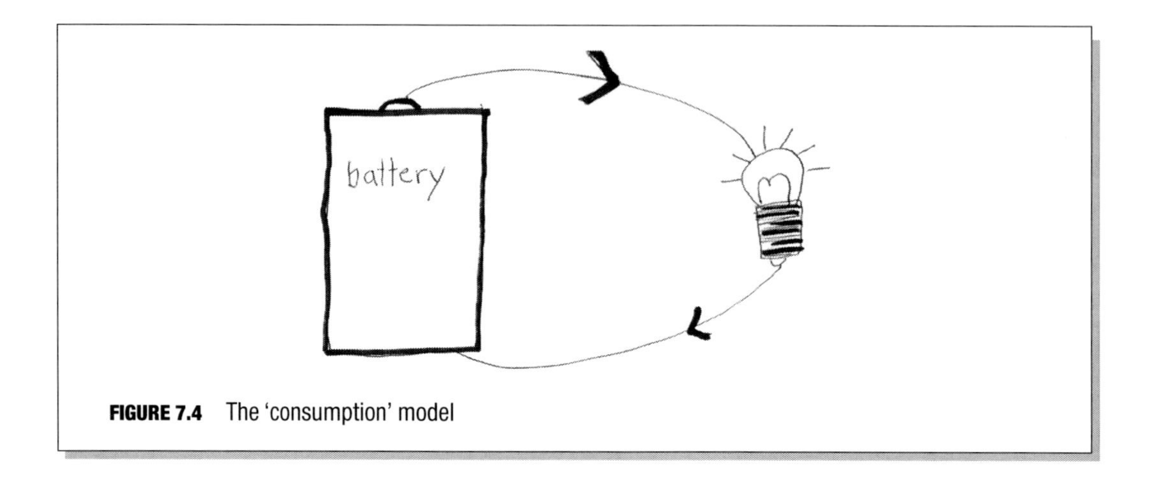

FIGURE 7.4 The 'consumption' model

NC Level 2: Assembles a circuit in which the switch turns the bulb on and off.

NC Level 3: Demonstrates that the metal parts of the home-made switch must be connected to each other for the switch to be closed.

NC Level 4: Explains that the bulb will not light when the switch is open because electricity cannot flow through the circuit.

NC Level 5: Checks the amount of current through the circuit when the switch is closed.

We cannot leave the topic of 'assessment of learning' without mentioning SATs, or 'National Curriculum tests' as the QCA now prefers to call them. It is worth noting that since 2003 the focus of tests has changed 'to focus on assessing children's understanding of the development of scientific ideas and the use of scientific evidence' (QCA 2003d). This will mean that Year 6 pupils taking the science test will need to interpret results from imaginary investigations (for example testing insulators and conductors or changing current by adding batteries and/or cells). This, however, reflects the recurring content of these tests since 1996: identifying faults (1996, 1998, 2002); interpreting circuit diagrams (all years); explaining the effects of switches at different positions in the circuit (1997); testing conductors and insulators (1998, 2001, 2002) and investigating resistance (2002).

Scientific enquiry

Although statutory tests may place more emphasis upon scientific enquiry than hitherto (see above), it is sometimes difficult to see how electricity can be taught through traditional 'fair test'-type science investigations. To do so seems at times somewhat contrived; many of children's early experiences of electrical components seem to fall under the general heading of 'exploration' – playing around to see what will happen. Some of the activities we use to develop understanding are really 'illustrative' rather than enquiry-led. Later on there tends to be more of a problem-solving approach (*Can you put in a switch to control both bulbs?*) and increasing links with D&T (for example the QCA/DfEE 1998 units 4c 'torches', 4d 'alarms' and 4e 'lighting up'). Whilst there are some 'solid investigations' in Year 6 (for example investigating the brightness of a bulb in various circuit arrangements) these tend to be the exception rather than the norm. Is this a problem?

Fear not! This mixed approach to teaching electricity is well supported by both research and inspection evidence. The AKSIS project found a number of different types of scientific enquiry appropriate to developing children's conceptual and procedural understanding in science, including 'exploration', 'problem-solving' and 'technology' (Goldsworthy *et al.* 2000a). Ofsted (2008: 8) advocates an approach 'focused on problem solving and scientific enquiry, and on developing pupils' understanding, rather than just transmitting knowledge'. The broad approach we advocate is to construct a whole-school teaching and learning sequence for electricity around a series of 'challenges' linked to the National Scheme of Work. These are supplemented with further suggestions from *Assessing Progress in Science* (QCA 2003c).

Unit 2F, using electricity

Activities prior to the challenges (see 'Assessment for learning' above):

- identifying and grouping electrical appliances around the home, classroom and school
- looking at battery appliances, disassembly/reassembly of a torch
- discussing safety issues.

Challenge 1: Can you make the bulb light or the buzzer sound?

Resources

A range of batteries/cells, matched bulbs/lamps and buzzers. Lengths of insulated wire with bared ends. No bulb-holders at this stage, since it is important for children to discover both terminals of the bulb. You may wish to use crocodile clips if children find connections difficult.

Children should draw a working circuit and annotate it, explaining the purpose of different parts (for example that the battery is to 'push' or 'drive' current around the circuit). Introduce vocabulary: 'cell' (a single 1.5 volt 'battery' – strictly speaking a battery is more than one of these, like a battery of guns), 'lamp' (the 'bulb' is actually the glass part – the whole component is called a lamp), 'wire', 'connection'. Find as many ways as possible to break the circuit in preparation for Challenge 2.

Challenge 2: Can you find the fault in the circuit? Can you make a fault?

Resources

Completed circuit, including bulb-holder or buzzer.

The fault can be:

- ends of wire not bared
- bulb/lamp not screwed in properly
- 'blown' bulb
- 'flat' battery/cell
- two cells opposing each other
- buzzer wrong way around, etc.

Challenge 3: Can you make something with your circuit? (for example a house with light, warning device, quiz board, novelty greetings card, steady-hand game)

Resources

As for Challenge 1, plus card, foil, sellotape.

This is a good example of a D&T activity used to apply children's understanding of circuits at the end of a unit (disassembling a torch is a way to use D&T for elicitation at the beginning). Illustrations and instructions for each of these 'toys' can be found in schemes such as *Nuffield Primary Science* (1993), *Collins Primary Science* (Howe 1990) and *New Star Science* (Feasey *et al.* 2000), together with D&T resources such as *Nuffield Primary Solutions for Design and Technology* (Barlex 2001). Each requires differing levels of scientific understanding (for example most incorporate some form of switch) and varying degrees of D&T capability.

Unit 4F, circuits and conductors

Activities prior to the challenges:

- Discussion: *Are all cells/batteries the same? What are the main differences between them?*
- Look at a mains plug and identify the live and neutral wires. Discuss the purpose of the earth wire (if there is a fault the electricity will flow to the earth rather than through you).
- Look carefully at a light bulb/lamp, and identify the filament and the two connections needing to be made to the circuit.

Challenge 4: Can you predict which of these circuits will work?

Resources

Drawings of circuits, some with only one wire, some with both wires at same end of cell, or same contact on bulb, some with open switches. Equipment as for Challenge 1 to test out predictions.

As an alternative to building the circuits, children could model them using an ICT simulation. *Yenka Basic Circuits* is a free download from www.yenka.com and enables children to put components together on screen, then test out their circuits. It could be used with any of the subsequent challenges, but remember that computer simulation is no substitute for hands-on experience.

Challenge 5: Can you make a circuit to test whether materials conduct electricity?

Resources

As for Challenge 1, plus a range of items/materials from around the classroom to test.

Introduce formal vocabulary: open, closed, terminal, electrical insulator, electrical conductor. This could be followed by a session identifying conductors and insulators in electrical fittings (e.g. plugs, cable, etc.). This challenge relates closely to *Assessing Progress in Science* unit 5.5 (QCA 2003c), which suggests that children write a plan for the activity and provides the following guidance on turning it into a 'fair test' investigation and assessing children's enquiry skills through it:

> Before they write their plans, encourage children to make predictions such as an ordering of the materials from the 'best' to the 'worst' conductor. Encourage them to describe the evidence they will look for to support or challenge their predictions. Look for children's questions which are framed with both an independent and a dependent variable. Some questions may be framed with only a dependent variable (DV) (for example 'does the bulb light?') while some questions may not be expressed in a testable form. Identify which children are aware of the independent variable (IV) (kind of material) in this investigation. Do they think of results as data that can be used as evidence in support of an idea? Or are they 'testing to confirm' their belief? Do any children reach a generalised understanding of metals as conductors? Do any move away from descriptions of the outcome in absolute terms to more comparative descriptions?

Challenge 6: Can you make a working switch?

Resources

A range of commercial and 'home-made' switches to provide ideas. Equipment as for Challenge 1 to test the switch.

Children could incorporate their switch into their working models (see Challenge 3 above), providing an effective link between science and D&T units of work. Detailed guidance (including sample lesson plans) on combining this unit with D&T units 4c 'torches' and 4e 'lighting it up' is due to be published by the QCA. There is also a very close link with the *Nuffield Primary Solutions* unit 'What sort of light will work for you' (Davies 2001), available at www.primarydandt.org/data/files/light_col-1848.pdf. There is also the option of controlling these models from the computer. Flowol 2 software can be used to simulate switching on and off different technological applications (e.g. traffic lights) with or without an actual model present.

Unit 6G, changing circuits

Challenge 7: How many ways can you find to change the brightness of a lamp or the speed of a motor? (for example, by changing number or type of battery, or number or rating of lamps)

Resources

As for Challenge 1, plus motor, different-rated lamps, ammeter to measure current.

This challenge links closely with *Assessing Progress in Science* unit 5.6 (QCA 2003c), which makes the following suggestions for probing questions to ask during the activity:

> *Can you think of some reasons why the brightness of a bulb in a circuit might vary?*
> *Does the position of the cell or battery in a circuit make any difference?*
> *What difference does the number of cells in a circuit make?*
> *Does the number of bulbs make a difference?*
> *Does the number of other components such as buzzers make a difference?*
> *Does the size of cell or kind of bulb make a difference?*

Some children will know that increasing the number of bulbs in a circuit has the effect of making each bulb individually less bright. Some may assume a difference in the brightness of two bulbs in the same circuit (indications of a *consumption model*, see above). Children may be aware of the effect of increasing the number of batteries but may be unsure about polarity (the way round you put the cells in series).

Challenge 8: Can you find two different ways of lighting two lamps in one circuit?

Resources

As for Challenge 1, plus bulb-holders, crocodile clip leads.

This is an introduction to parallel and series circuits. Children can be shown how to record their circuits as diagrams with conventional symbols (see Figure 7.5). They could relate this to discussing commercial circuit diagrams using examples from the home.

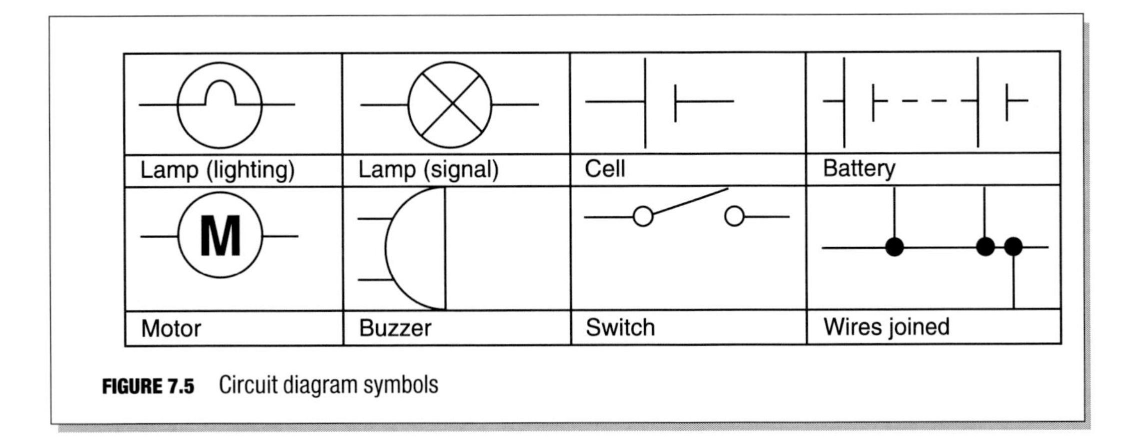

FIGURE 7.5 Circuit diagram symbols

Challenge 9: What will be the effect on current of changing thickness, length or material of wire?

Resources

As for Challenge 1, plus resistance wire (tungsten) in various gauges, crocodile clips, example of 'dimmer switch', ammeter. Use pencil lead to make dimmer switch.

This is a fair-test investigation and can be recorded in tables and charts. A particle model of electricity may be necessary to explain the findings (see below).

Challenge 10: Can you control two lamps each with its own switch? What about one lamp using either of two switches? Any other combinations?

Resources

As for Challenge 1, plus switches, crocodile clips, bulb-holders to rearrange circuits quickly.

This is a classic problem-solving activity, and children can have great fun considering the circuit needed for, say, a stair light that needs to be switched from either end. Increasing the complexity of the scenario will provide extension and challenge for higher attainers in this area and will develop creative-thinking skills. Again, control software such as Flowol 2 can enhance this activity, with or without actual circuits to control.

Developing children's understanding

Of course, any of the above challenges can be used to develop children's understanding of electricity but, as we mentioned in the introduction and elicitation sections, there are some particular concepts and models that children need to develop to make sense of what is going on inside a circuit. We as teachers need to be pretty sure of our grasp of these concepts in order to move children forward, even if we do not actually 'teach' the whole story to them. Summers *et al.* (1997) argue that teachers and older children need a particle model of electric current to understand what is going on at a microscopic level in a circuit; this is the 'big idea' that links the topic of electricity to that of materials. The particles in question are called electrons, which scientists believe are 'charged' bits of every atom and molecule of every substance. Electricity is essentially the movement of electrons from one place to another – even 'static' electricity involves transfer of electrons from one surface (e.g. a jumper) to another (e.g. a balloon), so that the charge is separated. A neat trick to show the effect of such charge separation is to hold a rubbed balloon near a stream of water. The water bends towards the balloon because of the attraction of opposite charges (the negatively charged extra electrons on the balloon 'pulling' the positively charged bits of the water molecules, if you want to know!).

A combination of hands-on experience and dialogue is a powerful way of helping children to reflect on and restructure their pre-existing ideas about electricity. For example, if a child has successfully assembled a circuit to make a bulb light, yet draws a 'source-sink' model (see above) an adult can ask questions which help to create 'cognitive dissonance' between the child's underlying concept and the evidence before them, e.g.: *How many wires did you need? Where do they have to join on to? Have you made a circle/loop? Are there any differences between the circuit you've made and what you've drawn? Can you make what you've drawn and show me how it works?* This is adopting an *interactive-authoritative* approach (Mortimer and Scott 2003), in which the accepted scientific version – that a complete circuit is needed – is being introduced alongside discussion of the child's own ideas. Similarly, for children drawing a 'clashing currents' model (see above), the introduction of a second bulb into the circuit can lead to some 'sustained shared thinking' (Sylva *et al.* 2004) through appropriate questioning: *Which way do you think the electricity is flowing to this bulb? What about the other bulb? What do you think is happening in the wire between the two bulbs?* Whilst not actually 'disproving' the clashing currents model, this discussion can raise uncertainties in the child's mind when they realise that electricity would need to be travelling in both directions at once in the wire between the bulbs! The introduction of a second bulb in the circuit (ideally of the same rating so that it gives the same brightness) can also challenge the 'consumption' model (see above). The dialogue on this occasion might progress something like this:

Adult: Which bulb do you think is getting the electricity first?
Child: This one. (points to the one nearest the positive terminal of the battery)
Adult: Tell me what you think is happening to the electricity as it passes through this bulb.
Child: Some of it gets used up so there's less for the other one.
Adult: Why do you think the other bulb is just as bright?
Child: Maybe it needs less electricity to work than the other one.
Adult: What if we swapped the bulbs round? How brightly do you think each bulb would glow then?

Once the child has realised that the bulbs are the same brightness whichever order they occur in the circuit, they may have their consumption model challenged, but the 'scientific' alternative – that there is the same electric current all the way around a series circuit (which could be verified by older children using an ammeter to measure the current at different points) – may still make no sense to them. At this point it be appropriate to introduce an *analogy* to help them visualise what's happening inside the wires. An analogy is a way of linking an idea or example from a different field, one which may be more familiar to the children, such as the flow of water through pipes. Powerful learning tools as they are, all analogies carry a health warning. De Boo and Asoko (2001) remind us that children may not be familiar with the 'domain' from which the analogy is drawn. It is not much use likening an electric circuit to a central heating system unless you have a class full of plumbers' children! Children may remember the event but not what it represents: 'Remember when Miss brought a bicycle into the science lesson?' Irrelevant or misleading features may be incorporated into the new way of thinking; in other words children often take analogies too literally or too far, and they can then become a barrier to further learning. With these cautions in mind, let us consider a couple of analogies for electric circuits and their potential for challenging the common alternative frameworks identified by Osborne *et al.* (1991, see above). Before selecting an analogy for use in your own teaching, ask yourself the following questions:

- Is it within children's experience?
- What do the components represent?
- What is not represented?
- What misconceptions does it challenge?
- What misconceptions might it reinforce?
- What are the other possible dangers of this analogy?

The rope (or hoop) analogy (see Figure 7.6)

Join two ends of a piece of rope to make a loop large enough for your class (or a group) to hold while standing in a circle. This represents the 'electricity' (strictly speaking the electric charge carried by electrons) that is already present within the wire, and that starts to flow once the circuit is connected up to a source of energy. Most children hold the rope loosely, palm up, allowing it to slip through their fingers. One child, representing the 'cell' – you could have more than one representing a battery – passes the rope through their hands so that it moves around the circuit. Alternatively, a small group of say four children could hold a PE hoop, which has the advantage that it is easier to hold loosely and therefore less tempting for everyone to become the battery, which could then be confusing. This makes the point that the cell/battery gives the 'electricity that's already there' a 'push/pull' to get it moving around the circuit (strictly speaking it gives energy to the electric charge to produce a current or flow). One or more children can now grip the rope lightly (avoid rope burns) to represent components that place a 'load' on the circuit (e.g. lamps, buzzers, motors). They do not 'use up' the electric current – there's still just as much rope after it has passed through their fingers as before – but they do take energy from it (represented by the warming of their hands) because they 'resist' the flow. So we have within this analogy both a challenge to the source–sink,

FIGURE 7.6 The rope (or hoop) analogy

clashing-currents and consumption models, together with an introduction to the key electrical concepts of charge, voltage (the 'strength' of the cell/battery in 'pushing/pulling' the charge around the circuit), current (the flow of charge) and resistance. Use your judgement and the age of children to decide how many (if any) of these terms to introduce.

The bicycle chain analogy (see Figure 7.7)

This is very similar to the rope analogy, though it is less kinaesthetic since only one person at a time can operate it. It introduces the notion of particles within the circuit so is probably more appropriate for older children. Turn a bicycle upside down (on a table if necessary for children to see) and rotate the pedals: these represent the cell/battery, giving energy to the charge (chain) to flow around the circuit. You can liken the individual links of the chain to free electrons moving from atom to atom, though this may be pushing the analogy a bit far (the electrons are not actually joined together). The rear axle and wheel represent the load (lamp, buzzer or motor) and you can increase the resistance by applying the rear brake gently. This can be used to introduce the relationship between voltage, current and resistance: the more resistance, the less current (slower movement of chain) given that the voltage (push on the pedals) remains the same. You can also talk about how the electric current (movement of charged electrons) transfers or 'carries' energy from

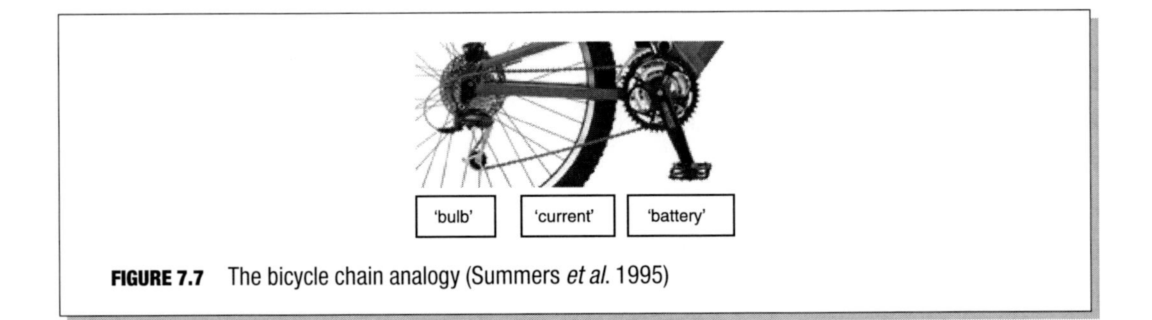

FIGURE 7.7 The bicycle chain analogy (Summers *et al.* 1995)

the cell/battery (pedals) to the lamp/buzzer/ motor (rear wheel), though this may be beyond the conceptual development of all but the highest attaining Year 6 pupils (it is certainly beyond the scope of the NC for science at KS2!)

Using ICT to teach about electricity

The most useful ICT applications for helping children develop their understanding of electrical circuits are probably modelling and simulation programmes, such as *Yenka Basic Circuits* (see above). This free download can be used with an IWB, so that children can come to the board, construct and manipulate circuits for different purposes, as well as monitoring the simulated current and voltage readings at different points in the circuit. Most simulations tend to focus on fairly low level activities that could be done more effectively using real materials – such as filling the gap in a circuit with conductors and insulators – though the BBC 'bitesize' electricity activities do include some opportunities to experiment with different numbers of cells and bulbs to investigate the effects (www.bbc.co.uk/schools/ks2bitesize/science/physical_processes.shtml).

Children in one North Somerset primary school used a digital camera to record their investigation into different ways of making bulbs brighter or dimmer in electrical circuits. They photographed each assembled circuit and imported the images into Powerpoint with captions to communicate their findings to the rest of the class. For example, Neesha, Jasmin and Aphra discovered that the physical size of the cells they were using made almost no difference to the brightness of the bulb. This led them to question why cells come in different sizes: does it make a difference to how long they last? A subsequent investigation – though one rather wasteful of resources so not carried out by the three girls – could be to conduct trials of different sizes and makes of cells to see how long each would keep a lamp alight, perhaps to test the advertising claims of a well-known expensive brand of battery! A datalogger with a light sensor could be used to monitor the decay in brightness of the lamp in each circuit, producing a number of line graphs for direct comparison. This could lead to a challenging discussion about what makes a battery go 'flat'; is it that it has 'run out of electricity'? Referring back to the dialogue section above, the teacher could introduce the idea that the chemical energy stored in the battery had all been changed into electrical energy – and subsequently light and heat – as an alternative explanation. Data loggers can also be used to monitor light levels in classrooms. Children could devise a way to investigate the amount of time that lights and other appliances are switched on or left on unnecessarily. They could even investigate how much electricity is used by ICT hardware and consider ways to reduce the school's electricity bill. Energy use is one of the key environmental topics that schools are asked to investigate to achieve 'Eco-School' status (www.eco-schools.org.uk): Eco-Schools report that some schools will spend four times more per pupil on energy than similar schools in the same region. The difference is often to do with how effectively schools manage their energy use. Surveys show that, through simple low-cost and no-cost measures, schools can reduce their fuel bills by up to 10 per cent.

Classroom management

One of the greatest barriers to effective teaching of electricity is resourcing; 'flat' batteries, 'blown' bulbs and loose connections can bedevil the most carefully planned of lessons. Our recommendation is to buy the old-fashioned 4.5 v bicycle light batteries (they are genuinely batteries consisting of three cells joined together), which have two copper strips (terminals) projecting from the top to facilitate easy connections. Although they are relatively expensive, these have the additional advantages of being relatively long- lasting, and of 'driving' 3.5 v bulbs quite 'hard' so they are very bright. When you start making circuits with children it is probably best to avoid crocodile clip leads and bulb-holders, lest the children come to believe that there is something magic in these components that makes the circuit work. They need to find the two terminal connections to a lamp themselves, before you introduce bulb-holders to facilitate easy connections, particularly if using crocodile clips. Older children will be able to make more permanent connections by using wire strippers to bare the ends of wire which can then be screwed into the bulb-holder terminals (so pliers/wire strippers and mini screwdrivers become very useful). Organise all your components into easy-access open trays, so children can collect and return the pieces they need, and encourage them to dispose of non-working bits rather than putting them back for someone else to struggle with. You may need to check the numbers of 'attractive' components such as motors, counting them in at the end of each lesson.

Effective teaching of electricity – as of many other areas of science – depends upon the following factors (Summers *et al.* 1997):

- controlling the scope of the session by restricting teaching to those aspects of subject knowledge with which you feel comfortable (for example not pushing analogies too far)
- controlling the content (try not to cover too much)
- getting the right mix between demonstration, explanation, exploration and investigation
- conceptual focus (trying to deal with only one concept per lesson)
- progressive development of ideas (see Table 7.1)
- use of visual aids (see analogies above)
- using a variety of approaches and contexts (see starting points above)
- linking experiences and discussion closely

- making new ideas relevant
- timing (making time for a plenary to discuss findings and new learning).

We also need to consider issues such as grouping (whole-class introduction and plenary, individual or paired practical activities), resourcing and health and safety. Electricity is one of the most overtly 'dangerous' of science topics, and it is worth starting each unit of work with a reminder of some basic rules for keeping safe (with the support of a video or DVD if appropriate). Children tend to know that electricity is dangerous; in discussion they might suggest that it can give a shock or kill. While they may know not to touch electrical appliances with wet hands, the dangers of long cables or pylons (e.g. when kite-flying) may be less familiar. Below are some safety tips for teachers to consider in planning a unit of work:

- Never use mains electricity (the types of power supply used in secondary science laboratories are not appropriate for primary).
- Never use rechargeable batteries (if 'short-circuited' – connected in a circuit without any other components – they may become so hot they burst into flames!).
- Check bulb voltage ratings (if you connect a 1.5 v lamp to a 4.5 v battery it will become very hot and not last long).
- Do not use a mains plug as part of a display (it may be too tempting for children to plug into a socket).
- Any mains electrical appliance brought in (e.g. a hair dryer) needs to be checked for electrical safety by a qualified person – usually the school premises officer.
- Never cut open batteries (they contain chemicals which may irritate skin or eyes).
- 'Button' batteries could be demonstrated but are not suitable for use by small children (swallowing hazard).
- Dispose of batteries carefully and recycle them if possible.

Further safety information can be found in *Be Safe!* (ASE 2001). There is a danger of making children so nervous about electricity that they refuse to engage in practical activities, so you may need to reassure them at the beginning that the equipment is safe to use.

Summary

In this chapter we have considered some of the main conceptual and practical barriers to teaching about electricity effectively. We have examined some common alternative frameworks held by children and the assessment-for-learning techniques we can use to elicit them. We have suggested some meaningful, everyday contexts through which children can be introduced to this topic, promoting the potential for links with D&T by using an everyday piece of technology such as a torch. We have considered the vexed question of progression in electrical skills and understanding, proposing a progressive sequence of 'challenges' to move children's conceptual and procedural development forward. We have explored the potential for making some of the abstract and difficult electrical concepts more concrete for children using a combination of practical activities, dialogic teaching and the use of analogies, whist being aware of some of the potential pitfalls in this style of teaching. Finally we have given some thought to appropriate uses of ICT and the safe organisation of classroom resources, to make our teaching of this topic as enjoyable and trouble-free as possible.

Discussion points

1. What are the main issues for resourcing practical electricity work? How can they be overcome?
2. What role is there for the use of analogies to help children understand electric circuits? What might be some of the dangers of this approach?

Further reading

Summers *et al.* (1997), *Teaching Electricity Effectively: A Research-based Guide for Primary Science*: this book is based on a research project to support primary teachers' understanding of electric circuits and help them to make effective use of models and analogies in their teaching.

CHAPTER

8

The Earth and beyond

Purpose of this chapter

After reading this chapter you should have:

- an overview of progression in the main concepts in relation to the relative movement of Earth, Sun and Moon
- an understanding of commonly held alternative frameworks in explaining night and day, movement of shadows, seasons and phases of the Moon
- confidence to use a range of illustrative activities, websites and enquiry activities to help move children's 'Earth and beyond' learning forward

Introduction

SHORT OF CHARTERING a spacecraft (which may one day become possible – watch this space!) it is very difficult for us to observe the ways in which the Earth, Sun and Moon move in relation to each other to give us day and night, seasons and lunar phases – the 'big ideas' in this topic. This is hardly surprising: most people believed that the Earth was flat and at the centre of the universe until the end of the 16th century, when global circumnavigation and Copernicus's observations of planetary motion challenged science and church teaching. A few decades later, Galileo famously got into trouble with the Pope for suggesting that his telescope observations supported Copernicus's ideas. It is very difficult to move away conceptually from our position on the surface of the Earth and to see it as part of a bigger system, and Piaget's observations of young children's 'egocentrism' (1929) would suggest that they may find this even harder than adults. We need as many models and kinaesthetic experiences as possible to help us envisage the three-dimensional movement of the solar system.

However, do not let this put you off teaching about the Earth and beyond: it is an extremely motivating topic that appeals to children of all ages, and a great deal can be done through various kinds of scientific enquiry – using secondary sources, illustrative activities, modelling, pattern-seeking and reference. You should find that your classroom rapidly becomes a rich treasure trove of astronomical charts, models of spacecraft and papier-mâché 'planets' hanging from the ceiling as children become enthused and fascinated by the topic. There are a number of ongoing space exploration missions that will make the news in the coming years, including a proposed return to the Moon for the first time since 1972 and possible future human travel to Mars. Our knowledge and understanding of the solar system and deep space are continually expanded, which is one reason why this topic is so captivating. It is almost impossible to avoid moving well outside (or beyond) the official curriculum, but try to ensure you devote enough time to tackling the 'tricky' ideas so that children do not emerge from their study confused, or with alternative frameworks reinforced.

Progression from the early years to the beginning of secondary school

Because the Earth and beyond does not feature in the NC for England until KS2, we could be forgiven for thinking that this topic is not applicable to children younger than 7. However, do children only start gazing up into the sky as they leave KS1? Surely the concept of day and night is highly relevant to the youngest of nursery children, who may count time to a waited-for event in 'sleeps'. Our whole notion of passing time is so closely related to the periods of rotation and orbit of the Earth around the Sun that no study of 'Ourselves' or 'Autumn' is complete without some link to these concepts, however implicit. Table 8.1 summarises the key concepts for children in their primary years with the related curriculum links and underpinning teacher knowledge.

TABLE 8.1 Earth and beyond: progression in key concepts

Key concepts	NC references	Teachers' background knowledge
The Sun is a source of light.	KS1 Sc4 4a, b	The Sun is a medium-sized star that produces light and heat energy from a process of nuclear fusion. It is ultimately the source of nearly all the light around us. Most combustible materials (e.g. wood) burn because of the energy stored in them from the Sun, via photosynthesis. 'Artificial' light sources transform electrical energy, much of which was generated from either fossil fuels or 'renewable' resources, again powered by the Sun. Only the other stars, nuclear power and volcanic eruptions have non-solar origins.
Day and night happen because the Earth spins on its axis.	KS2 Sc4 4c	The Earth's period of rotation is exactly 24 hours (give or take some slight 'wobbles'). This is a terrestrial 'day', made up of variable periods of light and dark, because only those parts facing the Sun are illuminated.
Shadows of still objects move during a sunny day because the Sun appears to 'travel' in an arc across the sky.	KS2 Sc4 4b	Of course, the Sun only appears to move; in reality it is us who move because of the rotation of the Earth. Because we move in an arc, the Sun appears to us to move in an arc, starting low in the east, rising to its zenith at midday GMT and 'setting' low in the west. The position of this arc in the sky changes constantly through the year (see seasonal changes below): it reaches its highest point at the summer solstice (21 June) and is at its lowest at the winter solstice (21 or 22 December). We can use this predictable movement to tell the time using a sundial – this will differ depending on our longitude because different points on the Earth's surface are directly opposite the Sun at different moments, giving us time zones.

The Earth, Sun and Moon are approximately spherical.	KS2 Sc4 4a	Nearly all heavenly bodies (planets, stars, etc.) are approximately spherical, which is because they are pulled together by gravitational attraction; a sphere contains a given mass or volume within the smallest possible surface area. A bubble is a useful (though potentially misleading) analogy.
We have years because the Earth moves around the Sun.	KS2 Sc4 4d	The Earth orbits the Sun once every 365 and a quarter terrestrial days. Because this period is rather inconvenient, we 'save up' the four extra quarter days and add an extra day (29 February) once every four years (the leap year).
We have seasons because of the tilt of the Earth's orbit.	KS2 Sc4 4d	This is one of the trickiest concepts in this topic, and strictly belongs in KS3. See the section on developing children's understanding on pp. 144–146 for further support. The Earth's axis of rotation makes a constant angle of approximately 66.5 degrees with its plane of orbit (i.e. 23.5 degrees from vertical). This means that as it moves in its orbit, the sunlight strikes any particular point on the Earth's surface at constantly varying angles. The higher the Sun's position at midday, the more intense its energy at this point, so summer tends to be warmer than winter.
The Moon has phases because we see differing amounts of the side lit by the Sun.	KS2 Sc4 4a	Another tricky KS3 concept! Half the Moon is always illuminated by the Sun (it is not a source of light). Because the Moon orbits the Earth (approximately once every 29.5 days – a lunar month), we see differing proportions of this lit half. For example, when the Moon is on the same side of us as the Sun, we see none of the lit half – a 'new' Moon.

Sources of further information

Farrow (1999), *The Really Useful Science Book: A Framework for Primary Teachers.*
Wenham (2005) (2nd edn), *Understanding Primary Science: Ideas, Concepts and Explanations.*

You will notice from the above that there is no mention of stars or planets at primary level – these appear at KS3, along with explanations for seasonal changes, phases of the Moon and eclipses. However, it is difficult to teach this topic without referring to them at all. Planets are like the Earth – large spheres of rock or gas orbiting the Sun, some with their own moons. Stars are like the Sun – intensely hot balls of gas in which nuclear reactions produce huge amounts of energy and new materials.

Cross-curricular planning

Although it is difficult to start a topic on the Earth and beyond from an everyday context, young children's familiarity with day and night, sleeping and waking, the Moon and the stars can be used to initiate a discussion about why it gets dark at night. Stories such as Jill Tomlinson's *The Owl Who Was Afraid of the Dark* (1998) or Martin Waddell's *Can't You Sleep Little Bear?* (2001) can be used to discuss children's fears and link the topic to that of light. Plenty of children's stories (for example Jill Murphy's *Whatever Next?* (1995b)), comics and films feature space travel. Older children might want to assemble a collection of images of space, spacecraft, aliens, etc., from various media sources and use them to discuss the differences between 'science fiction' and established scientific ideas in this area. There are lots of charts of the solar system available, and a globe used as part of a hands-on display can start children thinking about their position on it and the movements it might make through space.

For older children, making a table of the relative sizes and distances of planets from the Sun, then modelling them with different-sized beads, marbles and balls can offer a mathematical challenge and provide a graphic illustration of the sheer scale of the solar system.

The topic of the Earth and beyond has clear links with Religious Education (RE). Children's sense of awe and wonder at the night sky – perhaps as part of a 'night walk' on a residential school trip in a rural area with low light pollution – can readily lead to a discussion of 'the big questions' as suggested in the 'using dialogue' section on p. 142. Creation stories from different cultures can be compared with the current scientific story of the big bang, and children can also explore the origins of the signs of the Zodiac in the patterns humans have seen in the arrangement of stars. If your school is in an urban area with little opportunity to see the stars, a visit to a planetarium can be an excellent substitution for the night walk, and often raises some of the more mystical aspects of the cosmos. These links can easily be extended into History as children look at the different ways humans have interpreted the motions of the spheres over the centuries (see the 'day and night' section on pp. 142–144) including the appearance of astronomical signs at significant events such as Halley's comet at the Battle of Hastings.

A photograph of the Earth from space (particularly the iconic image of 'Earthrise' over the lunar surface taken from Apollo 8 in 1968, which is available to print out from the NASA website) is an essential resource if you want to use this topic as a way of addressing issues of Education for Sustainable Development (ESD). It is the fragile beauty of such images of a blue-green 'pearl' in space, suggesting a small planet with strictly limited resources, that arguably first kick-started the environmental movement in the late 1960s. By comparing photographs of the Earth with other moons and planets, children can come to appreciate the uniqueness of this environment in our solar system, as the only place that (we know) can support life through its liquid water and oxygen-rich atmosphere. The dangers of turning our own atmosphere into something like that of our neighbour Venus (full of carbon dioxide and sulphuric acid producing an inhospitable environment of intense global warming and acid rain) can be used as the starting point for an exploration of the possible effects of human influences on our environment. It is important here not to use shock tactics to frighten or indoctrinate children, but to enable them to collect data from various sources (a host of websites contain such data) and to evaluate them. The Association for Science Education (ASE) 'Primary upd8' service provides a digest of current science topics or controversies in the media and suggests classroom activities to accompany discussion. Barely a week goes by without some astronomical or environmental programme or article appearing, so there should be plenty of material to choose from.

Assessment for learning

Much assessment for learning in the topic of Earth and beyond can be done by asking children questions, or by listening to the interesting snippets of information they bring in from home, media and other sources. For example, if you are beginning to explore children's concepts about the relationship between our notions of time and the movement of the Sun, Moon and Earth, the following starter questions could be helpful:

How long is a day? (Explore the difference between daylight hours and period of rotation.)
How long is a month? (Explore the difference between calendar and lunar months.)
How long is a year? (Do children relate this to Earth's orbit?)
How can we work out what time it is? (This could lead to discussion of sundials.)

Young children will come up with a number of fascinating explanations for the difference between 'day' and 'night'. Here are a few examples, drawn from the SPACE research project (Osborne *et al.* 1993) and Year 1 children at Chandag Infants School, Keynsham, together with commentary:

- 'Night happens because we need to sleep.' (A typically 'egocentric' argument; external events are related to our needs.)
- 'The Sun goes down and down . . . under the hills and you can't see the Sun and then the Sun pops back up when it's morning.' (An anthropomorphic idea of the Sun 'hiding' from us.)
- 'The Sun goes down and the Moon pops up on our world, the Earth.' (This common notion – that the Sun and Moon are in some way interchangeable – derives from the remarkable coincidence that, although the Sun and Moon are very different sizes and different distances from us, they appear exactly the same size in the sky. This idea can easily be challenged on a clear day when both Sun and Moon are visible simultaneously.)
- 'The Sun gets covered up by clouds.' (Based on very selective use of evidence!)
- 'It's morning in a different place when it's night-time here. Because it's a different country and the Sun can't go everywhere.' (This idea is moving towards a more scientific understanding by relating day and night to the apparent movement of the Sun. This child is probably ready to be introduced to the notion that it is the Earth that spins, giving the appearance that the Sun moves.)

Making comparisons between day and night demonstrates some aspects of level 2 in NC science attainment target 4: physical processes (DfEE/QCA 1999), whilst linking cause and effect (the rotation of the Earth leading to regular periods of light and dark) demonstrates a level 3 understanding. The apparent movement of the Sun in an arc across the sky can be further explored with older children. Here are some suggestions for probing questions:

Which is the warmest room in the school?
Which is the warmest place to sit in our classroom?
Is it true for morning and afternoon?
Why is it warmer at one part of the day than another?

Two typical responses found by SPACE researchers were as follows:

- 'The Sun gets brighter/hotter during the day.' (With no mention of movement.)
- 'The Sun moves across the sky.' (With no mention of change of height.)

This concept has been tested on several occasions in KS2 SATs. Typically, children are asked to draw the position of the Sun in the sky at three different times of day, sometimes relating this to the direction and length of a shadow cast by a stick (see 'Scientific enquiry' below). An ability to describe and explain this apparent movement equates to NC level 4.

Modelling the Earth, Sun and Moon with Plasticine is an effective strategy for eliciting children's ideas about the shapes of these bodies. The Earth may well be represented as a sphere, whereas some children may model the Sun as a flat disc (as it appears in the sky) or the Moon as a 'banana' shape (deriving from standardised depictions of a crescent moon in storybooks). If you then introduce small model figures (e.g. Lego) and ask children to place them in two different locations on the Earth's surface, you can begin to find out their ideas about gravitational attraction and the concept of 'down'. These ideas can be further explored using drawings. Figures 8.1 to 8.4 show common representations found by Nussbaum (1985) in a study of American, Israeli and Nepalese children aged between 8 and 14 investigating the Earth's shape, the nature of sky and space and the 'down' direction of falling objects.

In Figure 8.1, the Earth is represented as flat, and the sky is a horizontal layer above it. The Earth may be seen as an island surrounded by a sea, or as extending infinitely in all directions. 'Down' is identified as being perpendicular to the surface.

In Figure 8.2, the Earth is seen as spherical, but we live *inside* the sphere on a horizontal flat surface with a dome of sky above us. It is impossible to live on the outside of the sphere, which may be occupied by 'space' and the Sun, Moon and stars. As in Figure 8.1 (idea 1), 'down' is identified as perpendicular to the surface.

Figure 8.3 represents a spherical Earth, surrounded by sky, with people living on the outer surface. 'Down', however, is considered to be Earth-independent so that a ball dropped at the South Pole would fall away from the surface.

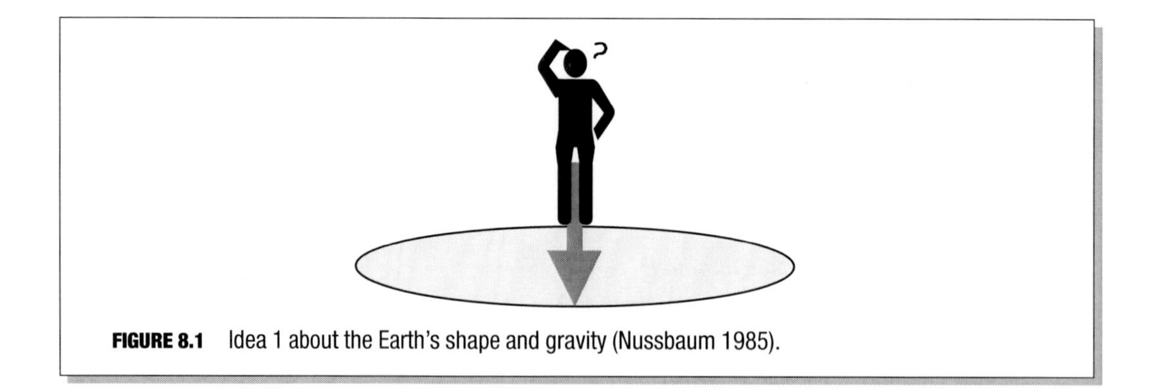

FIGURE 8.1 Idea 1 about the Earth's shape and gravity (Nussbaum 1985).

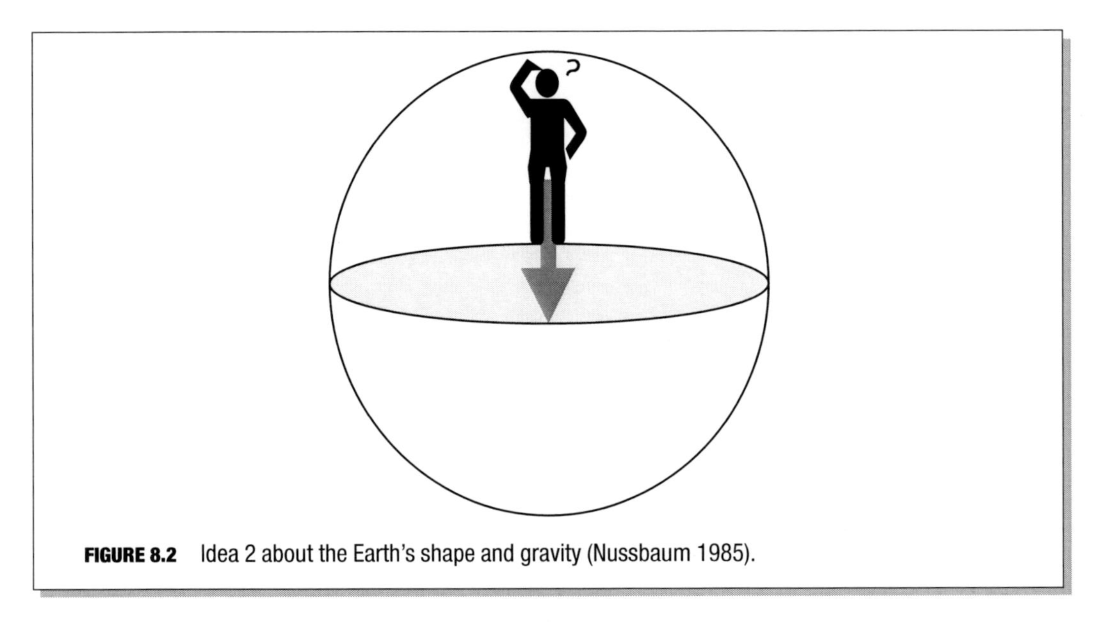

FIGURE 8.2 Idea 2 about the Earth's shape and gravity (Nussbaum 1985).

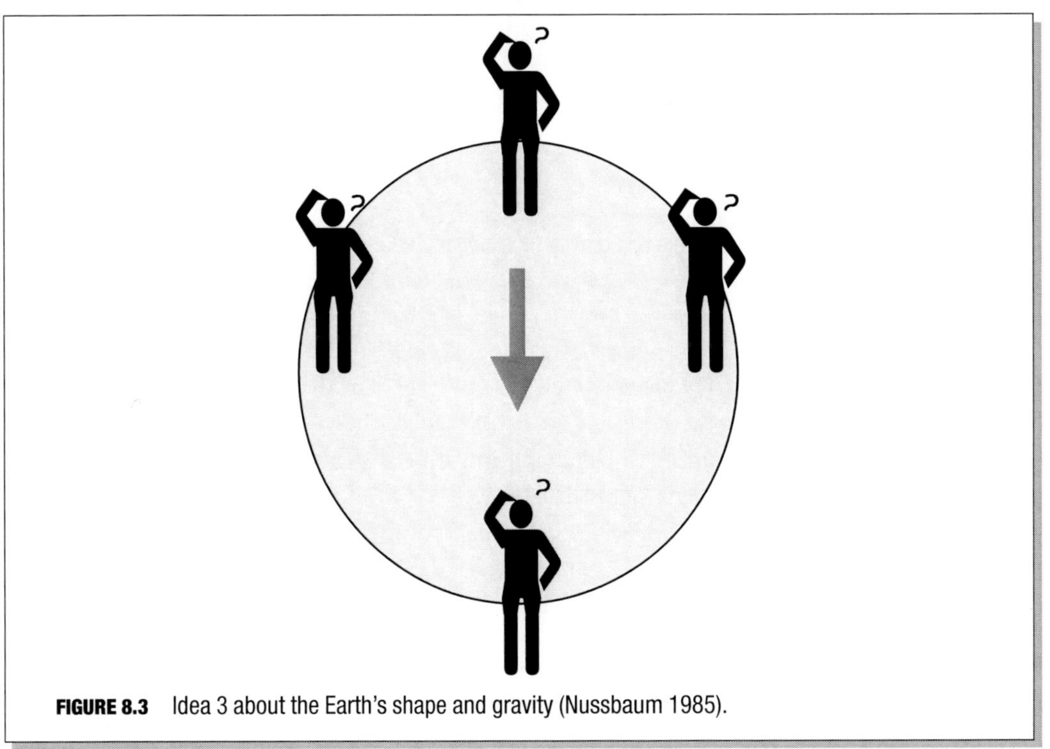

FIGURE 8.3 Idea 3 about the Earth's shape and gravity (Nussbaum 1985).

Figure 8.4 is closest to current scientific understanding. It recognises that the Earth is spherical, surrounded by sky, and that objects dropped at the surface fall towards the Earth (due to the attraction between objects with mass – the Earth has a large mass therefore pulls with a strong force). However, there are still some lingering features of the 'universal down' notion – 90 per cent of

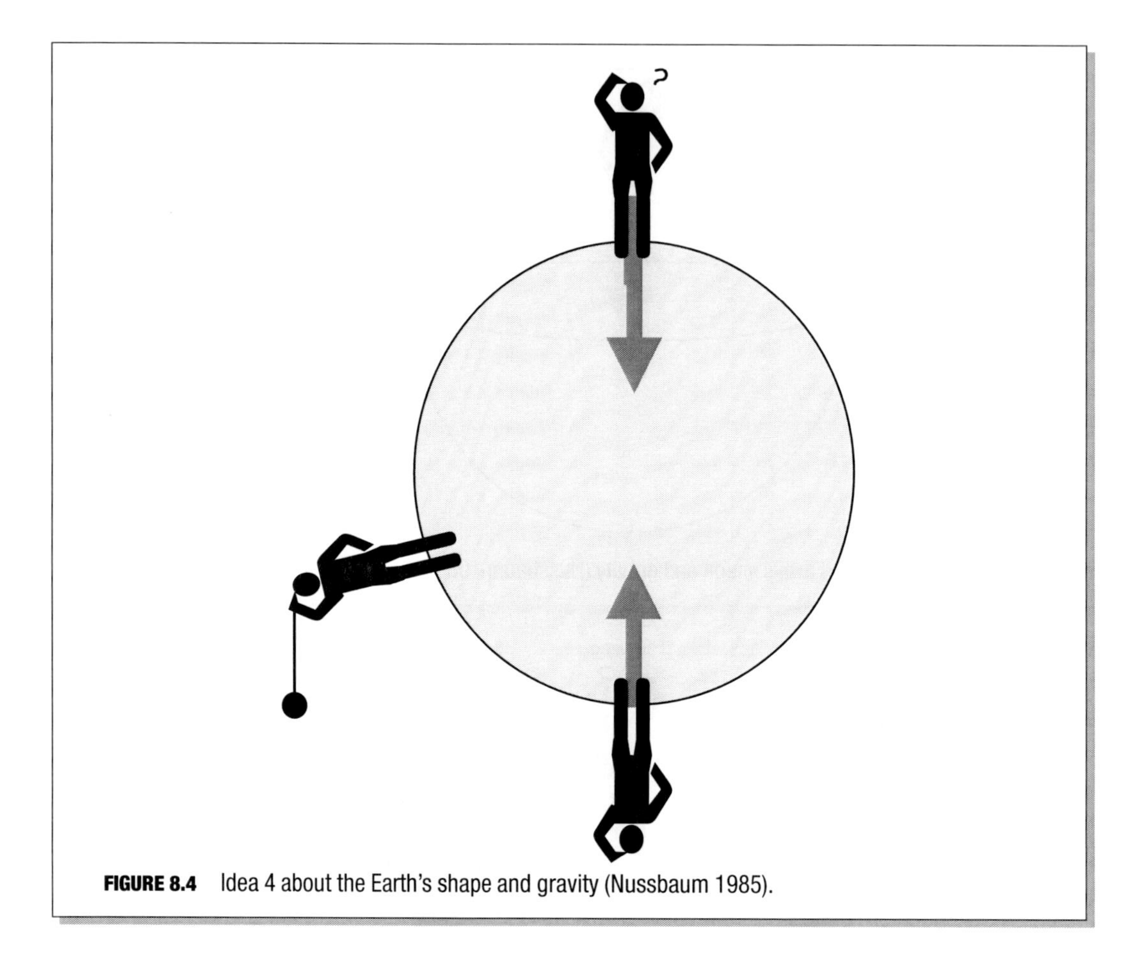

FIGURE 8.4 Idea 4 about the Earth's shape and gravity (Nussbaum 1985).

answers to a 1996 SAT question in which children were asked to draw the position of a plumb line held by people standing at different points on the Earth's surface showed it hanging vertically on the page, rather than towards the Earth. The ability to make generalisations about physical phenomena such as gravity is evidence of NC level 4.

Children's ideas about seasonal changes (Osborne *et al.* 1993) parallel many adults' alternative frameworks concerning this difficult concept, raising some doubts about the effectiveness of science education in this area:

- 'It's hotter in the summer because the Sun is closer to the Earth.' (Indeed, the Earth's orbit is slightly elliptical, but it is closer to the Sun during northern hemisphere *winter*!)
- 'It's hotter in summer because the Earth is facing the Sun.' (This notion is worth exploring further, since it could imply an appreciation of the 'height' of the Sun in summer, but may equally suggest that the child is confused about the Earth's rotation.)
- 'The Sun doesn't shine in the winter.' (Not a bad generalisation in England, but will not stand up to sustained observation!)

Children do not tend to mention changing daylight hours or 'height' of the Sun between seasons – perhaps these changes are too gradual or subtle to be easily observable. By contrast, the phases of the Moon do tend to be noticed and commented on by children, who may offer the following observations (Osborne *et al.* 1993):

- 'The Moon really changes shape.' (Influenced perhaps by storybook representations of the Moon. It is actually possible to see the whole disc faintly on a clear night, even when it is not full.)
- 'The Moon looks like it changes shape because of clouds getting in the way.' (Perhaps a confusion of time frames here, easily challenged by observing the Moon on a partially cloudy night.)
- 'The Moon looks like it changes shape because the Earth casts a shadow.' (This is another idea held by many adults; it confuses the Moon's phases with much rarer lunar eclipses, when the Moon does indeed pass through the Earth's shadow.)

If children are able to use simple models (such as those described in the developing ideas section below) to explain effects that are caused by the movement of the Earth (e.g. length of year), they can be said to be working at NC level 5 in this topic area.

Scientific enquiry

As suggested above, the topic of the Earth and beyond tends not to lend itself to 'fair test'-type investigations and is probably best taught through a series of illustrative activities (see below), and what Goldsworthy *et al.* (2000a) term 'reference' (for example compiling fact files for each planet on a database such as Information Workshop). 'Modelling activities' such as ICT simulations can also be extremely valuable in this area (Cox *et al.* 2004), particularly those which 'create frameworks for visualisation', such as the simulation of relative motion of Earth, Moon and Sun on the Fear of Physics website (www.fearofphysics.com/SunMoon/sunmoon1.html).

Perhaps the most common 'pattern-seeking' enquiry undertaken during this topic is an activity in which children place a stick in the playground on a sunny day, marking the position and length of the shadow every hour using either chalk directly onto the asphalt or marker pen on a large sheet of paper. They should notice a change in shadow angle, and this can be related to the study of sundials to tell the time, noting that a sundial gnomon is actually angled rather than vertical (in order to give accurate time at a particular location, the gnomon's angle should equal the latitude, for example, 51.5 degrees for London). The shadow-stick activity is really a 'pattern-seeking' enquiry (Goldsworthy *et al.* 2000a), particularly if the shadow lengths are recorded graphically via a spreadsheet, as in Figure 8.5 below.

Once children have identified the pattern observed and offered hypotheses to explain it, this activity can be followed up by simulating the Sun's 'movement' using a torch in the classroom (Figure 8.6).

They should notice that they need to move the torch in an arc to produce the same changes of shadow length observed in the playground, but of course this could reinforce the notion that it is the Sun that moves. So the third part of this teaching sequence should be to make a mini shadow-stick for a classroom globe, using half a matchstick. If the globe is then rotated in a strong unidirectional

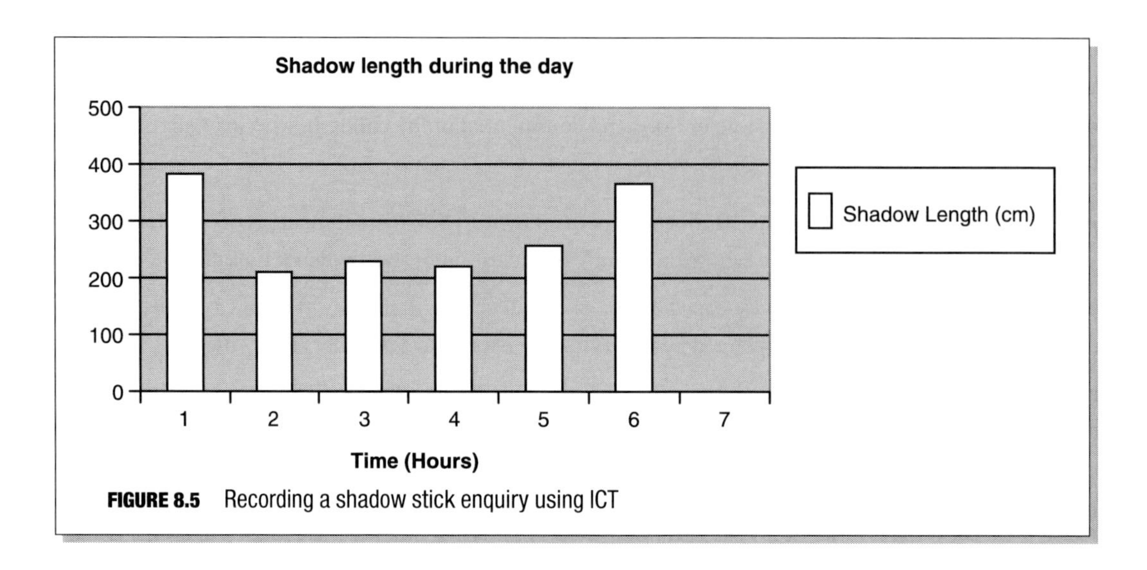

FIGURE 8.5 Recording a shadow stick enquiry using ICT

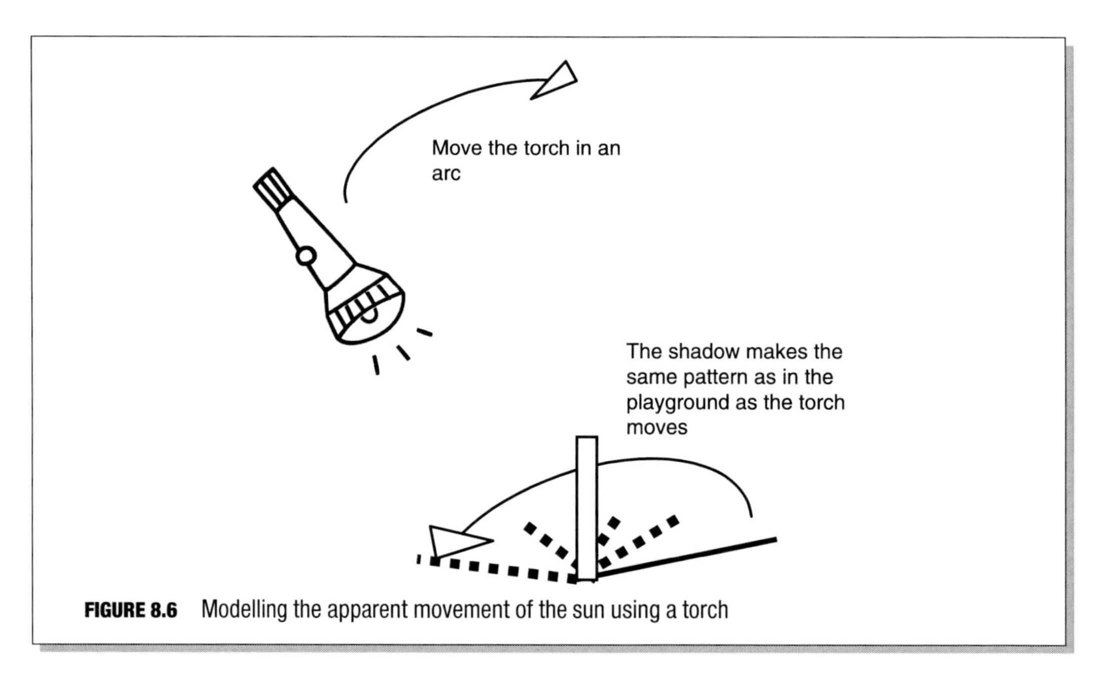

FIGURE 8.6 Modelling the apparent movement of the sun using a torch

light source (such as an overhead projector) the same pattern of changing shadow length can be observed (see Figure 8.7). Although not 'proving' that the children's observations of shadows in the playground are related to the Earth's rotation, this demonstration does at least provide some evidence in that direction.

Although not directly related to the key concepts in this topic, an enjoyable 'fair test' investigation, which could be undertaken at the end of a unit of work, involves simulating the impact of a meteorite (lump of rock) colliding with a planet or moon. Any observation of the Moon's surface

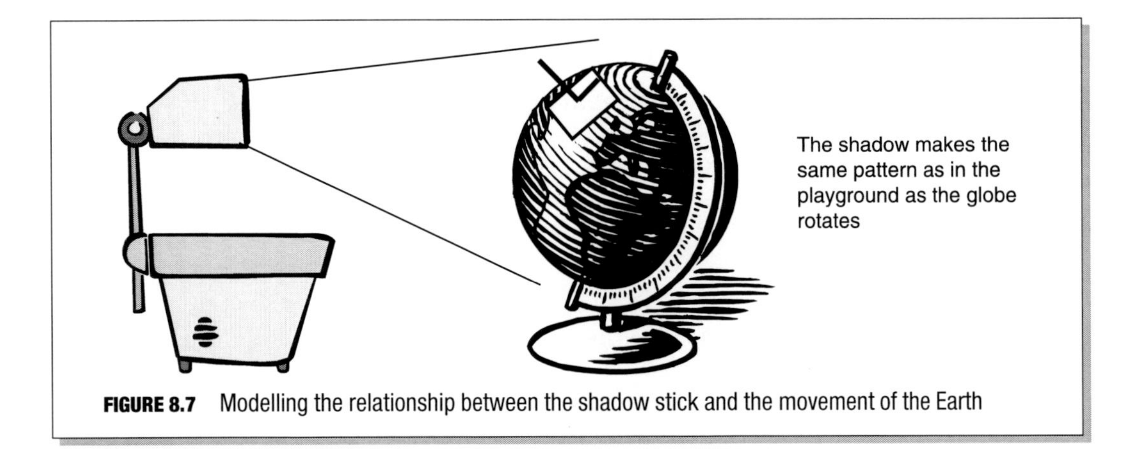

FIGURE 8.7 Modelling the relationship between the shadow stick and the movement of the Earth

will reveal craters caused by such impacts, so this investigation can be used as a model of a theory to explain them. A starting point is to drop a marble into a tray of sand. This will make a crater, and a little exploration will reveal that the higher the drop, the bigger the crater. At this point children need to be asked to plan the investigation, deciding on the independent variable (for example height of drop, mass or diameter of marble) and dependent variable (for example diameter or depth of crater). They should make a prediction (for example which mass will form the largest diameter crater) and consider some of the practical issues involved in testing this. For example, how can they change the mass without changing size? How will they measure the diameter or depth of crater accurately? Will they need to make repeat measurements? Once they start the practical part of the investigation, further issues will no doubt arise. Depending on the age of the children, you could extend the resources available, and hence the accuracy of measurement, as follows:

- Year 1/2: a range of different-sized spheres (including large balls), rulers with cm divisions only, metre stick without fine divisions, paper strips (for comparing length)
- Year 3/4: a range of marbles and other smallish spheres (e.g. golf ball, ping-pong ball), ruler marked in both cm and mm, tape measure, metre stick marked in cm, cm-squared paper
- Year 5/6: a range of marbles (or ball bearings) and other spheres, electronic balance, graph paper, string, callipers (or pairs of compasses) to measure the diameter of crater.

Recording, interpreting and explaining data from this investigation should also change with age. By Upper KS2 we would be expecting some kind of graphical recording (for example on a computer spreadsheet), together with a description and interpretation of the resulting scattergram and a hypothesis to explain the findings. (For example, marbles dropped from a greater height produce larger craters because they accelerate to a higher speed and therefore carry more energy to push sand particles aside.) Goldsworthy *et al.* (2000a) offer some helpful 'scaffolds' to move children on from describing to explaining results by focusing on the types of connective words used (explanations tend to use 'causal' connectives such as 'because', 'therefore'). Such an activity could be carried out during an English/literacy lesson.

Developing children's understanding

Using dialogue to teach about the Earth and beyond

Classroom discussion is particularly useful in helping children to express and restructure their ideas about the Earth and beyond, since the scope for investigative enquiry is limited and the scope of the topic is very broad, allowing for speculative and philosophical reasoning. Children as young as 5 or 6 are often asking the 'big questions' – Where did I come from? Has the universe always been here? – and a skilful teacher can turn these into open and thoughtful class or group discussions using a 'Philosophy for Children' approach (Lipman 2003). This will involve adopting an 'interactive-dialogic' style of teaching (Mortimer and Scott 2003) in which every idea expressed is valued equally, rather than the teacher imposing an 'authoritative' version of scientific truth against which children's contributions are measured. A similar approach can also be used to debate 'hot topics' such as the demotion of Pluto to a 'minor' or 'dwarf' planet in 2006. Should the discovery of other large objects such as 'Xena' further out in the Solar system lead to a smaller club of 'real' planets or should we allow others in? This could be a way into thinking about 'how science works'; for example, it could demonstrate how definitions in science can be open to debate. We probably need to use a more 'interactive-authoritative' approach to helping children talk through their ideas about day and night, the seasons and the phases of the moon. Listening to children's explanations and probing them before offering alternative models based on current scientific theories can help them to move forward in their understanding. Having some real objects at hand to model these explanations can help too, as described below.

A further use of dialogue in this topic is through the use of role-play. Neston Primary School in Wiltshire set up a 'moonbase' in their playground, with a live video link to the classroom. By sending groups of children on a 'mission' to the moonbase and observing them using the link, 9–11-year-old pupils were able to study group dynamics and how people respond to different situations (Davies and Heal 2006). For example, 'astronauts' in the moonbase were observed being given instructions from 'mission control' in the classroom by walkie talkie:

> Get some rocks out then test them please to see if they're limestone.

The 'astronauts' demonstrated effective listening skills and trust in following the instructions, which were monitored from 'mission control' by the video link. The school also applied to link up by radio for 10 minutes with the International Space Station (ISS) so that these skills could be applied in a real situation. Children asked questions such as 'how do you know what time it is on the ISS?', 'What does it feel like to take off in a spaceship?' 'How do you spend your time onboard the ISS?' and 'What is the ISS for?' They were given very clear answers from the astronaut concerned, increasing their confidence in speaking and listening in such a public forum.

Day and night happen because the Earth spins on its axis

In addition to the sequence of activities around shadow-sticks to challenge children's ideas about the 'movement' of the Sun (described above), there are a number of simulations available to engage kinaesthetic learners and to address our key concepts in this topic.

To help children relate day and night to the rotation of the Earth, we can seat them one at a time in a swivel chair whilst another child firstly walks clockwise around the chair shining a torch at its occupant (Figure 8.8). This simulates what appears to be happening from our Earth-centred view – that the Sun moves around us, and when it is behind us (on the other side of the Earth) we experience night.

The seated child needs to keep their head still and describe what they observe (the light from the torch moving across their field of view, then disappearing). Next, the child in the chair rotates anticlockwise whilst the torch-bearer stays still – this should produce a similar observation from the chair occupant.

This activity, whilst not disproving a model in which the Sun moves around the Earth, at least provides an alternative explanation for our observations. It can be linked effectively to an 'explanatory story' (Millar and Osborne 1998, Harlen 2000) of changing ideas about the universe – a good example of 'ideas and evidence in science' (DfEE/QCA 1999). Below is a brief summary of this story.

Ptolemy (Greek philosopher, circa AD 85–165)

- Earth is the centre of the universe.
- The heavens are perfect and unchanging.
- Heavenly bodies move in perfect circles around the Earth.
- Theory accepted by church and state for 1,400 years.

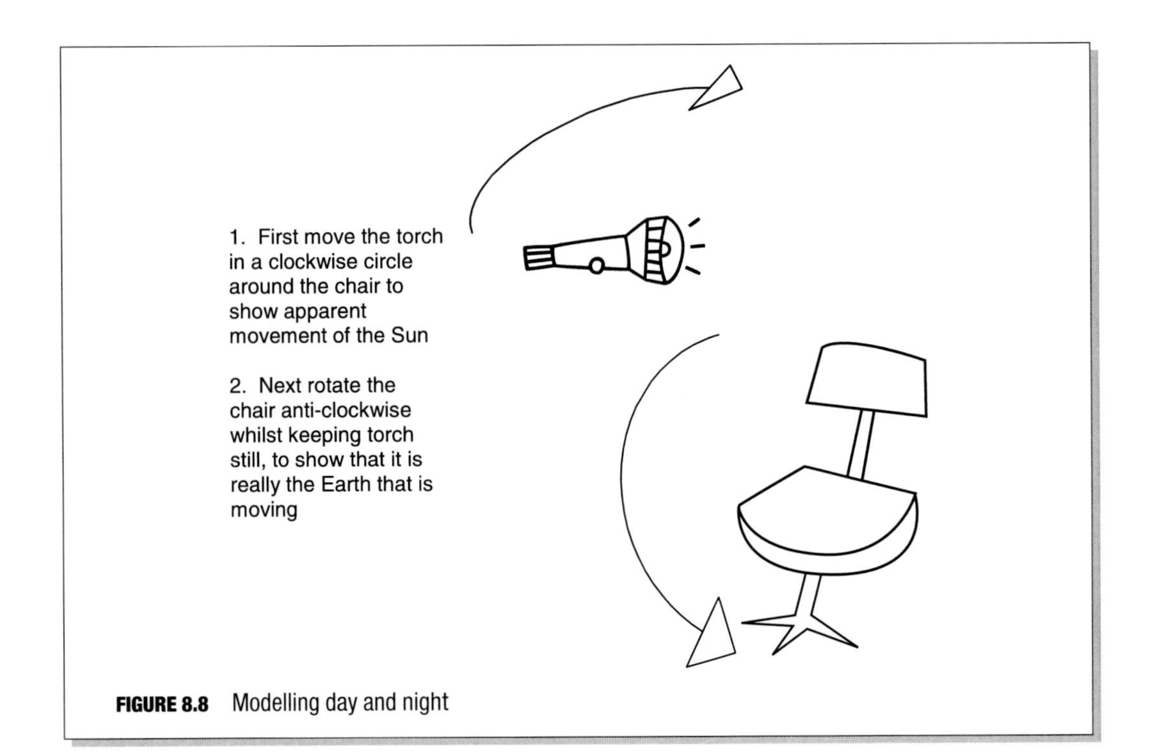

FIGURE 8.8 Modelling day and night

Nicolaus Copernicus (Polish astronomer, 1473–1543)

- Observed planetary positions and made mathematical models.
- Sun is the centre of the Universe; Earth orbits the Sun.
- Planets rotate in circles around the *centre of the Earth's orbit* (unwilling to use elliptical orbits to account for his observations).
- These ideas attracted many criticisms as they challenged accepted wisdom.

Galileo Galilei (Italian mathematician and astronomer, 1564–1642)

- Using the newly invented telescope, observed mountains on the Moon and spots on the Sun, showing that the heavens are not 'perfect'.
- Observed the moons of Jupiter and phases of Venus ('The mother of love has the same shapes as Cynthia!'), showing that not all heavenly bodies orbit the Earth.
- Assumed that Ptolemy must be wrong and that Copernicus must be right.
- These views conflicted with those of the Roman Catholic Church; Galileo was excommunicated and later repented (a fuller account appears in Poole 1995).

Albert Einstein (German mathematician, 1879–1955)

- Einstein's Special Theory of Relativity (1905) suggests that all motion is relative, there is no 'universal frame of reference'.
- Therefore, from our perspective, the Earth is the centre of the universe!

This brief narrative, which can be adapted and simplified for different ages of children, makes a number of important points about the nature of science. Firstly, it shows that ideas change over time, and that earlier 'rejected' conceptions may be revisited (Einstein's mathematics echoing Ptolemy's Earth-centred universe). It also suggests that scientists are influenced by the ideas of others (Newton described this as 'standing on the shoulders of giants') and by their own historical and cultural context (for example Galileo's devout Catholicism). Scientists too make assumptions: it is debatable whether any scientific observations are truly objective. Stories such as this can also be used to give children confidence that their own theories about the universe have been shared at various times by famous scientists, and that 'it's OK to change your mind'.

Seasonal changes occur because of the tilt in the angle of the Earth's axis

As suggested above, the 'reason for the seasons' is one of the trickiest concepts children are likely to discover in primary science, and really belongs in KS3. However, you may well find it difficult to escape from offering some kind of explanation to inquisitive Year 6 children, so the following activity can be used as a demonstration or, better, as a way for children to explain to each other, using the equipment as a visual and kinaesthetic aid to building a mental model. Using an overhead projector, or similar bright light source, to represent the Sun (it is preferable to have an omni-directional 150 W lamp as the Sun shines in all directions) you can show the effect on a globe whose axis is angled at 23.5 degrees to the vertical (as the Earth's is) using model Lego figures standing at various positions on the globe's surface. Starting with northern-hemisphere summer (Figure 8.9), with the axis tilting in the direction of the 'Sun', show that in this position the North Pole is in continuous daylight ('the land of the midnight Sun'), whilst the South Pole is in continuous darkness. By placing a figure on the UK (or another northern-hemisphere country) you can show that their shadow is relatively short and, if you have a figure that bends in the middle, you can make it bend over backwards in order to see the 'Sun high in the sky'. By rotating the globe from sunrise to sunset you can show that the day length is relatively long in this position.

Now move the globe to northern-hemisphere winter (Figure 8.10), preferably by making it orbit the 'Sun', spinning as it goes and passing through the autumn equinox, at which point the angle of the axis makes no difference to daylight hours since the line dividing the lit half from the dark half of the globe passes through both poles. Once you reach the winter position, draw

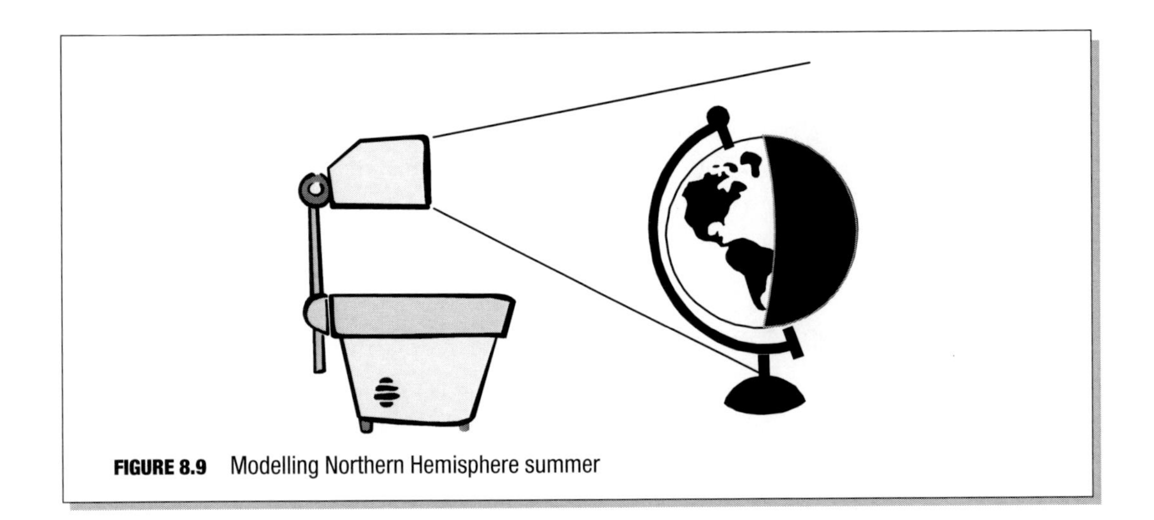

FIGURE 8.9 Modelling Northern Hemisphere summer

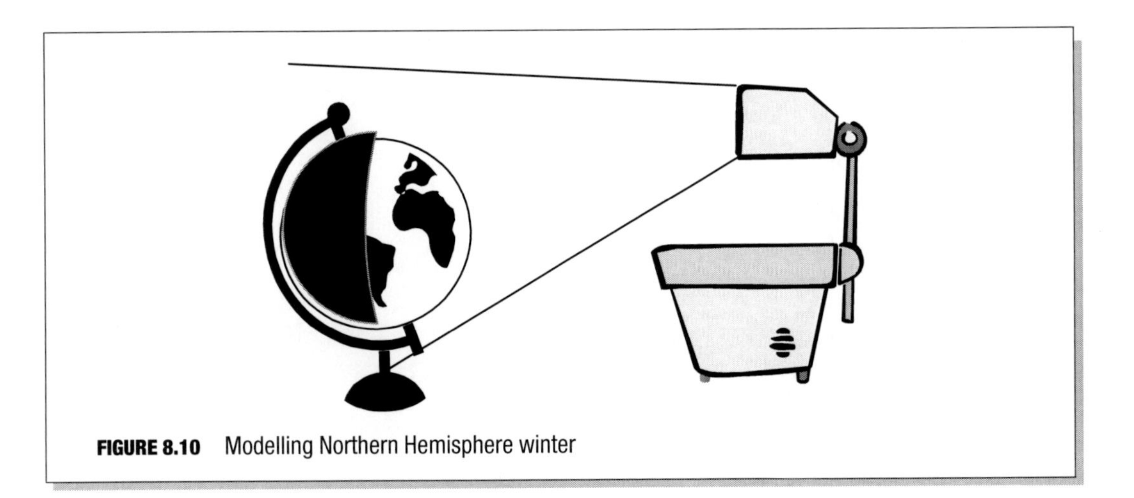

FIGURE 8.10 Modelling Northern Hemisphere winter

children's attention to the continuous darkness at the North Pole, and continuous daylight at the South Pole (the reverse of Figure 8.9). The Lego figure placed on the UK now casts a relatively long shadow, does not need to bend backwards to observe the Sun, and experiences relatively short daylight hours, whereas someone standing at, say, Cape Town, can be shown to have all the characteristics of summer that were demonstrated earlier. You may need to repeat the transition between summer and winter several times, partly to develop your own skills of demonstration and explanation, but also to help children to answer their own questions before trying it out for themselves. It can be supported by accessing one of several web-based simulations available.

While it explains changing daylight hours and 'height' of Sun, this model does not necessarily answer the question, *So why is it hotter in summer then?* to children's satisfaction. For this, you need to shine a torch or lamp onto a piece of squared paper at different angles (though the same distance), counting the squares to work out the area over which the beam is shed (Figure 8.11). This could be turned into an investigation, with predictions, careful measurement and graphical data presentation as with the shadow-stick described above. What it should demonstrate is that, shining down from directly overhead (at an angle of 90 degrees to the paper), the energy from the torch is concentrated into the smallest area, and that as this angle decreases so the area of spread becomes larger. Hence, taking this model back to the real situation it is intended to simulate, we can say that 'the higher the Sun in the sky, the warmer its rays'. This explains why summers, when the Sun traverses a much longer and higher arc, tend to be warmer than winters. It also shows that midday will tend to be warmer than either morning or evening and can be used to introduce PSHE discussions about preventing sunburn and skin cancer during the hottest parts of the day and year.

The phases of the Moon and the motion of planets

While seasonal changes occur over such a relatively long time-scale that it may not be practical to keep records over the period of a unit of work in science, children can observe a whole cycle of lunar

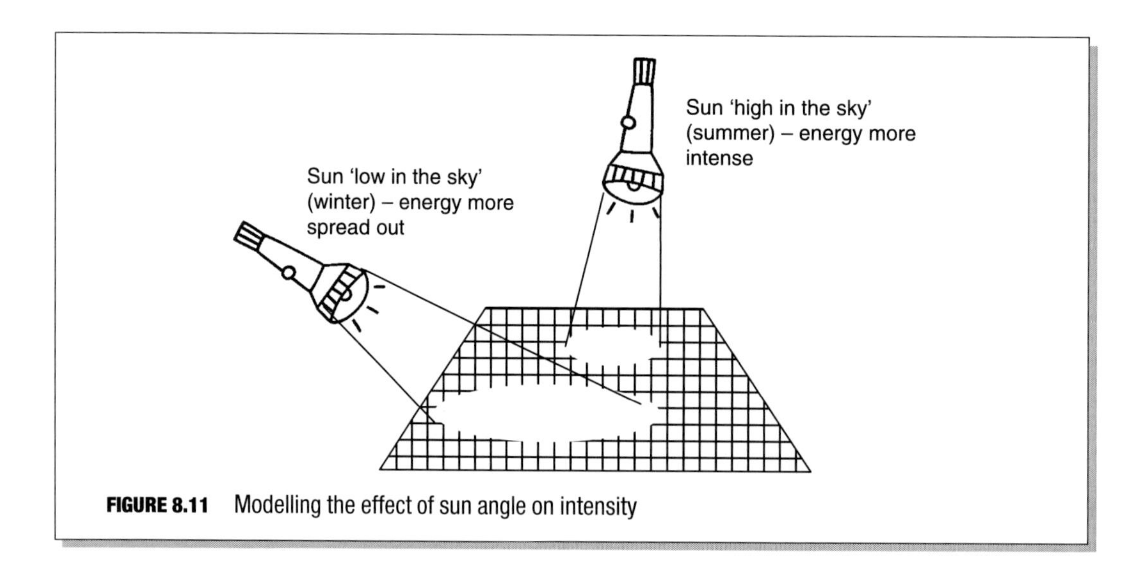

FIGURE 8.11 Modelling the effect of sun angle on intensity

phases over a month – provided the topic is occurring at a time of the year when they do not need to stay up too late to see it! Asking children to draw the 'shape' of the Moon in a lunar diary is an excellent way to start the discussion of what might be causing this phenomenon. However, to demonstrate the mechanism clearly, we can engage children in an elegant visual simulation using an overhead projector (OHP), a white ball on a stick (a polystyrene ball is ideal) and a swivel chair (Figure 8.12). A child sits in the chair, representing the Earth, and observes the ball held at arm's length and slightly above head height in the beam from the projector (a relatively dark room is required). By rotating slowly, a complete cycle of lunar phases can be observed, starting from the position where the ball is on the same side as the projector (though not blocking its beam – this would be a solar eclipse!). The rest of the class can see that half the ball is illuminated, but the child on the chair sees none of this 'lit half' – for them this is a 'new Moon'. Rotating a quarter-turn anticlockwise brings us to the 'first quarter' in which half of the lit face is visible to the chair's occupant. This is about seven days into the cycle. Turning further we pass through 'waxing gibbous' to 'full Moon' when the ball is on the opposite side of the chair from the OHP and the child can see the whole of the lit face (provided the beam is not blocked by their head – a lunar eclipse!). Completing the cycle, the white ball passes through 'waning gibbous' and 'third quarter' back to the new Moon position. Again, it may be necessary to repeat this several times to accommodate the child's mental model to this new representation, and you will certainly need to allow every member of the class to try it for themselves! A further refinement is to draw a face (either comical

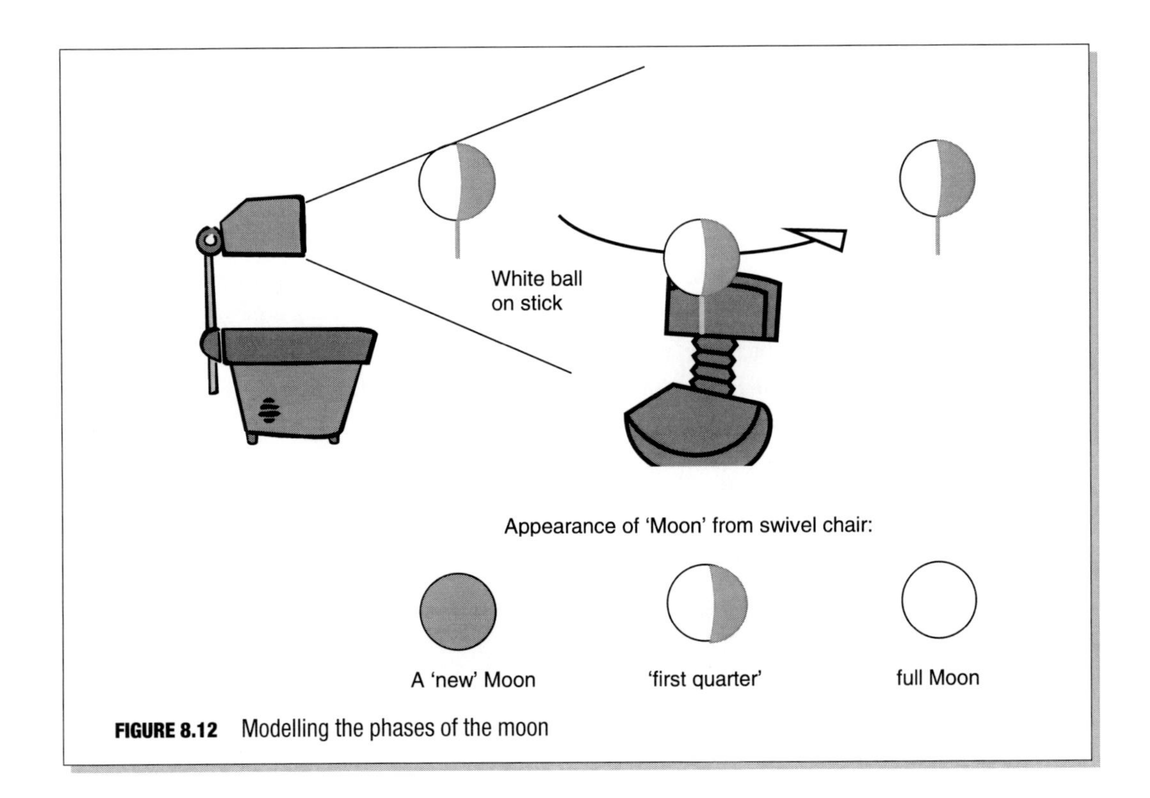

FIGURE 8.12 Modelling the phases of the moon

or representing the surface of the Moon) on the ball, and demonstrate that we always see this same face throughout the cycle. The far side of the Moon (not always the 'dark side' as we have demonstrated – Pink Floyd have a lot to answer for!) was only first seen by astronauts from Apollo 8 in 1968. This peculiar phenomenon occurs because the Moon's period of rotation is exactly the same as its period of orbit – it appears to have become 'locked into' a fixed synchronicity, possibly because of the Earth's gravitational pull on some massive features of the lunar surface (Galileo's Mountains).

The highly detailed simulations of seasonal and lunar changes described above can be generalised by letting children 'become' the inner solar system in the school hall. You can support this with simple models, posters or elaborate costumes; it can become a spectacular, if rather space-consuming, performance for assembly or parents. A child or group representing the Sun stands in the centre, perhaps shining torches in various directions. At its simplest, another two children represent the Earth and Moon – the Moon orbiting the Earth approximately 12 times as it orbits the Sun once. You can also introduce Mercury and Venus both orbiting the Sun within the Earth's orbit, and Mars outside it. If you want to introduce more mathematics, you could position the orbits at roughly the correct relative distances from each other (if Sun to Mercury is one unit, Sun to Venus is roughly two, Sun to Earth three, Sun to Mars five – the Fibonacci series, though this breaks down at Jupiter) and periods of rotation. You could add the outer planets but if you want to keep the orbit distances accurate you will need a very large playground! The modelling activity described in 'starting points' above is probably better for this purpose.

Using ICT to teach about the Earth and beyond

To help children visualise the three-dimensional movement of the Earth, Sun and Moon in relation to each other, it can be useful to show them a computer simulation, though this is no substitute for actually acting it out kinaesthetically in the classroom. Many websites contain such animations, though there are plenty of inaccuracies around – for example the Earth rotating at the same frequency as the moon's orbit, or in the opposite direction – so they are worth checking before using them with children. The interactive whiteboard (IWB) activity in the BBC's 'Science Clips' website (http://www.bbc.co.uk/schools/ks2bitesize/science/activities/earth_sun_moon.shtml) shows children how to set the period for which the simulation runs (in hours, days or months), allowing them to compare the rates at which day and night, lunar phases and seasons occur. The website http://www.ac.wwu.edu/~stephan/phases.html contains a lovely time-lapse animation showing a complete lunar cycle every couple of seconds; this can help reinforce the scientific explanation, as the pattern appears so beautifully regular and the 'dark' portions of the Moon are clearly visible throughout.

Another use of ICT to support conceptual change is the use of live 'webcam' pictures from different parts of the world to reinforce the idea of timezones. One site ('International Webcams') with links to webcams in Europe, North America, East Asia and Australasia is http://www.teleobjektiv.com/WebCam/index-webcam.htm. Children can find the cities on a globe illuminated by an OHP and relate the levels of daylight to the images they see on the computer screen. To help children understand how the angle of the sun in the sky affects the temperature on the Earth's surface – the explanation for seasonal changes (see above) – they can use a temperature or light sensor connected to data-logging equipment, demonstrating that the highest temperature and light levels occur when the source of light (e.g. a torch) is directly overhead. Another more sophisticated use of datalogging equipment could be to measure the speed of falling 'asteroids' (see 'scientific enquiry' above) using a pair of light gates attached to a datalogger with a timing facility. Finally, the 'Goldilocks' principle – the idea that planetary conditions including size, distance from sun, composition etc. have to be 'just right' to allow life – can be investigated using NASA's 'design a planet' site (http://astroventure.arc.nasa.gov/DAP/DAP.html).

Classroom management

Because so much of this topic is taught through demonstrations, models and simulations, it is essential to have a really good collection of resources so that several groups can be working simultaneously on the same or related activities. Of course, some of the class can be finding out information from secondary sources (books, websites, charts, etc.) and you can usefully employ discussion about the main ideas, but everyone needs to get hands-on with equipment as often as possible to aid spatial concept development. This should be supported by plenary sessions in which children explain concepts to each other using the models and simulations they have experienced. Below is a sample list of resources you may wish to accumulate:

- chart of solar system
- globes (including inflatable)
- Lego figures
- Plasticine for modelling shapes of the Sun, Moon and Earth
- powerful torches or lamps
- polystyrene balls
- OHP
- clocks and watches
- sundial, shadow-stick
- squared paper
- books on space
- compass
- videos of Earth, Moon, planets
- trays of sand, collection of marbles, metre rule
- data-logging equipment, including temperature and light sensors.

A room you are able to darken is desirable, though not essential provided that you have sufficiently bright light sources. There are few health and safety issues associated with this topic, although you may wish to remind children about not looking directly at the Sun (or the OHP in the lunar phases simulation).

Summary

In this chapter we hope to have communicated some of the excitement of teaching and learning about the Earth and beyond, a topic which remains on the cutting edge of science. It requires imagination and the ability to visualise in three dimensions, resulting in numerous alternative frameworks held by children and adults lacking the necessary information to help them 'decentre'. The more common of these ideas have been explored, relating them to historical precedents, and suggesting a series of discussions, demonstrations, models and simulations for helping children to move forward. The importance of scientific enquiry – in its broadest sense – in this area has been emphasised, offering the visual and kinaesthetic experiences children need to make sense of the counter-intuitive explanations for seasonal and lunar changes. We have suggested some useful cross-curricular links with RE, History and ESD, explored some possible uses of ICT to support children's learning and considered the issue of resourcing this topic.

Discussion points

1. What are the relative merits of computer animations and hands-on simulations to help children develop their understanding of how the Earth, Moon and Sun move in relation to each other?
2. How would you use this topic to teach about ESD?

Further reading

Arnold (2006) *Earth and Beyond*: this book gives plenty of creative ideas for teaching the Earth and beyond in the primary classroom.

Osborne *et al.* (1993), *SPACE Research Report: The Earth in Space*: this research report outlines the main 'alternative frameworks' held by children in this topic, enabling teachers to plan for appropriate interventions.

Poole (1995), *Beliefs and Values in Science Education*: this book includes the Galileo story referred to above, and other historical examples of how beliefs and values have influenced scientific endeavour.

CHAPTER

Humans and other animals

Purpose of this chapter

After reading this chapter you should have:

- considered how PSHE (Personal, Social and Health Education) and citizenship provide a context for learning about humans and other animals
- an awareness of strategies for eliciting children's ideas about humans, including annotated drawing, and for building on their ideas using visual models and secondary sources
- thought about scientific enquiries that are used to investigate humans, with a particular emphasis on pattern-seeking, and how these enquiries can be developed with primary-aged children.

Introduction

THE RELEVANCE OF THE TOPIC of humans and other animals to everyday life is immediately obvious, and children are fascinated by it. One could argue that it is more important for children to learn about themselves and how to ensure their physical, mental and emotional wellbeing than anything else in the school curriculum. It is clear that during their lifetimes, children in schools will be faced with many important and life changing choices about diet, exercise, drugs and sexual relationships. Understanding our bodies can help us in making decisions about what to eat and drink, how and when to use medicines and the kinds and amounts of exercise to take. The topic will also raise questions about sex and drugs that will need sensitive handling by teachers.

The fundamental importance of wellbeing has been recognised in recent government policy, namely the Every Child Matters: Change for Children Outcomes Framework (DfES 2004). Science education has specific knowledge and skills to offer in achieving the first two outcomes in particular: 'Be healthy' and 'Stay safe'. 'Be healthy' refers to aspects of physical, mental and emotional health, sexual health, healthy lifestyles and choosing not to take illegal drugs. 'Stay safe' includes references to safety from sexual exploitation, accidental injury, bullying and discrimination. We shall explore in this chapter how learning in primary science can contribute to achieving these outcomes.

The scientific study of humans and other animals raises ethical and values-based questions: Should all animals be treated with equal respect? Should we use animals as subjects for 'fair testing'? As adults we are bombarded with information on health in the media and need both biological knowledge and an understanding of research methods used in this field in order to evaluate and judge the different, often conflicting, sources.

This topic has several key concepts running through it leading to some 'big ideas'. Understanding these helps us think about *why* it is important for us to learn about various aspects of biology and how teaching and learning in primary science can contribute to building a deeper understanding of them.

Different animals have evolved different solutions to the problems of staying alive and reproducing, and part of the fascination of this topic is exploring the diversity of animal life and making comparisons between humans and other animals. We can ask questions about the way that animals, including humans, are constructed: *What do we look like inside and how do the parts work?* Relating the structure of parts of organisms to their function is a useful approach to understanding animals. Understanding the way that various organs and organ systems work and interact to keep us alive is the basis of this area of study. In primary science, children develop their understanding of what is happening inside our bodies.

Related to this, but with a different emphasis, is a consideration of health. What it means for humans to be healthy is based on social ideas and varies across different cultural and historical contexts. Does it mean just survival, or does it refer to some ideal model of physical and mental fitness? Looking at how ideals of body shape have changed in Western society in the past hundred years provides an example of how this is culturally defined. The challenges to health are also different for different groups of people: sedentary lifestyles leading to lack of exercise might affect one group of people, poverty may restrict access to certain foods for another group. There are workplace-related challenges to health such as back pain resulting from sitting at a computer all day, but there are also global challenges, such as HIV/AIDS and their complex relationship with sexual behaviour, and factors such as war. Questions about what we can do to keep healthy have both a social and a biological dimension. The biological dimension includes an understanding of what it means to be ill, including a scientific understanding of disease and the role of micro-organisms, but improving health often requires changing social structures too. This means that when teaching about health we need to link the science and the personal and social issues.

Another key area of interest is growth and reproduction. There are different solutions to this need to reproduce in the animal kingdom and studying different life cycles, such as those of butterflies and birds, as well as that of humans, is of interest in its own right as part of celebrating the diversity of species and understanding relationships between various organisms within ecosystems. There is an overlap here with the themes of chapter 10.

Reproduction is also about inheritable information, about how similarities and differences between living things can be understood, perhaps in terms of DNA and genetics and how these characteristics are passed between generations. This leads to ideas about evolution and natural selection that are fundamental to how we understand life. These issues are very much in the public domain through discussions about reproductive technologies such as in-vitro fertilisation, cloning and debates about the extent to which our genes or the environment determine how we are. Again, the science is clearly embedded in the social contexts. So, if a class of children is investigating variation in their hand spans, perhaps they could be challenged to think about why they might be different. This could lead to some interesting philosophical discussions and some deep thinking!

Progression from the early years to the beginning of secondary school

In the early years children become aware of their own needs and bodies, using their senses, developing physical skills and developing language, to name and describe parts of their bodies and actions. They develop awareness of other humans and of other living things and see that they have similar needs to their own. Good practice in personal hygiene and habits is encouraged in early years settings.

The *Curriculum Guidance for the Foundation Stage* (DfEE 2000a) has these goals for children:

- Dress and undress independently and manage their personal hygiene (personal, social and emotional development)
- Recognise the importance of keeping healthy and the things that contribute to this (physical development)
- Recognise the changes that happen to their bodies when they are active (physical development)

At KS1, children build on this by learning about their different senses, naming parts of their bodies and developing ideas that different parts of the body do different things. Teachers can encourage children to extend this beyond humans by providing a rich curriculum with experiences of a range of different animals. Children learn about how to keep healthy by thinking about what goes inside them – food, water, medicines – and how they use their bodies. This is further developed in KS2 when children learn more about what happens inside our bodies, identifying internal organs and their functions, mainly focusing on humans, but also relating their understanding to other animals. Ideas about why some choices are healthier than others are explored by learning about the effects, often invisible, that various actions, such as exercise or smoking, have on the human body.

This area of the curriculum is often one in which primary teachers feel relatively confident about their subject knowledge. One of the dangers of this is that children could be taught content that is more appropriate for secondary schools, such as details of the structure of the heart or the inner ear, that may not be very meaningful to most primary-aged children. Of course, if children are interested, there is nothing wrong with helping them to explore these ideas further, but primary teachers should avoid asking children to label complex diagrams, such as a cross-section of the eye, that are difficult to interpret, just because they remember these from their own science education.

It is helpful to see where children will revisit areas of the topics at different stages of education, both to understand what level of conceptual understanding might be expected for most children, and also to consider how to provide an extra challenge for children whose ideas could be extended further. Table 9.1 provides an overview of KS1 and KS2 based on the NC Programmes of Study (QCA/DfEE 2000). For convenience, this has been split into four themes relating to the 'big ideas': classifying animals, parts and functions of the body, staying alive and healthy, and growth and reproduction.

TABLE 9.1 Humans and other animals: progression of key concepts

Key concepts	NC references	Teachers' background knowledge
Classifying animals		
Animals can be classified into groups based on their observable features and evolutionary links.	KS1 Sc2 1c KS1 Sc2 4a, b	The accepted classification system used by biologists is to group animals according to a combination of observable features from the simpler forms to the more complex. Evidence about how they are grouped in terms of evolution is also taken into account. All animals, including humans, are grouped in a single kingdom: Animalia. The phylum '**Chordates**' – meaning having a form of 'spinal cord' – includes the following groups of animals that are vertebrates (with 'backbones'): ■ **Fish** ■ **Amphibians** – frogs, toads, newts; these animals have a stage in their lifecycle when the animals have gills and breathe underwater (tadpoles); they are cold-blooded ■ **Reptiles** – lizards, snakes, turtles; reptiles lay eggs in soft shells and are scaly; they are cold-blooded ■ **Birds** – characterised by being egg-laying and having feathers and wings ■ **Mammals** – includes humans, whales, dolphins, horses
Parts and functions of the body		
Different parts of animals have different functions. Skeleton and muscles act together to protect bodies and for movement. The digestive system breaks down food into pieces small enough to be absorbed into the blood and transported all around the body where it is used for energy, growth and repair. Teeth can be damaged if not properly cared for. The heart, lungs and circulatory system take oxygen to all the parts of the body and remove the waste product, carbon dioxide. Active muscles need more energy so the heart pumps faster to supply oxygen.	KS1 Sc2 1b KS1 Sc2 2a, g KS1 Sc2 2a, c–e	Complex animals are made up of systems, (e.g. the circulatory system) formed of various organs (e.g. the heart, arteries), which are made of tissues (e.g. muscle), which are made of various kinds of cells (e.g. heart muscle cells). In humans the main organs and their functions are: **Nervous system** – brain and spinal cord, nerves, senses. Information from the senses is sought and travels to the brain and spinal cord along nerves. The brain is a complex network of nerve cells whose function results in thinking, feeling, controlling movement and some hormones. The details of brain function are not well understood and it is a huge field of current research. **Digestive system** – mouth, teeth, stomach, intestines, (pancreas, liver), anus. These are concerned with absorbing food and water into the body. The digestive tract from mouth to anus can actually be thought of as being 'outside' the body, and its purpose is to break food down into molecules so it is small enough to pass through the walls of the intestine and into the bloodstream. The digestive system first breaks down food mechanically in the mouth, and different teeth have particular roles in doing this. The outer coating of

teeth is called enamel. Enamel can be damaged by acid, which is created in the mouth by bacteria, which feed on remnants of sugary and starchy foods stuck on and around the teeth. This mixture of food, bacteria and the acid they produce is called plaque. The acid will eventually eat through a tooth to cause a hole or cavity. It is therefore important to remove plaque regularly by brushing the teeth and also best to avoid eating too many foods that have a high sugar content. Saliva helps prevent tooth decay by neutralising the acid. Keeping the teeth clean and free from plaque also protects our gums. If left, plaque can harden into 'tartar'. This coating will make cleaning the teeth difficult as it can harbour more plaque, which attacks the gums and causes them to bleed (gingivitis). This is the beginning of gum disease which can lead to tooth loss. At various points in the digestive tract chemicals known as enzymes are released and these help break down particular kinds of food. Any undigested food is what forms the faeces (aka 'poo').

Circulatory system – heart, blood vessels (arteries and veins), blood. This is a transport system for taking food and oxygen to cells and removing waste. The heart acts as a pump to move the blood through the vessels around the whole body and back. It also plays a key role in defence against damage by carrying blood-clotting agents and against diseases, which may be attacked by white blood cells and antibodies.

Respiratory system – lungs, mouth, nose. Breathing and respiration are often confused. We breathe in air through our mouths and noses, which goes into the lungs. There are tiny blood vessels running close to the lungs and oxygen from the air goes into the blood, latching on to the red blood cells, and carbon dioxide dissolved in the blood goes into the air in the lungs and is breathed out. The purpose of this is to support a process called respiration that happens in all living cells. In respiration oxygen is used to release the energy in food (carbohydrates) and carbon dioxide is produced as a waste product. This is sometimes represented by the equation:

$$C_6H_{12}O_{16} + O_2 \rightarrow CO_2 + H_2O + \text{energy}$$

Excretory system – kidneys, liver, bladder, urethra. The function of this system is to remove certain unwanted or waste products such as urea (a waste product from breaking down proteins) from the body. This includes regulating the amount of water in the body. The urethra opens at the end of the penis in males and just above the vaginal opening in females.

TABLE 9.1 (Continued)

Key concepts	NC references	Teachers' background knowledge
		Skeletal system – bones, muscles, tendons. The skull and ribs protect the vital organs of the body. The skeleton provides a framework to support the body, and also something for muscles to pull on to produce movement. When a muscle gets a signal to act, it contracts and gets shorter, pulling on the bone it is attached to. Muscles cannot lengthen themselves, so they need another muscle to contact in the opposite direction to stretch them out again, and muscles are thus organised in pairs. **Reproductive system** – in males this is the testes and penis; in females the ovaries, uterus and vagina. Reproduction is explained below.
Staying alive and healthy		
Humans and other animals need food for energy, growth and repair. Exercise and eating a balanced diet help keep us healthy.	KS1 Sc2 2b KS2 Sc2 2b KS1 Sc2 2c KS2 Sc2 2h	Humans need a variety of different foods in their diets. Carbohydrates (bread, rice, potatoes, pasta, sugar) are the main source of energy; proteins (in pulses such as beans, and in meat, fish, milk) are the main building material of the body and are mainly used for growth and repair. Fats (oils, butter) are also a source of energy, but certain fats are needed in small quantities for specific purposes such as insulating nerve cells. Vitamins and minerals have a number of specific functions, for example Vitamin C has a role in strengthening skin, and the mineral iron plays an important role in red blood cells in transporting oxygen. Water is essential as a medium in which all the chemical processes of the body take place, and is one of the main constituents of the human body. (Some estimates suggest we are about 70 per cent water!) Exercise maintains and builds muscle strength, including the heart muscle and muscles around the lungs, and maintains the range of movement of various joints. If more energy is taken into the body, in the form of food, than is used, then the excess is stored as fat and this can have consequences for the health of the circulatory system.
Humans and animals may have other needs, including sleep and emotional needs.	KS1 Sc2 2e	Lack of sleep leads to poor mental functioning and general irritability – rest is also a need. If the emotional needs of humans are not met this may also have physical outcomes as well as emotional ones. It might be an interesting area of discussion to explore the emotional needs of other animals – what kind of care does a dog need compared with a tropical fish?

Drugs are chemicals (other than food) we put into our bodies that affect how they work. They may be helpful or harmful, and this may depend on how much is taken and when.	KS1 Sc2 2d KS2 Sc2 2g	Although we use the term drugs to mean illegal drugs in everyday conversation, medicines are drugs, though not all drugs are medicines. Different drugs act at different sites in the body, for example alcohol affects how messages are transmitted between brain cells. Some drugs, which may be used as medicines or not, affect the nervous system and may reduce feeling pain, slow down mental activity, or lead to hallucinations. Smoking cigarettes has a stimulant effect, increasing alertness, but the nicotine in tobacco is also addictive so that smokers may need to continue to smoke to feel 'normal'. Regular smoking leads to a build-up of tar on the lungs, reducing the area available for oxygen and carbon dioxide to be exchanged. Carbon monoxide in the smoke goes into the blood and prevents red blood cells from carrying oxygen as efficiently. It also increases the build-up of fat in arteries, which increases the risk of a heart attack. The effect of alcohol, as with many drugs, depends on the 'dose' – on how much is taken. It has a number of effects – it causes blood vessels to expand, leading to flushed cheeks, and this effect might be helpful in preventing heart disease. It also causes excessive passing of urine, leading to dehydration. Brain function is affected, and at low intakes this leads to a feeling of disinhibition which is often experienced as being pleasant, but as the levels of alcohol in the blood get higher mental function is increasingly affected, and can lead to risk-taking behaviour, impairment of coordination affecting speech and movement, and also judgement. High levels of alcohol intake also lead to liver damage. Dependency on alcohol is a serious condition and there may be unhappy consequences for individuals and their families.
Micro-organisms can be beneficial or harmful.	KS2 Sc2 5f	The role of micro-organisms in decomposition of matter is discussed in chapter 11, but they are also relevant to health as some are the causes of disease or illness. Good personal hygiene such as handwashing is important in reducing the transmission of micro-organisms (often called 'germs' in this context) between people. We need to store food in such a way that harmful micro-organisms do not grow, so we refrigerate or freeze foods at temperatures below which they can reproduce. We preserve foods in sugar or salt or vinegar – all chemical environments in which the cells of micro-organisms cannot survive. Processes such as bottling and canning (tinning) keep out the oxygen that micro-organisms need to live. However, some micro-organisms have a positive role in health. 'Bio-yoghurts' are marketed as having benefits because the digestive system contains some micro-organisms that are helpful to the processes of digestion, and the yoghurts might increase these.

TABLE 9.1 (Continued)

Key concepts	NC references	Teachers' background knowledge
Growth and reproduction		
Humans and other animals all reproduce, but they have different life cycles. The human life stages can be seen as: birth, childhood, adolescence, adulthood (parenthood), old age and death. In sexual reproduction, genetic information from both parents is inherited by the offspring. DNA is the chemical that carries this information.	KS1 Sc2 2f KS2 Sc2 2f	Different animals have different means of reproduction and have different life cycles. For some simple animals, reproduction means replicating themselves through cell division. Insects, e.g. butterflies, have life cycles in which the animal takes distinctly different forms, i.e. a caterpillar (larva), a pupa, a butterfly (imago). Birds and reptiles lay eggs from which smaller, immature versions of the adult hatch. Mammals give birth to live young. An essential feature of human reproduction is that it is sexual – that cells from the male with half of his genes fertilise cells from the female with half of her genes, so the resulting offspring has inherited genetic material from both parents. The cells with half the genetic information are called gametes. In the testes of the man cells divide in a special way to split the genetic information on chromosomes and produce sperm cells. A similar process happens in the ovaries of the woman producing the egg cells or ova. Bringing the two together is achieved by sexual intercourse when sperm from the man's penis travels up into the uterus. At the midpoint of the woman's menstrual cycle an egg cell will be released from one of the ovaries, travel down a fallopian tube (oviduct) to the uterus where one sperm cell may fuse with it, fertilising the egg cell. For a wonderful account of how this is achieved see Babette Cole's (1995) book *Mummy Laid an Egg.* The fertilised egg now has the full set of genetic information that is a unique combination of each parent. This cell divides repeatedly, forming more and more cells, all with the same genetic information and, in a process that is only partially understood, different cells become different parts of the developing fetus. This all takes place in the uterus (womb) of the mother until the birth of the baby. The DNA molecule can 'unzip' and make a copy of itself – this is the basis for reproduction and how information encoded in our genes is passed from generation to generation.

Sources to further develop subject knowledge

Section 2: 'Life Processes and Living Things', in Farrow (1999), *The Really Useful Science Book: A Framework for Primary Teachers.*
Health Education Authority (1998a), *A Parent's Guide to Drugs and Alcohol.* Abingdon.
Health Education Authority (1998b), *The Score. Facts about Drugs.*
National Drugs Helpline: 0800 776600.
Teachernet: www.teachernet.gov.uk/PSHE.
Healthy Schools: www.wiredforhealth.gov.uk,
American Society for Nutrition: www.nutrition.org.

At KS3, children go on to learn about the structure of cells and to explain how the body functions at the cellular level. For example, they would learn about how different types of cells go together to form different tissues, then organs. An example of this would be learning about red and white blood cells contributing to the tissue called blood. They study the processes of digestion in more detail, such as the names of the various enzymes involved in breaking down different kinds of food, and they identify various parts of the digestive tract such as the duodenum (small intestine). The children would also be expected to learn about the role of the lungs in more detail and the processes of gaseous exchange at the lungs where oxygen is taken in and carbon dioxide expelled. This is taken further into a consideration of respiration as the process by which oxygen is involved in releasing energy from food. They are taught more about various types of joints of the skeleton and how muscles act in antagonistic pairs.

The curriculum builds on that of KS2 as children encounter more information about the effects of smoking on the lungs along with the health implications for abuse of alcohol, solvents and other drugs. Other PSHE-linked work includes learning about the changes that occur during adolescence, about the human menstrual cycle and the development of the fetus in the uterus.

Cross-curricular planning

There are some obvious areas of overlap between this area of science and PSHE and citizenship, such as learning about personal health and hygiene, drugs, sex and relationship education and making informed personal choices about these issues. Science can also make a contribution to other areas of PSHE and citizenship including:

- communication skills and debating: for example, *Should crisps be allowed as break-time snacks?*
- social/moral issues: for example, *Should we care for farm animals as much as pets?*
- loss and bereavement: for example, understanding illness
- making choices: for example, *Why should we keep safe from the Sun?*
- meeting and working with people: for example, school nurse or dentist.

Clearly we *could* link science with PSHE and citizenship, but there are also reasons why we *should*. Scientific knowledge and understanding about health need to be understood in the context of ideas about relationships and personal development. For example, smoking could be taught just in terms of its harmful effects on the body, but it is better if children understand the reasons people might take up smoking, and how peer pressure might influence people's choices. This seems to be more effective in promoting health than a more didactic approach or using scare tactics, as it supports people in taking control of their own health, as far as possible given their social circumstances.

Making these cross-curricular links also provides an opportunity to learn about risk-taking and about how to weigh evidence and make judgements that are the basis for personal choices. It can both strengthen the science learning, by providing a real and motivating context, and support some of the aims of PSHE and citizenship, such as developing personal insights and understanding of relationships with others. Understanding how science can contribute to decision-making, at a social level as well as at an individual level, makes an important contribution to developing a better public understanding of the nature of science. Science does not provide cut and dried solutions to problems, but evidence that needs to be interpreted and judged. Some adults have responded to the lack of certainty provided by science by rejecting it altogether – teachers could encourage a critical, but not cynical, view of science.

A whole-school approach to PSHE and citizenship could provide valuable contexts for learning science. For example, recent national concerns about lack of exercise in children could be the basis for investigative work: children could devise a survey into how much exercise children at the school have and make recommendations based on the evidence and their knowledge and understanding.

Some form of orientation at the start of the topic will engage children's interest and help them to access their existing ideas. For example, to encourage children to think about what happens to food when you eat it, provide them with a tangible experience of eating a piece of bread and drinking some water, and ask them to feel, observe and think about what is happening. They might discuss their ideas in pairs and give feedback to the whole group. If you were about to begin some work on the heart and circulatory system, rather than assuming children will remember what exercise feels like, ask them to do some. Younger children could be encouraged to notice changes to their breathing and perhaps that they feel hot, or may be a bit flushed. Older children could observe their breathing and feel their heartbeat before, during and after exercise. You could make good use of a PE lesson to do this.

Other starting points could be making a comparison between humans and other animals and also plants. Comparing life cycles, or different ways of eating or moving, would also be interesting ways of approaching the topic. A resource bank of photographs and video clips of various living things would be useful in arousing curiosity and generating questions:

How do different animals move?
Why can't humans breathe under water?
Do dolphins lay eggs?
What do ducks eat?
Where do cows sleep?
Do humans have the same number of bones as a gorilla?

You might want to start this off with some questions of your own and invite groups or pairs of children to come up with more of their own. Perhaps a display of questions children have raised would make an interesting visual starting point to a topic.

Assessment for learning

For ease of reference we have spilt the topic into the four sections that mirror how they are likely to be split in school planning: classifying animals, parts and functions of the body, staying alive and healthy, and growth and reproduction. Elicitation is important at the beginning of a new topic so that plans can be made in the light of children's existing ideas, but ongoing formative assessment is also essential so that plans are adapted and changed to take account of children's learning. These suggestions could be used at various points in a teaching sequence to find out what ideas children are developing or to explore a different aspect of the topic with them.

Animals can be classified into groups

In discussions children could be asked to think of all sorts of different animals. They may tend to talk about mammals, and not include animals such as spiders or birds. It is very common for people not to include humans in the category of animals – this is often reinforced in everyday conversation. Think about signs on shops that say 'No animals allowed except guide dogs'. They may have a range of knowledge of various animals, or it may be quite limited. Are they able to give examples of different kinds of birds? Can they describe different sorts of beetles they have seen? Be aware that there may be colloquial or regional names for some creatures, for example woodlice are also known as cheese logs, pill-bugs, coffin-cutters, bibble-bugs and chooky pigs! Older children could be asked to sort photographs of a range of animals into groups, explaining the criteria they have used. Amongst various possibilities, they might classify them according to observable features, such as fur or legs, or according to where they live. It might be interesting to keep to hand some photographs of animals that are less easy to classify, for example, starfish and dolphin, and ask them where these might fit into their system.

Parts and functions of the body

A simple elicitation strategy when working with young children would be to play a game of 'Simon says . . . touch your elbow' – observing which children can identify and name which external body parts and noting any areas for development. Children could be invited to lead as 'Simon' providing a further insight into their confidence in naming parts of the body and making it easier for the teacher to make notes.

This topic is very accessible through the elicitation strategy of annotated drawing. Children can be given an outline of a human body and invited to draw on it: *What's inside me?*. This could be open-ended and general, such as the location and naming of any different parts the children want to show, or made more specific – for example, children could be asked to show their ideas about what happens to food and drink inside your body, or about what the heart does. The annotation could be labelling of names of body parts, or could be extended to include ideas about what the part does. An exciting variation on this is to make it human scale by drawing around a child to give a full-size outline of a body. A group can then work collaboratively to draw and annotate it with their shared ideas. This strategy can be used to develop children's ideas as well as elicit them, as children share knowledge and understanding, and providing secondary sources of information to use could extend this further.

Children's responses to this elicitation were analysed by the SPACE project (Osborne *et al.* 1990). This research found that young children focus on parts they can see or feel or hear, so external parts feature and there may be representations of a stomach, or a heart and perhaps some bones. These bones may not yet show ideas about joints, but be randomly scattered through the body and might be stereotypical cartoon dog bone shape. A common alternative idea is not to see blood as moving around the body contained in vessels, but that the body is a big bag of blood – an idea that makes sense of what happens if you cut yourself. Children's ideas about digestion also make sense in terms of what we experience when we eat and how we talk about food. There is often some awareness of food going down tubes, but these may be shown as ending in the middle of the body, rather than being seen as a continual pathway from mouth to anus. Food and drink may be seen as separate and may be shown as having a tube each from the mouth rather than all going down the same oesophagus. Again, it is possible to see how this idea develops from the experience of going to the toilet. Older children's drawings may show organs (heart, brain, muscles, stomach) as separate rather than interrelated systems, and they might be encouraged to think about this with questions such as *Is that part linked to any other parts?* This helps them to see the body as an integrated system so when they think about running, the role of the brain, heart and lungs are considered as well as the legs.

Older children may have ideas about the heart 'beating', and may know about blood travelling in veins. Veins are observable and are talked about while the term arteries is not in common conversation, and so children are often not aware of the distinction that veins carry blood towards the heart and that arteries carry blood away from the heart. They tend to have very vague ideas about breathing and what happens to the air they breathe in. If they are aware of muscles, they tend to see them as only being in arms and legs, and not as being needed for every movement.

Staying alive and healthy

One possible elicitation activity would be to ask children to sort different foods into groups. Examples of real foods are better than words or pictures as far as possible. It is important that the kind of food eaten by all the children in the class is represented. Children could sort the foods in as many different ways as they can think of. They might begin with categories such as 'I like/I don't like', but teacher questioning could explore this further – What is the same about those foods that you like? – to draw out common elements. It is important to remember that this is open-ended exploration of the ideas the children have about food, and to resist trying to impose classifications, such as carbohydrates, until you have a good understanding of children's starting points and of whether this would be helpful.

Various aspects of health could be explored through a true/false quiz about healthy lifestyles. However, the answers may not be clear cut. Adding a column for any comments might be helpful in promoting tentative responses. For example, in response to the question, *Is eating a bag of crisps bad for you?*, you might explore with the children ideas about how many bags should be eaten and how often, and what it is about crisps that might be an issue (the relatively high fat and salt content). Ideas about a balanced diet are quite subtle, and teachers need to be careful to promote positive ideas about food, rather than make it a source of guilt and concern that might support eating disorders.

Questioning is a very important elicitation strategy and can be used as a starting point for whole-class or group discussion. To give individuals time to organise their own ideas it is a good idea to identify key questions and give thinking time for these rather than expecting instant answers. Asking pairs of children to discuss their ideas is a useful strategy for this, and helps to keep all the children engaged. Recording children's ideas means that you can reflect on them and their implications for teaching. Having a record also means that children's ideas can be revisited and reviewed. You might scribe children's comments onto a flip chart, piece of sugar paper or interactive whiteboard, possibly including the child's name, or children might be asked to keep a record of their own ideas.

The following suggestions for key questions are based on the SPACE project research (Osborne *et al.* 1990):

> *Can you point to some parts of your body and name them?*
> *Can you think of any parts inside your body?*
> *What do you think those parts are for?*
> *What parts of the body are needed for moving/eating/breathing?*
> *How can you move different parts of your body?*
> *Can you feel any of your bones? Where are they?*
> *What kinds of food do you like to eat?*
> *What do you think happens to food and drink inside your body?*
> *What do you think is happening inside you when you move your arm?*
> *How do you feel when you are healthy?*
> *What can you do to keep yourself healthy?*
> *Why do you think people start smoking?*
> *What senses do you use when you eat your dinner/have a bath/go for a walk?*

Using 'person-centred questions' phrased as *Why do you think . . .?* helps to communicate that it is the child's ideas you are interested in, rather than a 'right answer' (Harlen and Qualter 2004).

The question *What keeps us healthy?* could be used as the starting point for an individual or group concept map for older children. A concept map is appropriate here because of the different interrelated ideas. For example, exercise could be linked to a healthy heart, to strong bones and to the need for eating foods for growth and energy.

In the SPACE project research, when children were asked what they could do to keep healthy, they often focused on food. They had ideas about fruit and vegetables as healthy, but had less understanding about balanced diets. They sometimes noted that exercise was important, often giving examples of adult forms of exercise, or doing specific exercises rather than running, playing and walking in everyday life. It might be a good idea to explore with children their ideas about what exercise is.

Research by Barnardo's (their website, 2004) into children's ideas about lunchtime food showed that what they had for lunch was helping to define them in the eyes of their peers. A lunch of burger and chips was associated with a boy who was a bit cool, a bit of a laugh, whereas children in their research thought a lunch of sandwiches and fruit would belong to a 'sporty girl who lives in a big house in London'. So making choices about eating is not just about having knowledge about a healthy diet, but about the images and social meanings attached to food.

Annotated drawing is useful too in exploring children's ideas about drugs, for example, 'Someone has dropped a bag of drugs. Draw what might be inside it'. This activity provides an insight into children's experience and opens up questions of how to define drugs. Medicines, tobacco and alcohol are drugs, though we tend to use the term as shorthand for illegal drugs.

Growth and reproduction

Questions and discussions are also a useful elicitation strategy in this theme. Questions could include:

What do you think makes you grow?
How have you changed since you were born?
What changes might happen to you as you grow older?

Children's ideas about changes that will happen at puberty can be explored in a similar way to other organ systems by drawing on an outline of the body. It is useful to provide two outlines so children can show changes for boys and girls. As with all records of elicitation this can be revisited later and amended so that the children can reflect on what they have learned.

Other fascinating insights into children's ideas can be found by asking them to draw a picture of what they think is happening inside an egg from a hen or butterfly. Again the SPACE research (Russell and Watt 1990b) analysed children's responses to this in detail and found a variety of alternative frameworks: some children drew a miniature version of the adult, some a complete animal 'in limbo' just waiting to hatch, wonderful drawings showed that some children imagine different component parts such as legs, feet, body and wings waiting to be assembled. Other children have a view closer to the scientific understanding of a gradual development from an undifferentiated mass to the formation of different parts. Exactly how this takes place is not fully understood and is one of the great sources of awe and wonder and questions in contemporary science.

Susan Carey's (1985) research into young children's ideas about human reproduction revealed stages in the development of their understanding. The first stage of understanding is that there was a time when they did not exist, then thinking of babies as 'manufactured'. This is followed by an awareness of the need for a mother and father and ideas about the baby growing in the mother's tummy. Then they move to ideas about a 'seed' and an 'egg' and by end of KS2 children may be aware of the role of sexual intercourse.

Assessment of learning

The elicitation/formative assessment strategies suggested in the earlier section can be used again later in topics in conjunction with ongoing observation and discussions with children as part of the evidence base on which summative judgements can be made. Teachers may also wish to plan specific assessments that they will use for both summative and formative purposes as recommended by *Assessing Progress in Science* (QCA 2003g). This suggests specific activities and indicators of 'levelness'.

For children to be judged as having attained NC level 1 they need to recognise and name external parts of the body such as the head or the arm. They can show through talk or drawings that they have observed features of a range of animals, such as the colour of a cat's coat, or that spiders have lots of legs.

At NC level 2 children would be able to list food and water as things animals need to live. They would recognise that living things grow and reproduce so they might be able to give examples of the offspring of different animals. Describing changes that humans go through as they grow from babies to children to adults would also be evidence of attainment at level 2.

Attainment at NC level 3 requires more detailed knowledge and understanding of what affects living things, so children might give examples of different kinds of food that are needed for humans to stay healthy. They would start to be aware of internal parts of the body, such as the heart, and to describe in simple terms how they feel exercise makes the heart go faster and breathing deeper and faster.

At NC level 4 children would be able to identify the position of the major organs in the human body, perhaps on themselves, or in a drawing, and use the scientific names such as heart, lungs, brain and stomach. They need to know that the heart acts as a pump and that blood travels around the body in blood vessels. They need to have more understanding of a balanced diet, for example they might explain how eating too much sugary food might damage teeth.

An explanation of the circulatory system that is characteristic of NC level 5 would demonstrate that that child had understood that the blood carries oxygen and other essential materials, such as food, and that the heart is the muscle that pumps the blood around the body. To attain level 5 they also need to describe the main stages of the life cycles of humans and point out similarities between this and the life cycle of flowering plants.

Scientific enquiry

In topics on humans there are opportunities to develop particular elements of scientific enquiry. Pattern-seeking and reference are two of the categories of types of scientific enquiry that were defined by the AKSIS project (Goldsworthy *et al.* 2000a) that will be explored in this chapter. Pattern-seeking involves observation, measurement and sampling, and there are links with data-handling skills in mathematics in its emphasis on constructing and interpreting graphs. These will be discussed here. Reference – the use of secondary sources of information to answer questions – will be considered in the next section.

In primary classrooms first-hand observation is a key aspect of scientific enquiry to develop in this topic area. Looking carefully at skin, ears, eyes, how our joints move, listening to a heartbeat and breathing with a stethoscope, and studying the different shapes of our teeth using a mirror provides valuable sources of evidence for discussion. This observation can be developed into more focused explorations into our senses:

Which smells do different people like and dislike?
Can we identify different surfaces better with our hands or our feet?
How far away can we hear a pin drop?
How do we feel after running on the spot?

Observation of different animal bones is fascinating. Children can make detailed observational drawings, making links with art. The artist Georgia O'Keefe has done some striking paintings based on animal skulls that the children could look at and respond to. Asking questions can support the exploration further:

Why do bones have holes in them?
Are they heavy?
What shapes are the ends?

These observations can be developed with measurements:

How big is my handspan?
Are my legs longer than my arms?
How many star jumps/bunny hops can I do in half a minute?
How fast is my heart beating?
How much puff do I have in my lungs?

When children are challenged to come up with different ways of comparing 'puff', they have some ingenious ideas, some involving balloons, others tape measures, so these are useful resources to have to hand. You can also buy lung-capacity bags to blow into – the visual impact of the large volume of air in our lungs is impressive. Measuring skills may need to be taught explicitly (Goldsworthy and Holmes 1999). Time spent, for example, on learning to use a stop clock reduces frustrations and will increase the accuracy of children's results.

In this topic some forms of scientific enquiry are less applicable. In particular, 'fair testing' by controlling variables, i.e. changing only one factor and keeping the rest the same, is often not possible for two reasons: ethical considerations and the variation and complexity of natural systems. Ethical considerations limit the extent to which variables can be controlled. For example, half of the class could have fizzy drinks with every meal and the other half water, and after half a term you could count how many fillings each group had. That, of course, would not be ethically acceptable if your hypothesis was that half of the class would suffer from tooth decay as a result of the investigation!

It is difficult to control variables in research into humans as the natural variation is so great. For example, if a medical researcher was testing a new treatment, they could not force the subjects to have an identical lifestyle or to have an identical attitude to the treatment – both of which might affect the outcome. They might select participants to reduce the variation, for example by having the same age band and gender. Another strategy is to have a sufficiently large sample so that all the individual differences become less important. Alternatively they might have a 'control' group, a group with a similar range of variation who are not given the treatment; the overall results are then compared.

Another strategy for investigating natural systems, and one that is more accessible to primary classrooms, is to carry out a survey and to look for patterns and correlations. A scientist might look for any lifestyle or genetic features that seem to be associated with high or low blood pressure. Of course, if there are multiple causes this becomes difficult to make sense of. A danger is that correlation is linked with causation when it may not be that clear cut. So, if there was a correlation between biting your nails and high blood pressure, it does not mean that nail-biting causes high blood pressure, rather than an alternative explanation, such as stress leading to both nail-biting and high blood pressure. The QCA scheme of work (DfEE/QCA 1998) suggests that Year 1 children could predict whether the oldest people will be the tallest and test their ideas by lining up in order of age. This needs sensitive handling, as do all comparisons of body size and shape, yet is an opportunity to think about diversity in a positive way.

Investigations also provide a good opportunity to develop mathematics – in particular children's data-handling skills – appropriate graphs can be drawn and examined together. (See Box 9.1 for information on constructing an appropriate graph.) Younger children can do this physically, for

BOX 9.1 Deciding how to represent data in graphs

Categoric variables

Eye colour is a categoric variable, which means it has no numerical value, and there are whole numbers of cases (children with that eye colour), so the data can be represented in a 'pictogram' (Figure 9.1). Since every case has an eye colour these are also proportions of the whole, so we can use a pie chart, although an understanding of angles is needed to construct one by hand (Figure 9.2). Pie charts and pictograms can help us see at a glance which are the most and least common or popular values, although pictograms are easier to construct and show actual numbers of cases more clearly.

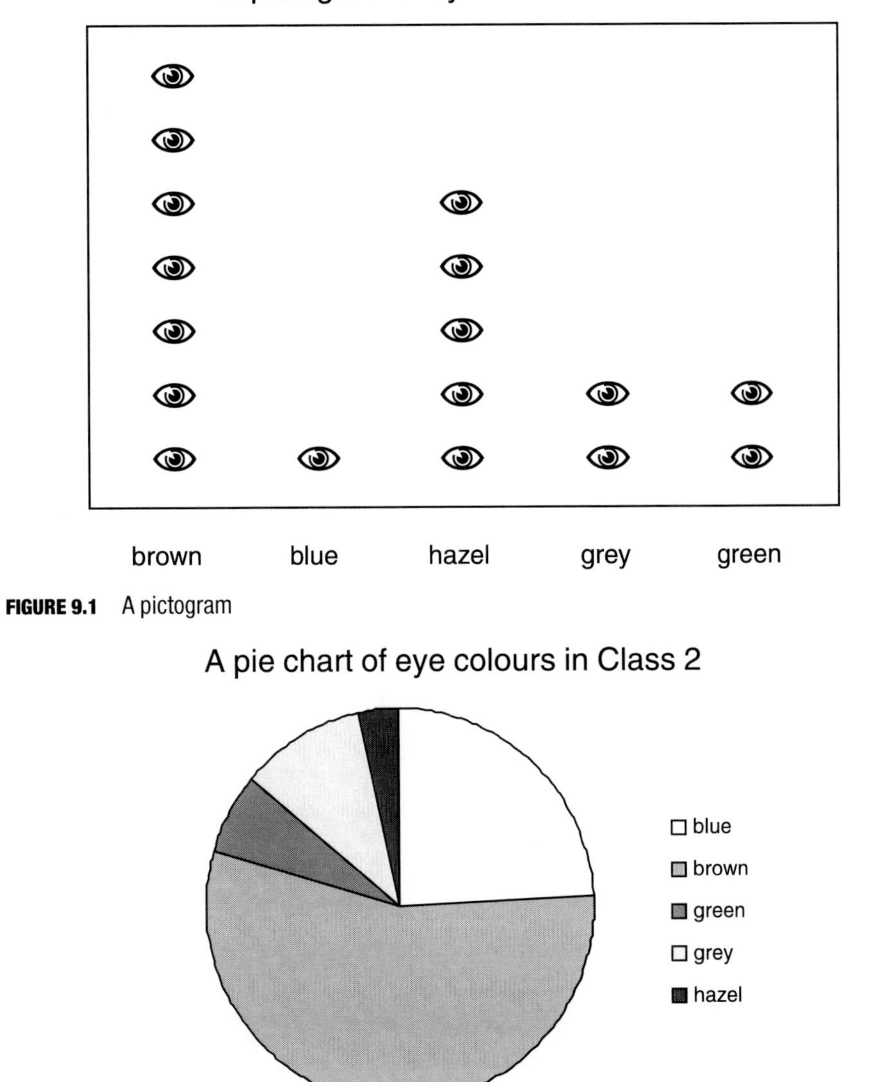

FIGURE 9.1 A pictogram

FIGURE 9.2 A pie chart

BOX 9.1 (Continued)

Discrete variables

Discrete variables, such as the number of brothers and sisters you have, are whole numbers; the numbers in between are meaningless, e.g. you can't have 3.5 siblings! This kind of data can be represented in a bar chart (Figure 9.3). There should be gaps between the bars because the spaces between them have no mathematical meaning. Bar charts help data to be interpreted and patterns to be identified.

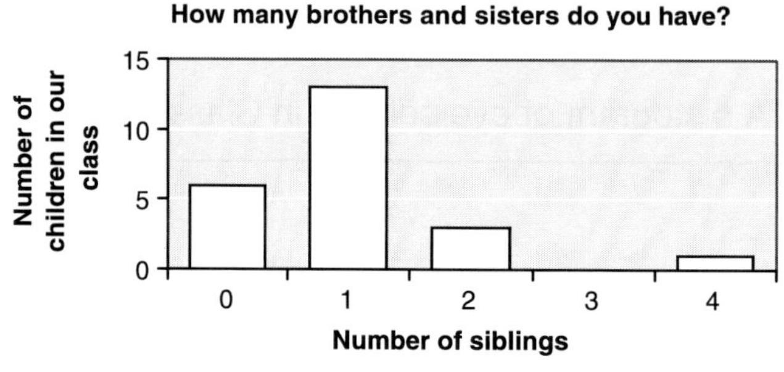

FIGURE 9.3 A bar chart

Continuous variables

Height is a continuous variable. If we want frequencies of various heights we need to use a histogram that divides the variable into class intervals (e.g. 5 cm). A histogram looks very like a bar chart, but the bars touch, showing that the variable is continuous (Figure 9.4). The histogram shows patterns in the data, such as the distribution, spread and centre of variation.

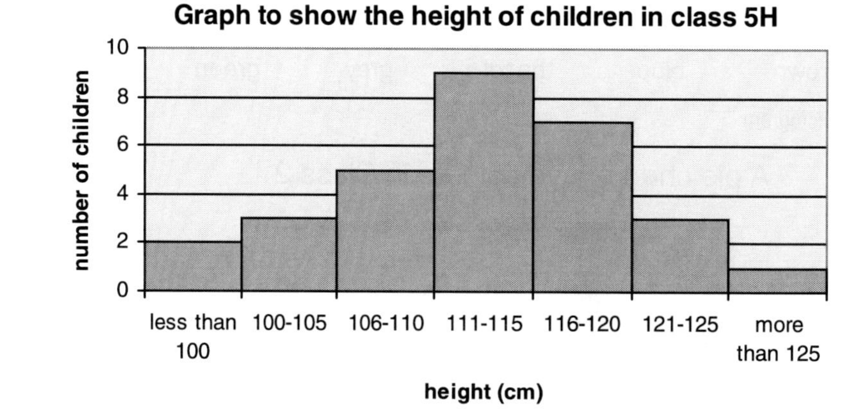

FIGURE 9.4 A histogram

If we want to show change in a variable over time (e.g. heart rate after exercise), the best option is a line graph (Figure 9.5). Line graphs can reveal trends in the data.

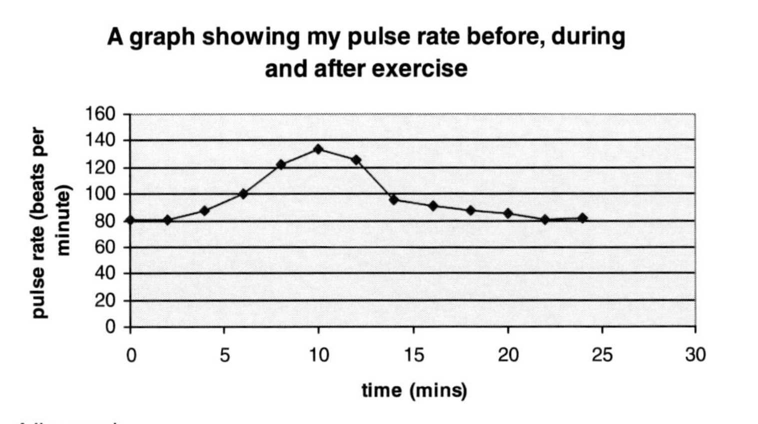

FIGURE 9.5 A line graph

If we want to plot two continuous variables against each other (e.g. height and weight), the most appropriate chart is a scattergram which shows strength of association between variables (Figure 9.6).

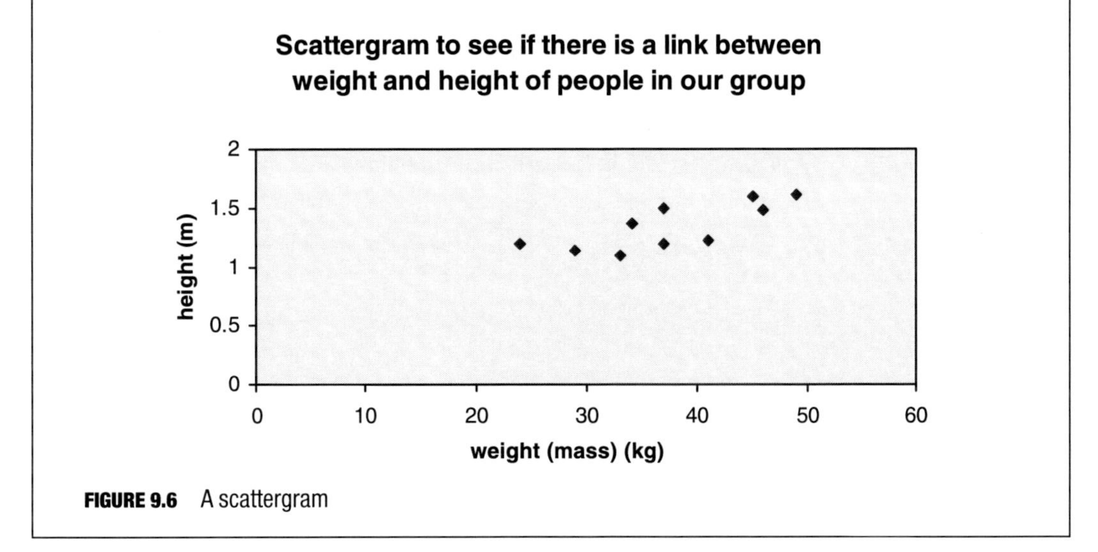

FIGURE 9.6 A scattergram

example by putting a block in the stack next to a picture of their favourite food, or visually, for example by cutting a strip of paper to match the length of their foot and comparing it with those of others in the group. Through constructing graphs children will understand the relationship between the data and the graph. See the section 'Using ICT to teach . . .' below for further suggestions on how to develop pattern-seeking activities.

Assessment of scientific enquiry

The topic of humans and other animals provides opportunities to assess children's attainment in scientific enquiry across all three strands of Sc1, but in this chapter we shall focus on the third strand, 'Considering evidence and evaluating'.

At NC level 1 children make simple observations and describe these, showing interest and sometimes surprise. For example, a child might do a simple drawing showing a chick hatching out of an egg. This is built on at NC level 2 when children need to have shown that they can make simple comparisons and say whether what happened was what they expected. In the context of humans and other animals this could mean they can describe similarities and differences between a bird and a beetle, or suggest reasons why babies need to drink milk rather than eat solid foods, for example, 'It hasn't got teeth yet: it might be sick if you gave it some apple.' With support they would be able to recognise some difficulties encountered in carrying out an enquiry. At NC level 3 this would have developed further with children making some general statements about simple patterns in results and suggesting simple explanations for these, such as 'Most children in Year 4 are heavier than children in Year 2 because they have been alive longer and have grown more.' They would also be able to make some suggestions about how the enquiry could be improved, such as 'We could have weighed people in Year 3 as well to make sure.' To attain NC level 4 children need to make generalisations that clearly link two factors in the enquiry. For example, 'The more I exercise, the faster my heart beats' or 'In my group, the older the child, the bigger their arm span.' With support they can use this generalisation to make further predictions. Explanations for results are related to scientific knowledge. For example, 'I think the heart beats faster because the muscles need more energy.' They can suggest how sampling children in other groups could improve the enquiry. NC level 5 requires a greater level of independence than level 4 in describing any patterns in data, developing generalisations and linking them to their scientific understanding of the enquiry. Children are more sophisticated in evaluating enquiries, for example they might discuss how different groups in the class who carried out similar enquiries got different results and suggest reasons for this.

QCA (2003g) *Assessing Progress in Science, KS2: Unit 8 Humans* includes an example of how assessment of KS2 children's investigation into the effect of exercise on pulse rate could be conducted and analysed to assess aspects of Sc1. The website www.azteachscience.co.uk contains some useful examples of assessments of scientific enquiry linked to topics on humans: Year 1 Ourselves, Year 2 Health and Growth, Year 3 Teeth and Eating, Year 5 Keeping Healthy.

Developing children's understanding

Alongside the first-hand observations and enquiries, which will contribute to developing children's understanding, teachers may want to introduce children to conceptual knowledge and understanding in different ways. One of the challenges of this topic is to help children to understand what they cannot directly see – what is happening inside living bodies. Using visual material such as pictures, video and three-dimensional models can help to develop explanations. Another strategy is to use models and analogies to help children relate new ideas to existing knowledge and experiences. The use of secondary sources of information is not only helpful as a teaching and learning tool, but provides an opportunity to evaluate them as sources of evidence, supporting some of the big aims of this topic – to take a critical approach to information. The use of information texts in English lessons can be made more motivating by linking them with research into questions raised in science lessons. Developing meaningful contexts for learning through links with PSHE can be supported by the use of stories and poems. Teaching about drugs and sex raises issues about how to approach these sensitive subjects and these will be considered in the section on class management.

Animals can be classified into groups

Visits to children's farms, wildlife centres, such as those run by the Wildfowl Trust, or zoos provide children with rich experiences of the variety of life and how different animals are cared for. They also raise issues for discussion: *Is it right that animals should be kept for us to look at or should they all be in the wild?* Try not to neglect the wildlife of the UK – there are links here with the study of habitats (chapter 11).

Children could carry out research into various animals using secondary sources and the results can be presented in various ways. For example, each group or pair of children could focus their attention on one animal and compile a factfile, perhaps presenting this to the rest of the class in the form of a PowerPoint presentation. A class information book could be constructed by making collections of photographs of the range of different ears, feet, body coverings and eyes that different animals have, and discussions could explore the variety of these and try to make links to how they function and to the environment they live in. For example, the kind of mouth could be related to what the animal eats. Again there are strong links here with the study of habitats. The website www.arkive.org is an excellent source of photographs and video clips of different animals and has particular information pages written for children.

Parts and functions of the body

Kress *et al.* (2001) describe how a teacher used hand gestures and drawings together with verbal explanations and reference to children's own bodies to help explain how the heart and circulatory systems works. This 'multimodal' approach to explaining about the functions of different parts of the body seems to be generally useful. However, choosing illustrations and three-dimensional models with an appropriate level of detail can be quite difficult as many include so much information it is difficult to make sense of it. It is possible to buy or make 'body aprons' – tabards worn by a child with organs, such as the heart, made of felt and labels that can be stuck on using Velcro. They have the advantage over paper versions of relating the position of organs to the real human body and of being more three-dimensional. They provide a kinaesthetic dimension as the child can feel the position of the various body parts.

Teeth are the first stage in the process of digestion. The 'big idea' of digestion is that food is broken down into small enough parts that it can cross the wall of the intestine, be taken up by capillaries and so move into the bloodstream to be taken around the body. This happens at a molecular level with different enzymes breaking down different types of food and this is addressed at secondary school, but the process begins with a mechanical breaking down of food in the mouth – by the teeth. Models of the ways in which different kinds of teeth work can be created: scissors for the slicing action of the incisors, forks for the canines which are designed for stabbing and tearing, a pestle and mortar for the grinding of molars, a squirt of water for saliva. Trying this model out on a banana is very popular!

Tooth decay occurs when bacteria (in plaque) break down sugars forming acids that dissolve the enamel and attack the gums. Brushing teeth reduces tooth decay because it helps stop the plaque layer from building up. Disclosing tablets can be bought from the chemist. When they are chewed they will turn plaque a bright red – it can be a striking demonstration of how much plaque remains even after teeth have been brushed.

Fen Marshall (2001) has developed some models and analogies to use with children to develop their ideas about the body. In groups, the children considered the similarities and differences between the model and what it represented: ketchup for blood, a camera for an eye, a tape recorder for ears, a balloon for lungs, and a bicycle pump for a heart. This provided a stimulus for discussion and sharing of knowledge, opportunities for the teacher to contribute new ideas, and for children to use secondary sources of information to further develop ideas and to resolve disputes.

The Internet and commercial CD-ROMs can be a useful source of illustrations, sometimes with the added benefit of simulating three-dimensional rotations or of animating processes. Of course, they can also be a source of non-fiction text that can be used in a similar way to books. The strategy of using a 'KWL grid' is useful in using non-fiction texts to support learning in science: the grid has three columns with the headings 'What I Know' (K), 'What I Want to Know' (W) and 'What I Have Learned' (L) (Wray and Lewis 1997). The first two columns are completed to set up the enquiry, for example into teeth, and then sources of information are used to try to extend the knowledge and answer questions. Any new information is recorded in the last column. Older children can refer to several different sources of information and can compare them.

Having existing questions to answer that the children have raised themselves is motivating, and also helps children with restructuring information from texts rather than copying it. Inviting a guest 'expert' provides another good secondary source for information, and again, having some questions prepared in advance makes the best use of these opportunities.

Staying alive and healthy

It is important to make sure that different foods are not presented as good or bad, or as healthy or unhealthy in themselves, but that a diet can be healthy or less so. What makes a diet healthy to some extent depends on the age of the person and their lifestyle. So what is healthy for an active, growing child may not be the same as for a more sedentary adult. Using a 'food pyramid' is a good visual means of exploring this message (Figure 9.7). Foods can be placed on the pyramid to show which food you should eat more of, and which should only be eaten in small quantities. This idea could be developed in all kinds of ways, using pictures, perhaps on an interactive whiteboard, or by placing examples of the foods on a big pyramid on the floor.

In one classroom, two trainee teachers brought in their lunchboxes – one full with chocolate, cakes and crisps and the other with a pork pie, chicken drumstick and cheese sandwiches. The class were highly amused by this and readily suggested their lunches were not balanced. A collaborative group activity to develop this idea would be to have a set of 'lunchboxes' made from laminated card with pictures of foods stuck on with Velcro (Figure 9.8). Groups could be given 'mixed-up lunches' and asked to share out the foods so that each person had a balanced lunch. Older children could examine food labels and make comparisons about the amount of energy or salt they contain or even use the nutritional information in a game of 'top trumps'.

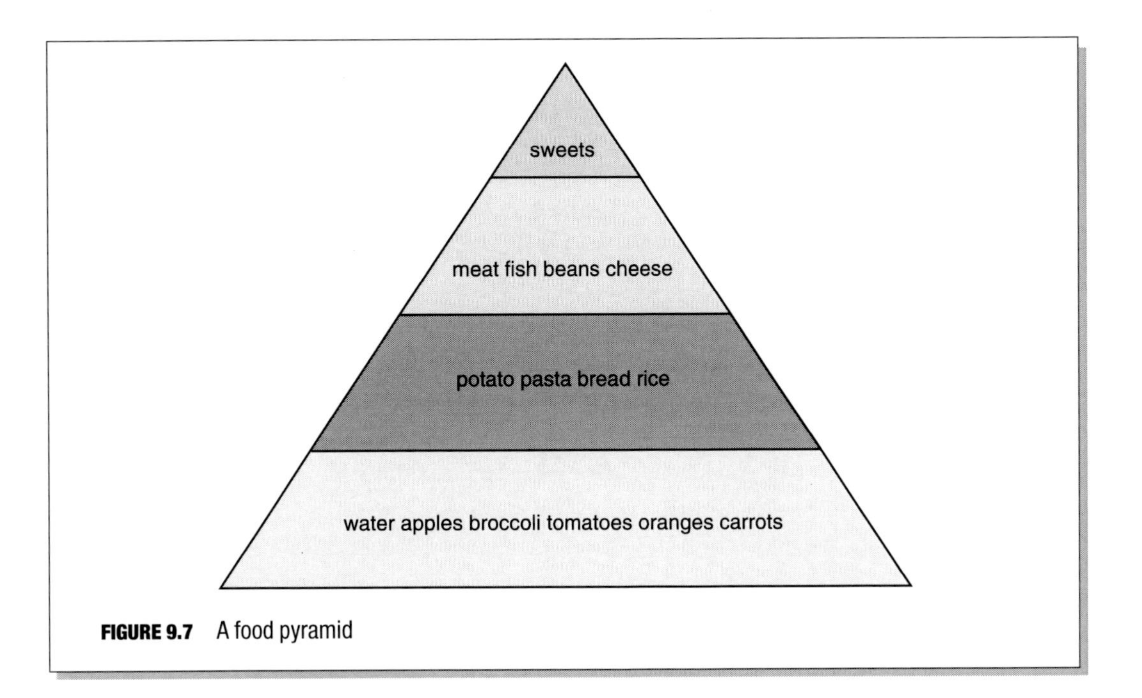

FIGURE 9.7 A food pyramid

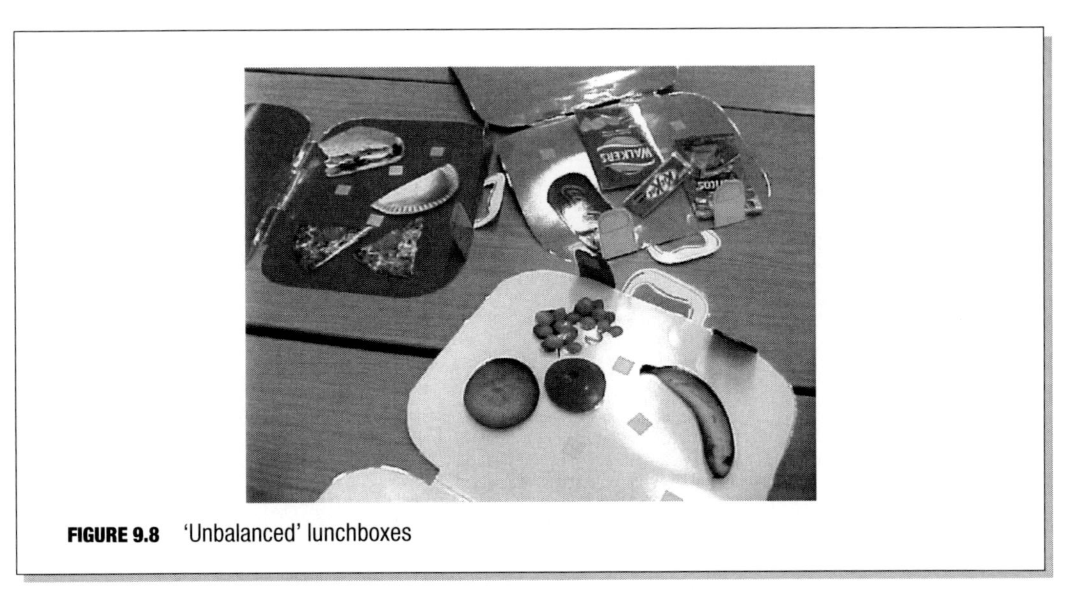

FIGURE 9.8 'Unbalanced' lunchboxes

Using biographical stories about scientists and medicine can also put science into a social and historical context. Mary Seacole's (1805–1881) and Florence Nightingale's (1820–1910) work as nurses in the Crimean War illuminates insights into the importance of hygiene and tells us something about attitudes to women at the time. The life of Charles Drew (1904–1950), an African American scientist responsible for the USA's 'Blood for Britain' project, which was set up to aid British soldiers and civilians during the Second World War is also worth celebrating.

Growth and reproduction

An experience such as having an incubator full of hens'eggs in the school and seeing them hatch is an exciting introduction to this topic. Butterfly and moth cocoons can also be bought and kept in the classroom, and the children can see the emerging butterflies and learn about their life cycle. Inviting a parent with a new baby into the classroom, and watching how it is bathed stimulates questions and discussion among young children (Figure 9.9). They could be asked to bring in photographs of themselves as babies and toddlers and to think about how they have changed. Children could be invited to make zig-zag books (folded paper strips) of annotated drawings that track the changes in their lives: *How have you changed since you were born? How do you think you will change as you grow up?* This provides cross-curricular links with history as it involves developing a sense of time and change over time.

It is not only non-fiction that provides useful sources of information. Effective use can be made of stories about caring for animals, growth and change, birth, death and illness, both as sources of information and to help to explore the feelings associated with these issues. Babette Cole has written some wonderful picture books that take a light-hearted but informative look at some of these subjects, such as *Dr Dog* (1996) and *Hair in Funny Places* (2001). Teachers often make use of television programmes or videos to help children learn about the changes they may encounter at puberty such as the Channel 4 *All About Us – Living and Growing* series.

FIGURE 9.9 Meeting a baby

Using ICT to teach about humans and other animals

We have discussed above how this topic can be explored through investigations involving data collection and analysis. Children can also be introduced to computer programs such as databases or spreadsheets and can use these to store data and present it as graphs. Using ICT in this way is a valuable skill and can speed up graph construction to allow more time for considering patterns in data. Asking questions such as:

Who was the tallest?
How many children had a handspan between 6 and 8 cm?
What is the most common eye colour in our class?

can help children understand how to interpret data presented in this way. This provides a good introduction to pattern-seeking enquiry. ICT is perfectly suited to supporting this kind of activity and there are a number of specially designed software titles that can be used. Information Workshop is one such piece of software that enables data to be stored as a number of records and fields. Once the data has been recorded time can be spent exploring correlations and connections between data. Data collected for a whole class could be gathered on a database. More complex questions to encourage searching for patterns might include: *Are people with the biggest arm span also the tallest? Can people with longer legs jump further?* This kind of question is best answered using a scattergram (Figure 9.6).

The outcomes of surveys are not always easy to interpret. This need not involve complex statistics, although older children could decide whether the mean, median or mode is the most useful average, but children can look at their results and think about them. Questions that might be useful in promoting this thinking could be along the lines of:

When the . . . increases, what happens to the . . .?
Some people say that children's hearts beat faster than adults'. Is this what our survey shows?
We predicted that . . . Is that what our survey shows?
Are there any trends in the data?
How big are the differences between . . . and . . .? Do you think they matter?
Can you suggest an explanation for this?
Could there be anything else that would explain our results?

Older children should be encouraged to make generalisations about results if appropriate: for example, 'The longer the legs, the longer the arms.' A further step is to qualify these generalisations if they need to in order to represent their results more accurately: for example, 'In most cases, the taller the person, the further they jumped, but some short people can jump a long way.' These are not trivial skills: they help prepare children for making sense of data and statements presented to them in later life. The publication *Getting to Grips with Graphs* (Goldsworthy *et al.* 2000b) provides many useful ideas for teaching children how to construct graphs and interpret data.

As a general rule, children at KS1 and KS2 are not required to learn about the internal structures of our bodies, but should instead focus on what can be observed externally. Taking photos can be a good way of focussing attention on the 'taken for granted' bits – eyes, ears, noses, fingers, skin, teeth, hair. Digital cameras, particularly those with macro setting, can highlight minutiae of finger-print patterns, eyelash length, ear shape, and so on. Digital microscope images of skin, finger nails, hair follicles can reveal fascinating detail.

If children wish to find out more about the internal workings of the body then a CD-Rom or on-line resource may be the answer. The BBC (www.bbc.co.uk/science/humanbody/) is a clear and well presented example and the American 'kidshealth' site (www.kidshealth.org) is worth a look.

Classroom management

There are two main management issues in this topic. One is to do with the teaching of 'sensitive issues', and the other concerns the particular information about health and safety that needs attention when teaching about animals.

Teaching about sensitive issues

'Sensitive issues' refer here to teaching about sex and illegal drugs. They are sensitive because there are moral and value positions attached to these areas that might also be linked to religious beliefs and customs. There is legislation around children's involvement in sex, alcohol, smoking and other drugs. Schools will have agreed policies on teaching about sex and relationships, and are likely to have clear guidance on what is considered appropriate teaching on drugs in their particular circumstances. Teachers need to develop these policies and then work within their boundaries. Parents have the right to withdraw their children from all or part of the sex and relationship education except for the parts included in the statutory NC, which is rather vague about how much detail is to be included. One of the implications of this is that it is important that parents be kept informed about what is happening and when.

A particular view of appropriate teaching is presented in *Sex and Relationship Education Guidance* (DfEE 2000: 5):

> It is lifelong learning about physical, moral and emotional development. It is about the understanding of the importance of marriage for family life, stable and loving relationships, respect, love and care. It is also about the teaching of sex, sexuality and sexual health. It is not about the promotion of sexual orientation or sexual activity – this would be inappropriate teaching.

This view of teaching about sex has a clear moral position, in that it is seen in the context of stable relationships, and the emphasis on marriage could be challenged. The guidance recommends that changes in the body related to puberty, such as periods and voice-breaking, should be taught at the end of primary education, and that how a baby is conceived and born, safe sex and contraception are to be taught at secondary school. There is a clear statement on homosexuality, which is to be welcomed as supportive of teachers and of equality:

> Young people, whatever their developing sexuality, need to feel that sex and relationship education is relevant to them and sensitive to their needs. The Secretary of State for

> Education and Employment is clear that teachers should be able to deal honestly and sensitively with sexual orientation, answer appropriate questions and offer support. There should be no direct promotion of sexual orientation.
>
> (DfEE 2000: 13)

Teachers are sometimes anxious about teaching sensitive subjects, and there are strategies that can be used to create a learning environment that feels safe for everyone:

- Set ground rules, for example no one has to answer a personal question. Specify names to be used for body parts.
- Use distancing techniques, for example role-play, stories, puppets, board games, video.
- Use boxes for anonymous questions, where children can write independently.

However, thoughtful discussion – in groups and circle time – is important too. Visitors, such as the school nurse, can provide useful sources of information, but it is a good idea to discuss the content carefully first, as there may be differences between their views and those of the school. A particular concern teachers may have about discussing sensitive issues is how to respond to 'difficult' questions or comments from children. If questions are too personal, teachers can remind children of the ground rules. Sometimes it is appropriate to either suggest that a child talks to their parents, or to alert the parents to an issue. If a comment or question is judged to be too explicit, then it should be acknowledged and the teacher should offer to talk about it later on an individual basis.

Knowledge that seems too explicit for the child's age may be a cause of concern, and if this is the case teachers need to follow child-protection procedures. Teachers have a duty to record and report any such concerns, but are not required to deal with them directly. The child-protection officer in the school (often the headteacher) will decide on any action that is needed. This topic may open up opportunities for children to disclose abuse, so it is important that teachers are prepared for this. When talking to children, never promise to keep something private, because if a child discloses abuse then this trust would have to be broken and this would be damaging.

Health and safety issues

If children are exploring their senses by tasting foods it is very important that all the surfaces and utensils are clean and that food has been stored correctly. Cheap plastic spoons could be used to taste small amounts of food and then thrown away so there is no cross-contamination between the children. You need to be aware of any food allergies and dietary needs, and children should not be made to taste anything they do not want to. Children need to wash their hands and dry them before tasting, and preferably after too. If mouthpieces of some kind are being used, such as to measure lung capacity, then disinfect shared mouthpieces with Milton. Any teeth that the children are going to handle should be sterilised in Milton.

Animal materials from butchers are safe to handle and cut up, again washing hands in soap and water after touching them, but children may not be happy about seeing or touching dead animal parts, and attention would need to be given to religious and ethical beliefs about animals and food. Bones can be prepared to use in the classroom by simmering them with calcium carbonate (washing soda), scrubbing them well, and then rinsing them and putting them in undiluted household bleach for a day to sterilise them. Dead mammals and birds are likely to be infected and should not be used, so if a child does bring one in, wrap it in newspaper and a plastic bag and dispose of it as kitchen waste. Explaining why this needs to be done is a teaching opportunity! There is detailed guidance in *Be Safe!* (ASE 2001) on keeping live animals in school.

Summary

In this chapter we have recommended that learning about humans and other animals can be linked with PSHE and citizenship because it provides real contexts for scientific learning that are relevant to the children. We focused on the elicitation strategies of sorting, annotated drawing and questioning, providing examples of how these might be used in various contexts in this topic. Humans and other animals as a topic lends itself to developing scientific enquiry skills of observation and pattern-finding, and effective use of links with ICT and maths can support this. Finally, we identified other teaching strategies that are useful in developing children's conceptual understanding, including using visual models and secondary sources of information, and provided guidance on teaching the sensitive issues of sex and relationships and drugs. Children applying their knowledge and understanding in one curriculum area to another consolidates learning and helps break down the compartmentalisation of science as a way of knowing that is separate from everyday understanding.

Discussion points

1. What science knowledge and understanding do children need in order to make choices about the food they eat?
2. List some of the ways schools could make a positive contribution to the health of pupils and teachers.

Further reading

Cole (1995), *Mummy Laid an Egg*: an ideal children's book for provoking discussion and questions – but be prepared to deal with some tricky questions sensitively.

Davies (2004), *Poo*: a delightful and informative children's book on a fascinating topic!

Goldsworthy *et al.* (2000b), *Investigations: Getting to Grips with Graphs*: this resource will give teachers a range of ideas about how to develop children's data presentation and interpretation skills.

CHAPTER

10

The green kingdom: plants

Purpose of this chapter

After reading this chapter you should have:

- an understanding of how children's knowledge and understanding of plants will develop from early childhood until the beginning of secondary education
- knowledge of research into children's ideas about plants and strategies for eliciting children's understanding of plants
- knowledge of a range of appropriate activities to teach about plants through an enquiry-based approach.

Introduction

ALL OUR LIVES DEPEND on them. Understanding and appreciating the life of plants is fundamental to the survival of our species and to sustainable development of the planet. This is an area of science that is relatively easy to resource, it lends itself to a range of scientific enquiries and it has great potential for developing children's creative and aesthetic responses to the world around them. This chapter will show how the study of plants in schools can and should be much more than growing cress and learning the reproductive cycle of a typical plant. Ways in which careful observation can be taught will be discussed, including the use of both digital cameras and more traditional aids. The chapter will also show how the diversity of plants can provide a range of opportunities for the exploration and investigation of life processes with contexts that have proven motivating to children: food, gardening and art.

It is impossible to imagine our existence without plants. It is a sobering thought that living things consume around 10,000 tonnes of oxygen every second. The planet's stocks would last only 3,000 years. Fortunately, plants have been replacing this amount, and more, for the last 400 million years. Most of our fundamental needs are connected to plants: oxygen, food, fuels, building materials, medicines. Many of our favourite luxuries from coffee to cola, cotton to cocoa, have all been provided by the green kingdom.

Plants are a vital part of every ecosystem, providing the food energy that every other species depends upon. If we are to understand anything about the big issues of sustainable development, preservation of biodiversity, famine and poverty, then we need a basic understanding of how plants live their lives. Good cooks are often also plant experts – they can name a wide range of plant species, identify varieties from subtle differences in appearance, recognise herbs from their leaf shape, and know if a fruit is ripe and fresh by its colour or its smell.

Gardening, visits to historic parks or botanic gardens, flowers on Mother's Day, autumn walks – all these activities are very much part of our culture. On a sunny Sunday thousands of us make the pilgrimage to the garden centre with the intention of beautifying our tiny patch of the Earth. The Eden Project in Cornwall has been a staggering success built on plant life. There is something deeply satisfying and intrinsically pleasing about growing plants, cooking them, eating them, smelling them or simply looking at them.

If we start soon enough, we can help children understand the importance of plants, know some details of their life and death and instil in children an appreciation of the diversity and beauty of this particular group of living things.

Progression from the early years to the beginning of secondary school

In the early years children will have had all sorts of encounters and experiences with living things in the classroom and environment. They will have used all their senses to explore plants, and begun to appreciate that they are all around us and can be put into groups and named – perhaps 'flowers', 'trees', 'grass', 'plants' (by which they may mean anything that does not fit into their other groups). They may well have grown plants indoors or in the garden, and may know that soil and water are important but have little conception of life cycles or the changes plants go through over time. During the Foundation Stage they will have had further opportunities to sow beans or cress seeds and watch seedlings develop, but probably not to mature plants.

At KS1, the study of 'green plants' is a strand of programmes of study for Sc2 life processes and living things. Plants also appear explicitly and implicitly in Sc2 in other strands including 'living things in their environment' (see chapter 11). As children progress, they will need further experiences of a variety of types of plant in order to develop their concept of plants to include grasses, trees, shrubs, 'flowers' and aquatic plants. They will certainly need to have the opportunity to grow plants from seed and to observe the growth in detail. They will also need to study plants in the local environment, for example, a garden, field, conservation area, hedgerow or wood. They will need to begin to see plants as part of the 'living things' group, different to animals in some ways, similar in others.

Although photosynthesis is not named in the curriculum at KS1 or 2, and children are not expected to know the details of the chemical reactions until KS3, children should be coming to a clear understanding that plants make their own food by the end of KS2, and teachers will need to understand how this happens. The key ideas about plants are outlined in Table 10.1. At KS2, some understanding of the concept of sexual reproduction as well as the mechanism for it is also developed, although the details at cell level (such as fertilisation as a fusion of gametes) are left to KS3.

TABLE 10.1 Green plants: progression in key concepts

Key concepts	NC references	Teachers' background knowledge
Plants need light and water to grow.	KS1 Sc2 3a	Plants needs a good deal of light once germinated, otherwise they will put all their resources into growing up and up, thus becoming leggy, yellow (as resources are diverted from producing chlorophyll) and eventually falling over. Classrooms are often too dark to sustain healthy plant growth. Plants need oxygen too, so too much water will drown them or encourage mould to grow. Too little water and the plant's cells will lose sap and go flaccid – the plant will look limp and fall over. As we need vitamins and minerals to supplement our diet, so plants need minerals, which they get from chemicals dissolved in water in the soil.
Flowering plants have leaves, flowers, stems and roots.	KS1 Sc2 3b	Plants come in every conceivable shape and size. Their sheer variety makes them fascinating and sometimes amazing. Observing their form and habit carefully is vital if we are to identify them. Leaves, designed to catch as much light as possible, can be little or large, smooth or rough, veined, ribbed, hairy, spotty, striped, fleshy, prickly, needle-like, jagged, split or holed. They can be every colour of green, red, yellow, purple, even black. Leaves are held on stems that are equally diverse – round or square, hollow or solid, horizontal, twisting or vertical, edible or poisonous. Roots can be delicate, thick and swollen or like branches of a tree. Plants store food as starch, and it is this fact we take advantage of when thinking of 'vegetables' to eat. Vegetable is not a scientifically useful word – it can refer to leaves (cabbage, onion), stems (celery, potato), roots (carrot, parsnip), flowers (broccoli) or fruit (marrow, pumpkin).
Seeds grow into flowering plants.	KS1 Sc2 3c	Germination of seeds requires an appropriate temperature, moisture level and oxygen, but not usually light. When conditions are right the seed will begin to absorb water, swell and burst its coat or testa. From the testa, one or two seed leaves will emerge. These are not true leaves but stores of energy in the form of starch. The radicle (root) heads for the soil and the plumule (shoot) goes in the opposite direction. The plant will rely on the stored food until it can produce its first leaves and begin photosynthesising food. If all goes well, roots will draw up water, leaves will develop on the shoot and the plant can grow. Once seed is produced, plants encourage their progeny to leave home – the adult plant does want to be overcrowded. Seed dispersal is a fun aspect of plant biology to study in the primary school as plants have evolved a variety of methods: **Wind dispersal** – the sycamore, ash and maple drop their winged 'keys' from a height, while the dandelion seeds are launched in feathery parachutes on a gust of wind. Poppies have long wobbly stems topped with 'pepper pots' that shake seeds out as they wave in the wind. **Water dispersal** – many water plants and shore dwellers (e.g. the coconut palm) have floating fruits that are carried by water currents to new desirable destinations.

TABLE 10.1 (Continued)

Key concepts	NC references	Teachers' background knowledge
		Hitchhikers – the 'sticky' cleavers and hooked burdock achieve dispersal of their seeds by hooking to the coat (or clothing) of a passing animal. **Edible fruits** – juicy fruits entice animals to eat them. The seeds pass through the digestive tract unharmed, and are deposited in a new location. Nuts lend themselves to being stored, buried and forgotten. **Exploding fruits** – some fruits, as they dry, suddenly explode open when ripe, expelling their seeds. The gorse, broom, wisteria and busy lizzie (impatiens, also a herbal cure for impatience!) are examples. Once the seeds find themselves in a suitable spot they may lie dormant for some time.
New material for plants' growth is produced in leaves (by photosynthesis).	KS2 Sc2 3b	Plants make their own food. Leaves are their factories in which simple raw materials are made, using the energy from the Sun, into new plant material. This food is then transported around the plant so new roots, stems and flowers can be made. Gardeners have 'green fingers', because they are stained by a pigment called chlorophyll, which comes from crushed plant cells. Chlorophyll is vital to photosynthesis. Photosynthesis literally means 'assembly by light'. In simple terms, carbon and oxygen from carbon dioxide gas and hydrogen from water are combined to make a sugar molecule of carbon, hydrogen and oxygen (carbo-hydr-ate) ('-ate' refers to oxygen). This can be represented simply as: $CO_2 + H_2O \xrightarrow{\text{ENERGY}} [CH_2O] + O_2$ This complicated reaction needs an input of energy. This energy comes from sunlight that is trapped by the chlorophyll and released at the right moment. There is excess oxygen in the reaction so some of it is given off as O_2 – oxygen gas – which enriches our atmosphere.
Roots have specific functions.	KS2 Sc2 3c	Roots have two main functions – to anchor the plant and to take up water and dissolved minerals to be transported through the stem to other parts of the plant.
The role of flowers and fruit in the life cycle of flowering plants includes pollination, seed formation, seed dispersal and germination.	KS2 Sc2 3d	Plants can reproduce sexually or asexually (without sex). The flower is the structure in which sexual reproduction takes place. 'Perfect' flowers have both male and female reproductive organs while 'imperfect' flowers have only male reproductive organs (stamens) or only female reproductive organs (ovary, style and stigma). Some plants have both male and female flowers, while other have males on one plant and females on another. Complete flowers have a stamen, a pistil, petals and sepals. Sepals are the leaf-like structures at the base of some flowers. Sometimes flowers are 'incomplete', meaning they lack one of these parts. Be aware of this when selecting flowers to use for a lesson.

Sexual reproduction involves the mixing of genes from a mother and father through the combining of sex cells or gametes (KS3 concept). At KS2 children will learn about pollen (male) and the ovum (plural ova) (female). The flower's anther makes pollen and the ova are contained within the ovary, usually found at the base of a flower. Plants have devised a wonderful variety of ways to get together these two cells through a process called pollination. Pollen does the travelling, therefore it is usually as light and small as dust – and can make some of us sneeze. Pollen is carried by the wind (in the case of grasses), by bees and other insects. The pollen is caught by the feathery or sticky stigma found at the centre of most flowers. Once on a stigma, the pollen grain grows a tube that finds its way through the stigma and style to the female ovum. The male sex cell, containing half the information to make a new, unique individual, will unite with the female half of the genetic information to produce a seed. This is called fertilisation. The ovary then swells and changes to become the fruit. A pea pod is the fruit and the 'pea' is the seed. The peas may look identical, but they will all grow into a unique individual with characteristics combined from their parents. The mother will be the same but the fathers could be different. Gregor Mendel discovered all about heredity and sex in peas in his ground-breaking work conducted, somewhat ironically, in a monastery garden.

It is easy to become pedantic about whether what we call a fruit is actually a fruit. For the purpose of primary teaching it is useful to categorise anything that contains a seed or seeds as a fruit. This is complicated by seedless fruits (e.g. bananas, cucumbers and grapes); seedless because humans have selected what would be naturally useless varieties. Tomatoes, pumpkins, peppers and 'green beans' are all fruits.

Life processes are common to all living things.

KS2 Sc2 1c

Although young children have trouble seeing plants as 'alive' in the same way as animals, they are classified as living things because they carry out all of the following processes:

Move	They do not get up and walk, but plants will move their leaves, stems or flowers (e.g. sunflowers) to find the light or a support (e.g. beans).
Respire	Within their cells, energy is released from food in the presence of oxygen. In plants they make this food themselves.
Sense	Plants can sense light, gravity and water. Some can sense if they have been damaged.
Grow	Cells can get bigger and also divide, so the plant gets bigger – usually growing for the whole of its life.
Reproduce	Making new organisms – plants can do this either sexually (flowers and seeds, etc.) or without sex (e.g runners or cuttings) (see section on reproduction above).
Excrete	Getting rid of waste gases, liquids and solids – oxygen is a waste product of photosynthesis.

TABLE 10.1 (Continued)

Key concepts	NC references	Teachers' background knowledge
		Nutrition — Plants use food they make themselves (see section on photosynthesis above) to get energy to do all of the above. Perhaps **MRS GREN** is a green-fingered gardener!
Living things can be grouped according to observable similarities and differences.	KS2 Sc2 4b	'Green plants' as they are referred to in the NC, or properly speaking 'Plantae', are one of the two main kingdoms of living things studied in primary school (Animalia being the other, of course). Scientists disagree about many things, and the definition of a plant is no exception. One way to identify a member of this kingdom is to check it out at cell level. A plant cell will have a cell wall made of cellulose, a sap-filled space within the cell and some tiny grains called chloroplasts, which contain the green pigment chlorophyll, which is vital for photosynthesis. If all these features are present then you probably have a plant. This knowledge about cells is, however, reserved for the KS3 curriculum. It is usually obvious to children that something green with leaves, a stem, roots and flowers is a plant, although we shall see below children are likely to hold alternative ideas about what is and what is not a living plant. To complicate matters, not all of the four main groups of plants have features that children usually associate with plants. **Mosses** are plants that, apart from being very green, have no flowers, stems or leaves. They keep low to the ground as they are non-vascular, which means they cannot transport water and food through their bodies. They reproduce by making spores, rather than seeds. **Ferns** are a group of plants that can transport liquids in vessels so have developed roots, leaves and stems – but they are non-flowering. They reproduce by making spores on structures usually found under their leaves. **Conifers** reproduce by making 'naked' seeds in cones (coniferous = cone-bearing). There are always exceptions in biology – the yew and the beautiful ginkgo tree from this group make seeds in soft 'berries'. **Flowering plants** are at the top of the evolutionary tree, so to speak. These are the plants that most children and adults will recognise as plants. **Seaweed, slime, mushrooms** and **mould** are the tricky things to classify. Seaweed and pond slime are called algae, which does not help say whether they are plants or not. If you want to study them in school, treat them as plants as they are green. Mushrooms and moulds are fungi, which have their own kingdom. Fungi cannot photosynthesise – they feed off dead or living things. Lichens (studied in detail by the young Beatrix Potter) are a curious group, and are actually two organisms – algae and fungi – living in perfect harmony.

Sources to develop further subject knowledge

www.enchantedlearning.com/subjects/plants.

Johnsey *et al.* (2000). 'Functioning of Organisms: Green Plants', in *Achieving QTS: Primary Science Knowledge and Understanding.*

During KS3 children will learn about photosynthesis and summarise it as a word equation. They will also be taught that nitrogen is a requirement for plant growth, the role of root hairs in absorbing water and minerals from the soil and that plants carry out aerobic respiration. If teachers want to differentiate for higher ability children at KS2 it is better to concentrate on broadening the children's understanding of plant diversity rather than introducing these new concepts.

Cross-curricular planning

We have identified a number of ways in which plants are very relevant to adult lives – farming, cooking, gardening, appreciating nature – but how can we connect them to children's experiences and interests? To orientate children to such topics a number of starting points can be suggested:

- looking at a collection of plants, for example a bag of 'vegetables' from the local greengrocer
- a trip to a local park, woodland or allotment
- a visit from a gardener or farmer
- a visit to the supermarket
- a classroom display that focuses on plants as food.

The above suggestions can lead to some interesting cross-curricular projects, but we can also find a strong justification to place learning in science in a cross-curricular contex by looking at the current direction of our educational priorities. Arguably the key intiatives of the decade in schools are associated with the health and wellbeing of children (e.g the National Healthy Schools Programme) and of our planet (e.g the Eco-schools project). In addition, Personal, Social and Health education, as defined by the National Curriculum, particularly 'Developing a healthy, safer lifestyle' DfEE/QCA 1999: 137) and the 'Every Child Matters' agenda, when considered in combination, provide a compelling framework of curriculum initiatives and legislation which make learning about the plant kingdom seem not only a good idea, but an imperative if we are to prepare children to make informed decisions about their future. Specific science-based questions can lead to some issues of global importance. Teachers might use some of the following questions to promote a class discussion:

What does 'Eat 5-a-day' mean?
What counts as a fruit or 'vegetable'? Why?
Where does the school get our fruit from?
How does it get here?
Can we grow our own? Is that a healthier option?
What other benefits might there be from growing food in school?
What problems would we have to overcome?
Where would we get the water and soil?
What should we do with the waste?

As this kind of enquiry unfolds, so skills and knowledge from many areas of the curriculum and themes such as economic awareness and sustainable development become central to the curriculum. It is the aspiration of many schools to plan meaningful learning around life skills and relevant knowledge. Perhaps the most fundamental way to learn about plants is to grow them. Setting up and maintaining a garden, allotment or conservation area has huge potential for learning across the curriculum from reception to Year 6. Organisations such as Learning Through Landscape, Love School Grounds, Eco-schools and Growing Schools can offer plenty of advice.

At Batheaston school near Bath, all children follow a seven-year programme of growing food (http://www.batheastonprimary.co.uk/ecology.html). Year group gardening projects include:

- Growing the ingredients to top a pizza
- Growing and learning about the use of herbs, field crops such as potatoes, corn and wheat
- Growing and eating 'superfoods' such as blueberries and broccoli
- Foods from another country
- A self sufficient fruit and vegetable allotment.

Apart from this programme, other foods and plants are grown to relate to other projects – e.g. the butterfly garden, the 'Withy Dome'. As part of the school's ongoing involvement with the community, there is a 'Grandparents Flower Garden', where older relatives and friends work with the children to grow cut flowers. Exciting elements of this work include the Produce Sales, where families can purchase school-grown foods, thus providing opportunities for the children to learn about 'economic well-being', and how to return profit to investment for future gardening work. The school cook prepares seasonal dishes from the produce that the children have grown. Composting, recycling, crop rotation and organic methods are other important aspects of this project work.

Batheaston school also recognises other ways that their outdoor facilities contribute significantly to the teaching and learning of the wider curriculum:

- Maths calculations about the costing, selling, profit and reinvestment are involved when the children sell vegetables, flowers and herbs they have grown in the class gardens
- Personal, Social and Health Education (PSHE) and organisational skills are involved in the caring for school animals, rotating land used to meet with organic criteria
- Play opportunities are offered around the school's bark trail and the withy dome
- The conservation area and outdoor classroom provide inspirations for creative writing.

A wholly integrated approach to cross-curricular work may not be possible in every school, but the creation of links between subjects usually is. Indeed, the linking units of work, for example between science and D&T, is welcomed by the QCA. Design and make assignments (DMA) provide opportunities for the knowledge and skills gained during science lessons to be applied in the real context of making a product. For example, linking 'Growing plants' (science unit 1b) or

'Ourselves' (unit 1a) with 'Eat more fruit' (D&T unit 1c) would give children the opportunity to apply knowledge about fruits to making a fruit salad in food technology, which in turn would lead to a kinaesthetic way of learning more about the structure of fruits. The first lesson could be an exploration of fruit and vegetables using the senses of taste, smell, touch and sight. Recording is achieved through using digital cameras, children's drawings and notes. The lesson might conclude with the compilation of a display of photographs and pictures of the foods and children brainstorming all that can be made with fruit and vegetables. Later lessons would then be planned for the designing and making of a fruit salad.

The art curriculum also offers potential for connections. After observing and exploring the diversity of colours and patterns in plants, flowers and leaves, art-exploration activities that incorporates colour-mixing and matching could follow. Many artists have used plants as inspiration for their work. The style of work of Georgia O'Keefe (1887–1946), in which she painted large-scale depictions of flowers seen close up and cropped, has potential for the primary classroom: work that is developed from observational drawing and sketches into large-scale paintings and pastel images could make a striking display. The work of painters Van Gogh and Monet, textile designers Kaffe Fassett and Cath Kidston or botanical artist and author Beatrix Potter all offer inspiration for further creativity.

Assessment for learning

As suggested above, an ideal way to begin a topic would be to use a collection of plants. This collection can also be used to elicit children's ideas. The collection should be carefully selected to include some specimens that would be likely to cause questions to be raised. Rymell (1999) asked children *What defines a plant?* Their responses revealed a range of definitions based on different experiences:

> It's quite small, not high up.
> That's [dandelion] a weed not a plant.
> It grows in the ground.
> It's like a plant; it needs watering.
> A plant is . . . a flower that grows in the garden.
> A fungus is not a plant . . . because it has a trunk like a tree [i.e. trees are not plants].

An elicitation collection would therefore include plants such as those children might know as weeds (e.g. dandelions), plants not in flower, a tree (or at least a picture of one), grass, a cactus, a tiny seedling, even an air-plant. The inclusion of a mushroom, a fruit and a cut flower in a collection would further challenge children's ideas. Adults or children could note comments in a floor book or concept map. You may find that, to some children, 'plant' may mean 'small or medium-sized green-leafed thing', which excludes trees, grasses and anything too far removed from a pot plant. 'Plant' may include or exclude 'flower'. 'Flower' and 'weed' may be mutually exclusive groups. Fruits and vegetables may be separate groups, perhaps not connected to plants. Fruits will include only obvious contenders, such as apples, oranges and grapes. Plants may not be seen as living because they do not move in ways obvious to a child. Although sunflowers turn their heads through 180 degrees during a day and some climbing plants can grow up to a metre a day in the summer, these changes will not be discernible to a child who cannot remember if they have had lunch. A plant's lack of apparent growth, 'feeding' and 'breathing' will all contribute to a child setting them outside a concept of 'living thing'.

The QCA (2003e), when analysing KS2 test responses, found that at the end of primary schooling many children did not correctly identify 'reproduction' as a distinguishing feature of all living things and that teachers can 'extend their understanding of reproduction by teaching explicitly about the stages of the life cycle of plants, including trees'. The QCA goes on to suggest that teachers could:

> . . . use ICT and video to extend children's knowledge of life processes and to give them opportunities to consider whether, and perhaps how, these are carried out in a range of living things; use discussion and argument to help children generalise their understanding of life processes to unfamiliar organisms.

In this context 'unfamiliar organisms' could mean trees, moss, seaweed or fungi.

The same QCA report noted that more could be done to help children understand how organisms are adapted for survival (see chapter 11). In the plant kingdom there are wonderful examples of how plants cope with a range of conditions: cacti storing water in their stems which are protected by leaves adapted into spines; onions exuding chemicals when damaged to ward off attackers; dandelions producing tall flower bearing stems to give their parachuted seeds a chance of a good launch into the wind.

Russell and Watt (1990b), in their SPACE research on growth found that KS1 children usually identified only three conditions for growth: water, sun and soil. Very few children mentioned all three. Soil was typically viewed only for support, rather than a source of water and dissolved minerals. At KS2 children mentioned water, soil and sun (distinguished between sunlight and heat in some cases). Few children at KS1 or KS2 mentioned air or gas as a requirement for growth.

Russell and Watt also found that children held a number of alternative ideas about how and when growth occurred. Growth was often seen as an 'unfolding' of material in a seed, rather than understanding that plants generate new material from water and carbon dioxide. Twenty-five per cent of KS2 children thought growth occurs in plants during the night rather than understanding it as a continual process. This is understandable, as children will witness that plants have 'magically' grown overnight.

Dale Tunnicliffe (1999) found that children were unlikely to understand the internal structure of plants, particularly trees. Her elicitation technique, of asking children to draw the 'insides' of a tree, revealed 'inappropriate connections' with the internal organs of humans. The children's drawings showed a wonderful array of muscles holding up 'limbs', hearts pumping water up the trunk and holes to allow the tree to breathe. It is not a requirement of the primary curriculum to know the internal structures of trees, yet it is a fascinating insight into how children can apply knowledge quite logically from one context to another.

Summative assessment (assessment of learning)

In NC terms, at NC level 1 children are expected to recognise and name the external parts of a plant. They communicate observations of a range of plants in terms of features (for example size and shape of leaves). At NC level 2 they are able to describe the basic conditions plants need in order to survive (food, air, water, light). At NC level 3 they distinguish between living and non-living things with reference to basic life processes (growth, reproduction) and they can explain changes in living things (for example lack of light alters plant growth). Children attaining NC level 4 will 'know and understand life processes from the KS2 *and* KS3 curriculum' (DfEE/QCA 1999: 77). This is a difficult statement to interpret as children are introduced to all life processes in KS2. A QCA report analysing end of KS2 NC tests (QCA 2004) indicates that 'pupils need to learn the life processes and relate them to the mnemonic *MRS GREN*' (see Table 10.1 above). They also need to have opportunities to relate the processes to the particular parts of the plants that carry out that function (for example, flowers – reproduction, leaves – nutrition). NC level 5 requires that children demonstrate 'an increasing knowledge' of life processes and of plant organs, again with content drawn from the KS3 programme of study (for example, the function of root hairs). Also at NC level 5 children will compare the life cycles of plants and animals and understand the importance of classification.

Scientific enquiry

Scientific enquiry may well emerge from an elicitation activity. In one school, a group elicitation session with a Year 6 class revealed a whole range of ideas and vocabulary associated with the topic of plants from being able to list just water and light as the needs of plants to citing 'photosynthesis' and 'oxygen' as key vocabulary. Further exploration showed that one child had some understanding of the process of photosynthesis while the rest of the group were happy just to use the word. One group said of a plant, 'it's a living thing' and 'the flowers grow from seeds, need sun and water and absorb the Sun'. Such comments suggest the teacher could explore the children's use of the word 'flower' to mean plant, whether the 'Sun' is understood as providing light energy and whether the function of leaves and flowers is understood. During the elicitation, the children in this case also raised some questions that they wanted to answer:

> *What would happen if we broke the veins of a leaf?*
> *How long would a plant live without food?*
> *Could you put a plant back if you uprooted it?*

These questions then lead to some fascinating and worthwhile scientific enquiries but need to be developed further to move them from exploration to other investigations. For example, *What would happen if we broke the veins of a leaf?* could remain a simple exploration, could be developed into a pattern-seeking enquiry to find *Do all leaves have visible veins?*, or could be developed into an enquiry to test a prediction such as *A leaf will die if its veins are broken, but the plant would survive. How long would a plant live without food?* could be developed into a reference search *Do plants need food?* or a fair-test enquiry: *Do some plants last longer than others without soil/light/water?*

A second way of initiating enquiry is through observation. Picture the scene: a vase of daffodils on each table, children drawing with crayons or pastels as the spring sunshine streams through the Portakabin window.

Teachers will be familiar with 'observational drawing' as a way of getting children to look more closely. Drawing leads to learning – the process of in-depth observation and careful recording is a fundamental way of knowing and has a long tradition in botany and biology. The children's author Beatrix Potter (1866–1943) was a skilled artist and created a large portfolio of botanic drawings before turning to the telling of tales. The knowledge she gained from drawing can be seen in her children's books where Jeremy Fisher and friends can be seen sitting on very accurately portrayed mushrooms. Skills need to be taught and the skills of observation and recording through drawing are no exception.

The drawing activity described above is considered step by step in Box 10.1, while Table 10.2 below shows how a number of other scientific enquiries are possible.

BOX 10.1 Observational drawing

Setting up the task

- Is the lighting and background suitable? Bright light and an uncluttered background are ideal for scientific observation. Has the Sun stopped streaming in? Does light need to be shed on the subject? Is the child inadvertently blocking light from the object?
- Do the children know how to use magnifying aids? Do they know that you have to move the object (or the lens) until the image comes into focus?
- Are appropriate drawing media and tools available? This depends on the type of drawing required. If colours are to be matched, can the paints or pastels be mixed or blended? If fine detail is required are sharp pencils or small brushes available?

Making observations

- Has each child had the opportunity to handle or be close to the objects? The learning experience will be a richer one if the child could look at, feel and smell the flower too. It may serve to focus attention on the specimen, rather than the vase.
- Have the children's observations been focused by discussion? What do they notice? The texture of the leaf, the colours, the cross-section of the stem or number of structures within the flower? How do they describe the feel of the sap exuding from the cut stem?

Recording

- What are the children to focus on? It is a tall order to ask for a drawing of all the flowers in a vase. A hand-held card frame – rather like a camera viewfinder – might help here. You might direct them to look particularly at: a visual element such as colour, texture, form, pattern (e.g. by sketching 'swatches' of pattern and colour, specimens could be compared); structure, such as leaves, anthers, petals (e.g. by enlarged line drawing of these dissected parts); variation and diversity (e.g. by six sketches of leaf shape).

Considering evidence

- Will there be time to share observations, to celebrate the work and to discuss what has been learned?
- Ask the children to say one thing they noticed, that perhaps no one else noticed. Make a record of questions about the plants that have been raised. Are the stems of other plants hollow? Do other plants have six anthers?

TABLE 10.2 Scientific enquiries: plants

Related QCA unit	Key concepts	Suggested enquiries	Possible multi-media outcome
1b Growing plants	Treating plants sensitively. Where plants grow. Why we grow plants. Change.	Observations of growing plants. A local survey: what kinds and numbers of plants, grasses and trees can be found on the school premises? How do we use the plants? Green plants need light: is this true? Ask the class how we could test this statement and support them in planning their own investigations.	Labelled drawings and photographs to show the parts of plants and what plants need to grow A diary or journal: *My Plant Diary* A big book of the class investigations
2b Plants and animals in the local environment	Where plants (and animals) grow and live. Comparison of two habitats. Flowers produce seeds.	A plant survey of two contrasting sites (e.g. two schools swapping data and photos via e-mail). Fruits investigation. Collecting seeds from flowering plants and fruits. *How many seeds? How are they arranged? How are they dispersed? How do they germinate?* Use reference sources to discover the life cycles and cultivation of crops such as rice, bananas and potatoes.	An information sheet on the two locations A poster or display of the variety of fruits and seeds
2c Variation	Recognise similarities and differences between plants (variation and diversity).	Observe and draw contrasting plants e.g. tree *vs* pot plant or conifer *vs* deciduous. Observe and draw/photograph a range of leaves, stems and roots.	A 'coffee-table' book entitled *Our Green Kingdom* to show the variety of plants in the locality
3b Helping plants grow well	Recognise that plants make and provide us with food. Recognise that plants need light, water, warmth.	Visit an allotment and survey the food plants growing. *Do we eat the roots, stems or leaves?* Observe celery sticks in dyed water. Compare a plant growing well and one not. Raise questions such as *Do you think the more you water a plant the bigger it will grow?* Support children in planning different investigations. Observe patches of grass in light and masked (dark). Test children's ideas about what will happen.	Produce a leaflet or web page about looking after plants Group presentation (e.g. PowerPoint) of *Our Plant Investigation* A food-technology activity.

TABLE 10.2 (Continued)

Related QCA unit	Key concepts	Suggested enquiries	Possible multi-media outcome
4b Habitats	Plants and animals depend upon each other and are suited to their environment. Feeding relationships and plant nutrition.	Sort and classify plants and animals through discussion (specimens or photographs). Survey how plants and animals depend on each other. Research and model food chains and food webs.	Make a key to distinguish common plant and animal species. Notes on how plants and animals interrelate. Plans or cross-sections of habitats
5/6h Enquiry (environmental)	To fully plan and carry out an investigation.	Plan and carry out a survey to find out how dandelions growing in two locations differ. Investigate the best house-plants to keep in school.	Scientific report to be published in the school's *Journal of Science.*
6a Interdependence and adaptation	Plants make new material using air, water and light How animals and plants are interdependent How animals and plants are suited to their environment.	Investigate the effects of 'plant foods' on houseplants. Use primary and secondary sources to investigate the populations in a local habitat and discuss how changes in populations will affect other organisms (e.g grass, rabbits and foxes). Identify plants and animals with a key. Use primary and secondary sources to investigate how plants overcome challenges in order to thrive e.g. getting water, getting light, protection from primary consumers.	Create complex food webs. Discuss the findings of an investigation. Write an evaluation of the investigation.

Developing children's understanding

Living things can be grouped according to observable similarities and differences

If you feel your class does not have a clear idea that plants are living things that carry out the same processes as animals then it would be worth spending time making that point through a sorting activity. Provide children with a range of items that includes some non-living things (e.g. stones, classroom objects), plants and animals (or representations of animals, ensuring the children understand the picture or toy is meant to stand for the real thing). When they have sorted the collection, discuss the common processes of living things and how plants and animals are similar.

If children are clear about plants being alive then move on to simple classification within the plant kingdom. Provide specimens for children to discuss and group according to similarities (e.g. tomatoes, Brussels sprouts, peas, beans, lettuce, cabbages, carrots). Encourage them to say why they have grouped the plants together. Ask them to construct an identification key to help other children identify the plants.

Plants need light and water to grow (KS1), and the effect of light, air, water and temperature on growth (KS2)

Growing cress does not feature in the suggestions in Table 10.2. Whilst it is undoubtedly an easy and cheap way of allowing children to grow plants, most children have had such an experience by the time they reach KS1. Many other seeds will germinate within 7 days (try broccoli or begonias) and can be used to illustrate variety and diversity. Rice is one of the most important crops in the world; it can be germinated from brown cooking rice and grown in a 'paddy field' (from *padi*, meaning rice in the Malay language) in a bucket.

Seed germination offers scope for the gathering of good numerical data for older children to work with. If seeds are sown in groups of 10 in a petri dish or similar (see the very useful Science and Plants in Schools (SAPS) website, www-saps.plantsci.cam.ac.uk, for detailed guidance on this and other investigations), the data generated can lead to calculations and graphs exploring the rate of germination and growth rates of roots and shoots. Another great SAPS idea is to sow seeds in 35 mm film containers that have lids on, a hole punched in the side or coloured cellophane over the top. The seeds will use their store of energy to grow in search of light. If there is no light they will grow upwards quickly in an effort to find it. This has the effect of making the shoots look spindly and yellow (etiolated). If light is coming in from one side the shoots bend to that source. Shoots that grow in light will be strong with green 'seed leaves' as the stored energy is used to make chlorophyll to enable the plant to make its own food. This film-pot technique also allows the variable of light colour and light direction to be explored.

Flowering plants have leaves, flowers, stems and roots (KS1), and their roles in growth and nutrition (KS2)

At KS1 children are required to know the names of the external parts of a plant. Children will be familiar with leaf, flower and probably stem, but roots will need to be investigated as, of course, they are not usually visible. Some opportunities for children to uproot and examine the root systems of plants such as grass, dandelions and potted plants can be provided to address this. At KS2 the emphasis shifts to considering the functions of plant structures. A classic primary demonstration is to put a stick of celery or a carnation flower stem in coloured water that can then be seen drawn up through the plant. This demonstrates one function of the stem, but does little to develop an understanding of the role of roots in the process of taking water from soil to leaves. A similar investigation can be done using a rooted plant (e.g. radish or cress seedling) compared with another without water. Put the roots of one seedling in a small tub of coloured water and another in a similar tub without water. Leave over playtime. *Can the 'dry' seedling be revived? Have the roots taken in any of the coloured water?* This will also demonstrate the concept of a plant being supported by water in the plant (turgidity), as the 'dry' seedling will be very floppy. Roots also have the function of anchoring the plant. This could be shown by a model-making activity using art straws or pipe cleaners to make stable tree models anchored by their roots in a sand or soil tray.

Recognising that seeds grow into flowering plants (KS1), the flower's role in the life cycle of flowering plants includes pollination, seed formation, seed dispersal and germination (KS2)

To ensure children understand the part seeds play in the life cycle of plants, it is advisable to involve children in opportunities to grow plants from seeds they have collected themselves, which will then set seeds in a reasonable time. One of the best plants for this is the sunflower, which produces hundreds of seeds from the 'composite' flower-heads, which in fact consist of hundreds of florets, or little flowers. One problem with sunflowers is that the growing season is spread across the summer holidays, although this might be an opportunity to plan work between two teachers. Some seeds, such as mustard or peas, will germinate early in the year and produce seeds that can be dried and are ready to sow again before the summer break.

At KS2, children should begin to learn from secondary sources the processes of pollination and fertilisation. They should have the opportunity to examine a range of flowers to understand the similarities and differences between flower 'designs'. Role-play is a fun way to learn about pollination – tennis balls can represent pollen grains that can be transferred between flowers and from anthers to stigmas by willing pollinators (bees or butterflies).

New material for plants' growth is produced in leaves

Children need to begin to understand the function of leaves as the 'food factories' of the plant. These factories need a supply of raw materials: carbon dioxide from the air, water and light. A bottle of fizzy mineral water is a useful visual aid to demonstrate this concept. It contains all those ingredients a plant needs to make its own food: water, carbon dioxide and dissolved minerals.

Using ICT to teach about plants

We have discussed above how to go about setting up observation and drawing activites. To complement drawing activities children could also make digital images on the same themes in order to develop a 'picture library' of the plants in a collection or in the local environment. The resulting images can be sorted, collated and manipulated to show similarities, difference and patterns in plant structures. Figure 10.1 shows, for example, four images that show leaf veining and patterns. In Figure 10.2, children have observed fruit and recorded their selection with a digital photo.

Most cameras have a 'macro' setting that allows close-up images to be taken from a few centimetres away. When displayed on a class screen, small plants (try daisy flowers) become wonderful

FIGURE 10.1 Digital images taken in the classroom to show the variety of leaf veining

things. Digital microscopes, such as the Intel Play QX3 model, can further enhance observations by allowing children to magnify plant parts. The surface of a leaf, pollen on stamens and root hairs all become remarkable structures when magnified 10 or 60 times. Images can be captured to produce a labelled PowerPoint slide show (see Figure 10.3), a textbook or PhotoStory about plant growth and reproduction.

FIGURE 10.2 Children's recording with a digital camera: a group of 'scwoshy' fruit

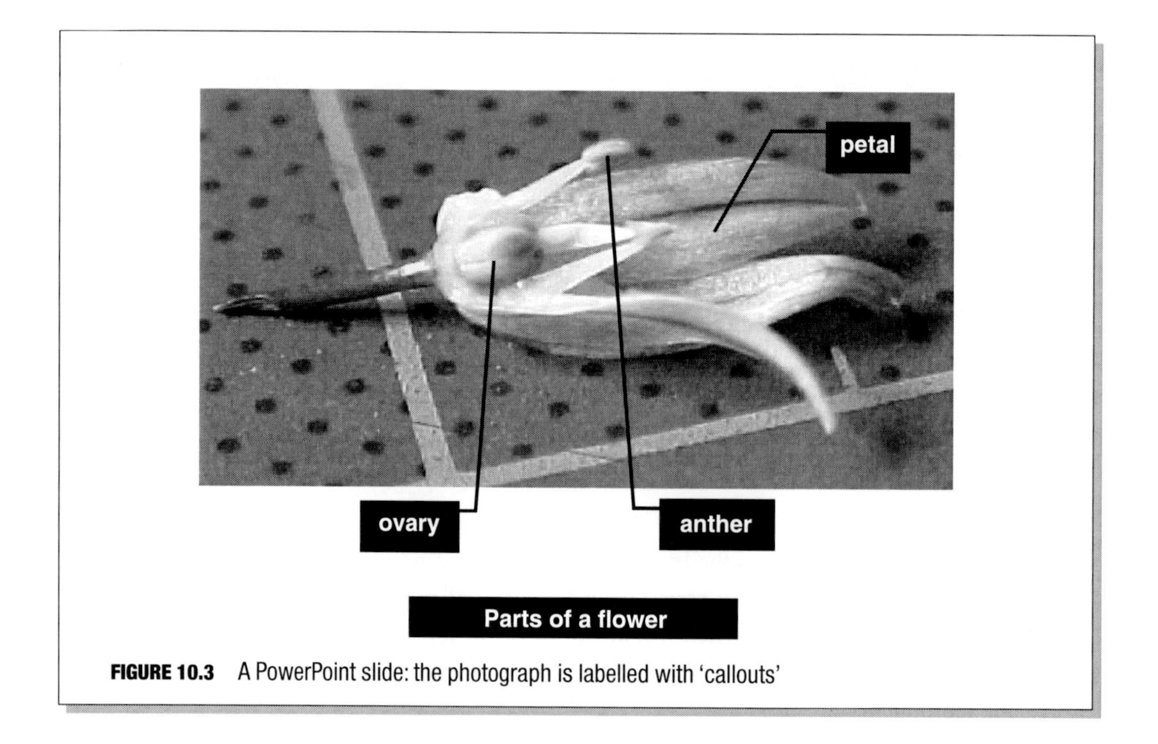

FIGURE 10.3 A PowerPoint slide: the photograph is labelled with 'callouts'

Timelapse video is one of the most powerful ways to illustrate that plants move and grow. It is possible to make using digital videos cameras or digital microscopes, although the task presents a number of technical difficulties. Fortunately there are lots of ready made time-lapse images that teachers can access. The best sources are:

The BBC http://www.bbc.co.uk/nature/animals/planetearth/hd/ – look for the high definition 'Planet Earth' downloadable clips (e.g. the flowering Baobab tree and jungle regeneration).

Plants in Motion: http://plantsinmotion.bio.indiana.edu/plantmotion/starthere.html – this site provides a very good array of material (e.g. a passion flower opening, plant stems growing 'away' from gravity and toward light).

Google video – search term 'time lapse plants' gives lots of suitable material.

Classroom management

It will be apparent from the above discussions that timing and preparation of resources will be an important consideration when working with plants. The spring and summer terms will be the best time to study plants, as they will germinate more readily and receive more light if they are growing on the classroom window sill. If there is not enough classroom space to keep trays of seedlings, then a good solution is to sow seeds in soil or water-soaked cotton wool inside small plastic bags. The bags can then be stuck to a window with waterproof tape. If the bags are sealed they cannot be spilled and will not need watering, as a little 'water cycle' will be created in the bag. This technique has the added advantage of ensuring the plants get maximum light. If you wanted to engender in your class a caring attitude to plants, children could carry the bags around with them, safety-pinned to their sweatshirts!

The start of a new topic is often the time when children's interests are captured. With preparation on the part of the teacher, children could have access at that point to seeds, germinated seeds, seedlings and mature plants rather than waiting a week or two for tiny seeds to germinate. A good deal of practical work on this topic is likely to be organised as group work. One way to ensure this is effective is to provide sufficient material for children to handle. Within a class of children it is very likely some parents will be gardeners and will be happy to donate material for study. Cut flowers are often used as specimens – but the greengrocer will also be able to provide leaves, roots, stems. School grounds may also be a good source of material. Even if only grass and weeds, a certain amount of investigation can be done: see the DfEE/QCA (1998) science unit 5/6h on dandelion growth, for example.

One strategy to focus children on research using a mixture of primary and secondary sources is to divide the class into groups and to assign them different aspects of the same topic to investigate.

Theme	Examples of aspects for each group
Diversity of plants	Tall, tiny, prickly, edible, poisonous
The parts of a plant	Stem, root, leaf, flower
Plants we eat	Fruits, stems, leaves, roots
Plant reproduction	Pollination, fertilisation, fruits, seed dispersal, germination
Growing plants	Vegetables, fruits, flowers, weed control

You may need to support groups to subdivide their tasks further: for example, each child may research one example, or one child might write an explanation while another draws a diagram. A significant plenary then needs to be planned to allow each group to feed back on what they have discovered. This is also a time when the teacher could make note of the contributions children make to the research. The final stage may be a class presentation, display or book publication that draws together the information (see Table 10.2 for more ideas on this).

Health and safety

Most plants are very safe to handle, particularly if you make use of food plants such as beans, peas, mustard, rice and radishes. Bought seeds are likely to have been treated with pesticides, so ensure children do not put them in their mouth, even if they look like food, and ensure they wash their hands after handling them. Health-food shops will sell untreated seeds and sprouts such as mung beans and rice.

The following common plants or parts of plants are poisonous:

- holly
- privet
- red kidney beans (before cooking)
- rhubarb leaves
- tomato leaves
- potato leaves
- yew
- mountain ash seeds.

Be Safe! (ASE 2001) provides a more comprehensive list of poisonous species.

If you think a child has swallowed any poisonous plant material, keep a sample of the material and seek medical advice immediately.

Summary

In this chapter we have seen that the green kingdom is very significant to our lives and, if taught in an appropriate way, we could initiate a child's lifelong interest in growing and enjoying plants. Even though plants share the same life processes with animals, children are likely to have a number of alternative ideas about plant life and do not necessarily appreciate the range and diversity of organisms that make up the kingdom. We have shown how children's ideas can be starting points for scientific observations and enquiries to enable a better understanding of life processes, plant structures and their functions. Finally, we have offered advice on how to use resources and organise teaching in appropriate ways.

Discussion points

1. How could the cross-curricular topic of food meet the NC requirements for Sc2 'Green plants'?
2. How could an inner-city school teacher make plants seem relevant to children?

Further reading

Science and Plants for Schools (SAPS) website, http://www-saps.plantsci.cam.ac.uk/: the 'Mainly Primary' section of the website brings together items that are suitable for the Primary curriculum. Other sections detail activities that might be useful in science clubs or with older or more able pupils. All link in some way with plants and many of them are fun!

Teachers TV: Science Tube – Green World (http://www.teachers.tv/video/12097): a 15-minute programme for KS2 about how plants adapt to their environments, and how they are essential to our lives.

CHAPTER

11

Living things in their environment

Purpose of this chapter

After reading this chapter you should have:

- an appreciation of how the study of living things in their environment will progress from early childhood until the beginning of secondary education
- knowledge of key concepts and how children's understanding of these develops
- knowledge of how to teach about living things in their environment, including how the topic relates to citizenship and ESD.

Introduction

THIS CHAPTER CONSIDERS the phrase 'think local; act global' in the context of science in the primary school. The initial focus of this chapter will be the use of local settings and frequent outdoor explorations to develop understanding of living things in their environment. We will suggest a range of sensory activities to engage children's interest in the natural world and suggest appropriate steps to move from explorations to systematic investigations of plants, animals, habitats and ecosystems. We will then consider how a scientific understanding of the interdependence of living things within a local ecosystem can lead to a wider understanding of global issues such as conservation and sustainable development.

Progression from the early years to the beginning of secondary school

Children can find 'living things in their environment' one of the most interesting and rewarding aspects of science, not least because it can involve lots of practical outdoor work. The key concepts of this area of science are concerned with the diversity and quantity of living things in particular places, the ways in which living things interact with each other and how animals and plants are adapted to survive and thrive in their environment. As children come to understand that animals are intimately connected to the places where they live, they will begin to appreciate that ecosystems need to be left undisturbed, protected or managed.

Good early years settings will make the most of the outdoors by encouraging children to play outside. They will also encourage children to experience and notice their outdoor environment. This may take the form of 'Earthwalks' or 'welly-walks', where children might discover the sights, sounds, smells and textures of a field or wood, or of digging and planting a small garden. In one reception class, children planted seeds in trays and nurtured them until they were big enough to plant out. Unfortunately, many of the plants were either eaten by slugs or wilted over the weekend. New seeds were planted and watered more carefully. The teacher discussed with them what to do about the slugs. The children noticed some plants had not been eaten, so it was decided to grow more of these.

Early years practitioners will also make good use of incidental events, such as finding spiders lurking in the outdoor sandpit or snails slithering up the window, to develop young children's knowledge and understanding of living things.

At KS1 (Sc2, 5a–c) children will find out about different kinds of plants and animals in the local environment, and will identify similarities and differences between local environments and the ways in which these affect the animals and plants that are found there. They will also be taught to care for the environment.

At KS2 (Sc2, 5 a–f) this work is developed to consider how different plants and animals are found and are adapted to their environments. Children learn that feeding relationships within a habitat can be illustrated in the form of food chains, starting with green plants. They are also taught about beneficial and harmful micro-organisms. Through this programme of study children will learn about how to protect the environment.

In KS3 (Sc2, 5 a–f) the curriculum includes 'the importance of sustainable development', how predation and competition for resources affect the size of populations, that food webs are composed of several food chains, that food chains can be quantified using pyramids of numbers and that toxic materials can accumulate in food chains.

At KS1 and KS2 teachers should take advantage of the opportunities for cross-curricular application of skills and knowledge. We shall see below that to study an ecosystem requires skills that may be developed in mathematics or geography contexts. Surveying, mapping and finding out about the rocks, soils and weather – all contribute to an understanding of the habitats that living things populate. The key concepts taught at KS1 and KS2 are identified in Table 11.1, along with some notes to inform the teacher's understanding.

Cross-curricular planning

The most obvious way to start work on living things in their environment is to go outside. There is a realisation among many teachers that children simply do not get outside enough. It would seem a reasonable suggestion for children to work outside at least once every month – perhaps this should be a feature of the school timetable. There is a strong tradition of outdoor activity in Scandinavian countries, even in their winter months, so we in the UK should not use the weather as an excuse for staying indoors.

A walk outside can provide a sensory experience that contributes to an understanding of living things and their needs. Even if the school lacks a pleasant environment, there may be some

TABLE 11.1 Living things in their environment: progression in key concepts

Key concepts	NC references	Teachers' background knowledge
Biodiversity: that there are many different kinds of plants and animals.	KS1 Sc2 4a	There are an estimated 100 million different types of animal and plant life on our planet. About 1.4 million are known and half of these are insects. It is exciting to think that there are plenty of species out there to be discovered by today's primary children. There is also diversity within species – just look at the diversity of Homo sapiens in your school, road, town or country. Species are incredibly important because they are irreplaceable. This is a fundamental piece of knowledge needed to comprehend the fragility of some ecosystems. Biodiverse ecosystems are important to preserve for a variety of reasons. Rainforests, for example, harbour species that may be useful to us but are as yet unknown. Diverse populations tend to be better at surviving changes, such as the introduction of a disease or pest, and they also tend to be more beautiful places.
Ecosystem	KS1 Sc2 5b	An ecosystem is a community of plants and animals and the environment that supplies them with water, air and other elements they need for life. Ecosystems can be studies on very different scales, from a slice of mouldy bread, to a single tree, to a forest, to the Pacific Ocean.
Interdependence	KS2 Sc2 5d	Each living thing depends on others to survive. Species are unable to survive without others (e.g. bean plants cannot grow without special bacteria). This interdependence includes food (one eats another), provision of shelter (e.g. hermit crabs use the shells of other species), dispersal of seeds and the control of competitors. Competition can come from other individuals from the same species (the population) or from other species.
Adaptation	KS1 Sc2 5b KS2 Sc2 5b	Animals and plants are adapted to survive and thrive in specific environments. Children can look for adaptation in the behaviour or physical features of organisms. For example, animals that live in cold climates are large and have a small surface area to volume ratio to ensure minimal heat loss (e.g. polar bear). They have thick layers of fat or fur for insulation. They have a white coat in winter for camouflage and may hibernate during the coldest months. A dandelion can survive in a meadow grazed by animals (or a lawn) because it has a short stem and grows close to the ground. It quickly grows a flower on a long stem, which then waves in the wind to release parachuted seeds. The seeds germinate quickly to colonise pastures new.
Energy transfers through a food chain	KS2 Sc2 5d, e	Food chains indicate feeding relationships, as energy transfer, between organisms from producers (green plants) to consumers (animals). Arrows indicate the passing of food

	KS1 Sc2 5c	(chemical energy) from one living thing to another and therefore the direction is important. The chain generally begins with a green plant (e.g. stinging nettle → tortoiseshell butterfly caterpillar → sparrow → sparrowhawk), or with dead organic matter (detritus) (e.g. leaf litter → earthworm → blackbird → fox). Older children will be able to understand the more complex representation of a food web. Food chains need not always include whole animals (e.g. grass → cow (milk) → human). A common mistake in making food chains is to use the arrow to mean 'eats' (e.g cow → grass), which is wrong because the energy transfer is from grass to cow.
Sustainability	KS2 Sc2 5a	Sustainability has a special meaning in environmental contexts. One way to describe it is to think of a bank balance that lists all the resources the planet has. Most resources are finite. The list would include soil, water, air, fossil fuel and all our different species. If we are to behave in a sustainable way then the bank balance should be just as healthy when we leave this planet to our children as it was when we inherited it from our ancestors. Unfortunately, current generations are likely to leave less soil, clean water, fossil fuels and species for future generations – our level of consumption is not sustainable – it cannot go on like this forever. Governments around the world agree that we need to concentrate our efforts on saving the planet from destruction. Their plans were thrashed out in the Rio Earth Summit (1992) and published in Agenda 21.
Materials are cycled in an ecosystem	KS2 Sc2 5a	When plants or animals die or are eaten then the materials that made up their bodies remain in the ecosystem and some are used to make other plants and animals. If plants and animals are poisoned then these chemicals may pass to the next animal in the food chain.
Micro-organisms are living organisms that can be beneficial or harmful	KS2 Sc2 5f	Micro-organisms such as bacteria and some fungi cannot be seen individually with the naked eye yet are present almost everywhere in their millions and billions. We may be able to see groups or 'colonies' of them. Many micro-organisms are completely harmless and some are beneficial, such as those that help break dead organisms down into useful materials. Some are not helpful, such as the mould that appears in a damp bathroom. Some are harmful, such as those that cause disease and food poisoning. (See also chapter 9.)

Sources to develop further subject knowledge

Summers *et al.* (2000), *One Small Step: Understanding the Science of Environmental Issues.*

Johnsey *et al.* (2000), *Primary Science Knowledge and Understanding.*

possibilities for starting points. One urban school with a small concrete playground noticed how gulls congregated on the rooftops during playtime. The children observed that the gulls came to feed on the scraps of snacks left by the children. This led to work finding out if gulls were welcome visitors and then thinking about how to discourage them.

Most schools are more fortunate, with a patch of paradise, at least for insects and other invertebrates, not too far away. The aim of any initial outdoor activity should be to 'orientate' children to the idea that walls, fields, trees, hedges and ponds can be habitats for a diverse range of plants and animals. It should also contribute to their awe and wonder at the bounty and beauty of living things, as they begin to appreciate the complexity and abundance of life.

The range of activities we call 'Earthwalks' can be used to encourage children to explore natural environments using all their senses (see Box 11.1). They also perform the function of engaging children with a place at a kinaesthetic and emotional level which we think is a prerequisite for thinking about ecosystems as places to enjoy and look at.

BOX 11.1 Earthwalks

Earthwalks is a general term we give to a range of sensory activities that can be used to encourage children (and others) to explore their environment.

The Earthwalks activities can be adapted and used in any setting, in the built and green environments: they are as useful for exploring walls and buildings as they are for a woodland. The aim is to encourage children to become involved in a place, to get to know what is there, the sights and sounds, the smells and textures, and to view it closely from different perspectives. From these initial, broad explorations, questions may arise that could be followed up with investigations to find out more. The activities are very touchy-feely and sensory. They can be easily adapted to suit children of all ages. Be aware of general health and safety precautions for working outside (ASE 2001). Some of our favourite activities are as follows.

Squirrels hide their nuts

As you set out on the walk give each child two acorns (or any small biodegradable object). Ask them to hide them and not tell anyone else where they are. On the way back from the walk ask the children to find them again. Who are the lucky squirrels? What would happen to the acorns that have been lost?

Hug a tree

Find some trees. Work in pairs. One child has their eyes closed or wears a blindfold (place a paper towel inside the blindfold to prevent any risk of contracting conjunctivitis). Child 2 leads their partner to a tree, invites them to touch, feel, smell the tree, get to know it well, its girth, texture, etc. The child is then led away from the tree and twirls around a few times. The blindfold is removed and the child tries to find 'their' tree. How do they know it? Now swap roles. Remind children to visit their tree again another time, if possible.

Skywalks

This activity encourages children to look skywards. Give each child a safety or flexible mirror. Remind children they should never look at the Sun. Get the children to walk in a crocodile with one hand on the shoulder of the person in front and the mirror under their chin, so that they can see whatever is above them. Lead the children along slowly, get them to look in their mirrors. Stop under a branch, invite the children to observe one of the reflected leaves closely, get to know it. Then ask them to look upwards into the tree. Can they see 'their' leaf? This technique can also be used to look at carvings on church ceilings, etc. Alternatively, if it is dry, take a lie down and survey the sky above.

Opposites

This activity uses touch. Pairs of 'opposites' e.g. rough–smooth, warm–cold, hard–soft, are printed on card and each pair is given two words and an egg box. They are not to tell anyone what their pair of words is. The children then collect six things in their egg box: three things that are in keeping with one word and three for the other word. The children then show their objects to another pair of children and let them handle them. Can they guess what the descriptive words are? Now the other pair has their turn.

Pick and mix

This is another activity designed to encourage children to look closely at an object. Each child chooses a similar small object (e.g. a stone, conker, leaf, etc.) and examines it carefully. They then put their objects into a bag. Later that day the children see if they can remember their object well enough to find it again amongst all the similar but different objects.

Matching colours

Obtain some colour charts or strips from a DIY store. Invite children to find little stones, leaves, etc. that match the colours on the card. The range of colours and tones can be varied according to age and environment studied. The links with art and colour-mixing are strong.

Nature palette

Stick a small piece (3 cm by 2 cm) of double-sided sticky tape on a piece of card shaped like an artist's palette. Ask children to find tiny pieces of petal, grass, leaf, etc., and to place them onto the sticky tape to make a picture. Share their pictures with each other. Again this activity encourages children to observe different colours and materials in their surroundings.

Sound symphony

Each child will need a pencil and a small piece of card. Ask children to sit or stand separately, be absolutely quiet and still for one minute. Invite children to record, in pictures or symbols, the sounds they can hear. Ask children to identify sounds they like, sounds they dislike and whether some sounds seem out of place. Discuss findings. Children are rarely given the opportunity to actively listen to the sounds around them.

Nature mini-safari

Children work in pairs. Each pair has 1 metre of string and several matchsticks. Children stake out points of interest along their string trail with matchsticks and study the ground so they become experts and know this small patch of the world better than anyone else. Then invite an adult or another child to be taken on a mini-safari with an expert guide.

Shake-down

Put a white sheet under and around a bush, give it a little shake and see what comes tumbling down! A pooter can be used to collect small invertebrates for a closer look.

Perfume potion

In a small container select leaves and other fragrant items that give a pleasant odour (you may need to crush leaves). Give the new perfume a name and pass it around for others to experience and even dab behind their ears!

Photo-quiz

Each member of the group takes a digital photo of part of the environment from an unusual angle, and then shows others the photo. They have to work out where the photo was taken and what the subject of the picture is.

Science, citizenship and sustainable development

In NC terms, children should be taught to care for and protect the environment as part of science, yet this requirement hides a far more complex range of issues. Such learning could be completely passive (knowing what to do) or fully active (actually caring and protecting). Imagine a scenario where a class discovers that a local ecosystem (perhaps a neglected school conservation area) is not biodiverse, that a habitat, for example, a pond, is polluted and in need of management. To be active, children will need skills beyond science to make the case for action and to decide what action to take. To act on scientifically gathered information, children will need skills and knowledge developed through citizenship. Taking action to protect or develop habitats connects science to real and motivating contexts. The QCA citizenship scheme of work offers teachers some useful guidance on how to go about this. 'Animals and us' (unit 3) is explicitly linked to the QCA science scheme of work and outlines how . . .

> Children learn about their basic human needs and the needs of animals. They learn that humans have a responsibility of care towards different kinds of animals – including pets and wildlife. In later sections of the unit they learn about the role of one or more local and/or national voluntary organisations concerned with animal welfare . . . Children learn about the effect that their choices and behaviour can have, at both a local and a national level. (www.standards.dfes.gov.uk)

In the later citizenship unit 6 'Developing our school grounds': 'The children develop ideas and discuss and consult on them with different members of the school community. They work in groups, democratically agreeing priorities for change, and come up with a plan for their implementation' (www.standards.dfes.gov.uk). As children become more environmentally aware, they will need to refer to some guiding principles to inform action. The concept of sustainable development and the actions we all need to take to achieve sustainable development are very clearly laid out in the Earth Charter:

> Earth, our home, is alive with a unique community of life. The forces of nature make existence a demanding and uncertain adventure, but Earth has provided the conditions essential to life's evolution. The resilience of the community of life and the well-being of humanity depend upon preserving a healthy biosphere with all its ecological systems, a rich variety of plants and animals, fertile soils, pure waters, and clean air. The global environment with its finite resources is a common concern of all peoples. The protection of Earth's vitality, diversity, and beauty is a sacred trust. (www.earthcharter.org)

The charter goes on to identify four principles, which are:

1. Respect Earth and life in all its diversity.
2. Care for the community of life with understanding, compassion and love.
3. Build democratic societies that are just, participatory, sustainable and peaceful.
4. Secure Earth's bounty and beauty for present and future generations.

We think science in primary schools has a responsibility to address these principles and can do so by teaching science in a way which helps children to understand some of the key concepts needed to appreciate the beauty and complexity of living things in their environment. Scientists are often 'blamed' for the demise of our planet because they are the ones who discover new ways to use our finite resources. However, it is also scientists who draw our attention to the consequences of our actions, and their research offers us choices about our future. In many cases, scientists can be the 'goodies' rather than the 'baddies'. One starting point for environmental science might be to learn a little about the lives of scientists who have made a contribution. Children will come to know the names of the men who have contributed to the physical sciences, yet the names of some great women who have contributed to environmental science are not well known. Three such examples are Rachel Carson, Wangari Maathai and Jane Goodall.

Rachel Carson (1907–1964) was a scientist from the USA who is credited with being a founding campaigner of the 'green' movement. Her book *Silent Spring* (2000, first published in 1962) is still considered a classic and drew attention to the damage pesticides were doing to our environment, particularly in relation to human health and song birds – hence its title. She advocated more careful use of and better research into pesticides and, in spite of some rampant sexism, took this campaign right to the top – to the President of the USA. Her biography shows what can be achieved by someone who has not only the scientific understanding but also the determination and skills to communicate her views to the general public. Her books are also considered very good literature – one is called *The Sense of Wonder* (1998, first published in 1965), which is described as 'words and pictures to keep your child's inborn sense of wonder alive'. Learning about Rachel Carson may inspire children to ensure influential adults hear their views.

Professor Wangari Maathai (born 1940) received a Nobel peace prize in 2004. This is particularly notable as she is the first African woman to be awarded the prize. She received her prize 'for her contribution to sustainable development, democracy and peace'. She is a highly qualified scientist, a commissioner for the Earth Charter Initiative and a politician who, in 1976, initiated a massive tree-planting campaign through Kenyan women's groups in order to conserve the environment and improve their quality of life. Her campaign began when she planted trees in her own back yard and realised how trees could provide a family with shade, fuel, food and income. In spite of being frequently told that she should be at home looking after her husband, being harassed at public meetings and physically attacked by opponents, Professor Maathai has become internationally famous for her work. Her example may inspire children to do their own planting or to learn about how plants can be used to reclaim and stabilise soil.

Dr Jane Goodall (born 1934) is world famous for her observations of chimpanzee behaviour. She made careful study of the lives, loves, 'wars' and peace of chimps in Tanzania and was the first to observe chimps as tool-makers. She also revolutionised the way such science was carried out by considering the chimps' emotions and personalities when interpreting their actions. As well as writing scientific papers, she has written children's books including *Chimpanzees I Love: Saving Their World and Ours* (2001) and *My Life with the Chimpanzees* (1996). She has set up the Jane Goodall Institute that works towards 'creating healthy ecosystems, promoting sustainable livelihoods and nurturing new generations of committed, active citizens around the world' (www.janegoodall.org).

The work of these scientists and others like them can be used to illustrate the positive contributions that science can make to sustainable development. It also shows us that scientists sometimes need to communicate their message to a wide audience, present convincing arguments and have more than a little persistence. Through combining science, citizenship and communication skills, science can be taught in a way that reflects the work of 'real scientists'.

Finally, the therapeutic benefits of the natural outdoor environment should not be underestimated. One of the five outcomes of the Every Child Matters agenda (DfES 2004) is 'Being Healthy', which encompasses mental and emotional health. Hearing birdsong or the gurgle of a stream, witnessing the visually restful colours of autumn, smelling the strong garlic odour in a spring wood; all promote our feeling of well-being in some small way.

Assessment for learning

After children have been orientated to the topic, perhaps by doing some of the activities outlined in Box 11.1, you will want to find out their level of understanding. Asking some of the following questions could start a discussion:

Where do plants and animals live?
Why do they live there?
What kinds of plants and animals would live in these places: the air, water, land, underground?
Can you think of animals that could live here (e.g. school grounds) and those that could not?
How is . . . adapted to live in the sea/soil/cold climate?

Children might think that animals make a conscious choice to live in a certain habitat – 'the worm lives under the soil because it's dark and the worm likes it like that' (Nuffield Primary Science 1995), rather than that the worm is adapted to live in such a habitat. Children's thinking might turn the concept of adaptation around and say something like 'the bear grows a warm coat so it can live in a cold place'. Of course, polar bears cannot decide whether to have a warm coat or not. It is more correct to say 'only bears with thick warm coats can survive in cold climates'. Children may also think that if a habitat is destroyed then the living things can just go and find somewhere else to live. This might be the case with a few species, but the majority do not have the ability to do so.

Seasonal change

What do you think this place is like in the night?
What is this place like in the summer?
How is it different in the winter?
Do plants and animals live here all the time?

Children may have a stereotypical view of ecosystems (for example, the Arctic is always cold and the desert is always hot) or of seasons (for example, it is always sunny in summer but never in winter). Seasonal changes may be overlooked apart from the very obvious such as leaves falling in autumn and new plants growing in spring. A popular idea among children is that all plants die during the winter (Nuffield Primary Science 1995).

Food chains

What do you think this animal (example) eats?
Is this animal (example) eaten by anything?

Children's food chains are likely to reveal a number of alternative ideas such as confusion with life cycles (egg > chick > hen) or with how food is produced (chips > potatoes > plants). When questioned about the numbers of living things involved at each level of a food chain, children may think consumers (animals) rather than producers (plants) constitute the largest population. This may be true in some cases – for example, insects on a tree – but in all cases plants will make up the largest amount of 'biomass' or living matter (Leach *et al.* 1996). The QCA (2004) reported that when drawing food chains children should 'pay attention to the arrow direction', i.e. indicating food and energy transfer from producer to consumers. Children may not have a clear understanding that plants make their own food through photosynthesis (Driver *et al.* 1985) (see also chapter 10).

Some children may believe that all ecosystems are controlled or created by people – of course many of those that children know about have been. KS1 children may think that all living things depend on human care (Leach *et al.* 1996). Again this is an understandable alternative idea given most children's experiences of animals.

Micro-organisms and biodegradation

If we left a leaf/apple core on the soil, what would happen to it?
What do you think happens to plants'/animals' bodies when they die?
What would happen to this plastic bag if we left it buried in the soil?
Why do things rot in the ground?
What does 'recycle' mean?

Children may not have any conception of rotting or decay. They may therefore explain the 'disappearance' of leaves and animal bodies by saying 'something ate it', or 'it blew away'. Others may have some idea about things rotting but have no idea what causes the process. Very few children at KS2 are likely to understand the role of micro-organisms in decay (Driver *et al.* 1985). When children were asked to think about why a chicken sandwich left in a warm place in the classroom had gone smelly, 40 per cent thought it had been contaminated by the warm temperature itself, 70 per cent of children mentioned something about 'bugs' or 'germs'. Others thought it had been ill when alive, the ink on the wrapping had contaminated it, or it had been deliberately poisoned or had BSE (Grace 2000).

Summers *et al.* (2000) have produced a useful research-based guide on teachers' subject knowledge of environmental issues. They report, perhaps not surprisingly, that not all teachers fully understood concepts related to environmental issues. As with children's learning, it is useful to know which are the common alternative frameworks, in order to provide a focus for learning. For example, Summers *et al.* (2000: 8) found that few teachers understood that:

- A species is unable to breed with another species and produce fertile young
- Most species in ecosystems require very particular living conditions in order to survive

- Potential consequences of unsustainability include ecosystems suffering a loss of species and population decline.

Summative assessment (assessment of learning)

At NC level 1 it is expected that children will recognise and identify a range of common animals. At NC level 2 they will also recognise that different living things are found in different places, and at level 3 they will identify some ways in which an animal is suited to an environment. To reach NC level 4 children must describe feeding relationships between plants and animals in terms of food chains. NC level 5 is attained if children can explain that different organisms are found in different habitats because of differences in environmental factors (the availability of light in a woodland means only certain species of plants will be found – bluebells, for example). The QCA (2003e) document *Assessing Progress in Science, Key Stage 1 and 2: Unit 2 Living Things in Their Environment* provides further guidance for teachers.

Scientific enquiry

After children have spent a little time in the local area getting to know it through the Earthwalk activities described above (Box 11.1), the next task of an environmental scientist is to survey the ecosystem to be researched. Children can do this in a range of ways for a variety of purposes. Table 11.2 describes a variety of survey types. The final type, managerial, shows how science can become a starting point for the promotion of values and attitudes relevant to ESD. Children might also need to be taught how to use some survey tools or how to apply some techniques such as those outlined in Table 11.3.

TABLE 11.2 Ideas for ecosystem surveys

Type of survey	Activities	Outcomes	Learning outcomes
Descriptive	Make an annotated sketch of the ecosystem including details such as some plants, animals, water, soil, walls. Make a drawing or painting on a footprint-shaped piece of paper to show what is on the ground beneath your feet. Write a paragraph about 'a day in the life of a tree' including details about the air, water, rain, sunshine, animals and plants that it comes into contact with. Note the 'good' and 'bad' aspects of the environment.	A collection of sketches that can be made into a book for children to compare. A display of footprints across the classroom wall. A collection of 'The secret lives of trees'. A list of likes and dislikes about the environment from the perspective of the children and imagined views of animals and plants.	Children will find out about different kinds of plants and animals in the local environment, identify similarities and differences between local environments and ways in which these affect animals and plants that are found there.

Type of survey	Activities	Outcomes	Learning outcomes
Spatial	Use simple mapping techniques to make a plan and cross-section of the ecosystem on which the positions of different types of plants and animals found can be plotted. Mapping techniques include measuring dimensions (including depth of ponds, height of trees, depth of soil) and finding north.	A scale plan and cross section of the ecosystem. A wall display of the plan or cross section e.g. 'our pond' showing above and below ground and water level.	Children will identify similarities and differences between local environments and ways in which these affect animals and plants that are found there.
Physical	Use simple scales or measuring devices, including data-loggers, to record the factors and gradients of the physical environment such as temperature, wind, light and sound levels. Note could be made of the materials found, e.g. wood, stone, soil, etc.	A list of non-living parts of the ecosystem. Notes about how wet or dry the soil was in different areas. Graphs or contour maps showing key measurements.	Children will identify similarities and differences between local environments.
Numerical	Use sampling techniques to estimate the populations of different species. For example, use a metre-square quadrant placed on the ground randomly, and count the grasses, daisies, spiders and ants within. Repeat and multiply up to find the estimated population. Estimate the numbers of birds visiting the area during one day by making observations each hour. Sweep different parts of a pond and identify the living things found.	A 'pyramid' of numbers showing the different populations of plants and animals. A food chain showing the relationships between plants and animals found in the habitat.	Children will identify similarities and differences between local environments. Children will learn that feeding relationships within a habitat can be illustrated in the form of food chains starting with green plants.
Temporal	Study a single plant and how it changes over time. Study an ecosystem over time, making a record of its appearance, the weather, plants and animals to be seen.	A 'tree diary' from spring to summer. A set of photographs and captions showing changes in the environment and populations during a school year.	Children will learn about seasonal changes in the environment and how this affects populations.

TABLE 11.2 (Continued)

Type of survey	Activities	Outcomes	Learning outcomes
Managerial	Find out from adults how the ecosystem is cared for and managed. Find out what information exists about the ecosystem and what information would be useful to help maintain and improve the biodiversity of the ecosystem.	A fact-file presentation dossier that can be presented to the school governors or parent–teacher association about a local environment and what needs to be done to improve it.	Children will learn to discuss and consult with different members of the school community. They will learn to work in groups, to democratically agree priorities for change.

TABLE 11.3 Teaching survey skills

Tool/technique	Teaching point
Hand lens, magnifying glass, two-way magnifiers	Ensure the object is well lit. Keep it still and move the lens between eye and object to focus
Line transept	Take a standard length (e.g. one metre) of string and plot each plant or animal touching the string.
Quadrat	Drop the square or hoop after taking a random number of steps in a random direction. Count the populations of plants and animals within the area.
Pooters, brushes	Show children how to collect small animals without harming them using a small paintbrush or pooter to suck the animal into the collecting jar. Reassure them it is not possible to suck the animal up into their mouth!
Collecting bottles	Ensure animals are not left for long in 'bug jars' and that they are replaced where they were found.
Nets	Sweep through water in the same way each time and for the same length of time. Avoid stirring up silt. Show how to tip the animals into a white shallow tray to observe the contents.

The kinds of initial surveys described in Table 11.2 could lead children to be able to ask questions about the ecosystems studied, such as those posed by the DfEE/ QCA 1998 Science Unit 5–6h:

> *Do you find more small insects on the top or the underside of leaves?*
> *Is there any difference in the length and width of leaves on the top, middle and bottom of a shrub?*
> *Will we find different kinds of animals if we take a sample of water from the top, middle or bottom of our school pond?*
> *If we make small patches of bare earth in different locations, e.g. under a tree or near a wall, will there be a difference in the type of plants which first grow there?*

These are pattern-seeking enquiries that are best answered by analysing the findings of a survey rather than carrying out a 'fair test'-type investigation. As they work to find answers to such questions, children should be encouraged to suggest reasons for their findings using scientific knowledge where possible, for example 'There are fewer animals in the middle of the pond because there is less food.' They should also draw conclusions recognising limitations in evidence, for example 'On the whole, there were fewer insects on the tops of leaves but they may have flown off when we came near.' The raising and answering of such questions will provide opportunities to develop children's understanding.

Developing children's understanding

The needs of life

In 'life processes', children will have learned about some of the MRS GREN (see Table 10.1) processes common to all life, and within this strand there is an opportunity to learn about the needs of life: air (oxygen), water, food and a place to live (habitat) where they can be safe.

In order to understand the needs of life, the best approach is likely to involve encounters with real animals – whether as pets, working animals or in a zoo (Figure 11.1) and the people who look after them. Ask parents whether they would be willing to bring in pets or discuss the work they do with animals. Some animals, particularly invertebrates such as giant African land snails, can be safely kept in schools. The Consortium of Local Education Authorities for the Provision of Science Services (www.cleapss.org.uk) offers advice on this.

FIGURE 11.1 Getting to know a goat

It may be possible to set up a hide in or near the classroom so children can do some bird-watching. A bird table could be set up outside the classroom near a window that is blanked out apart from a small viewing hole. Morning is usually the best time to catch birds feeding. The birds will need to get used to the table so do not expect immediate results. Some research into the foods and habitats that local species prefer will help children develop their understanding of the birds' needs and may help them in attracting more species.

Adaptation

Children's work in this area can begin by looking at some animals and plants in detail. First-hand observation should reveal plenty about the organism (for more details about plant observation see chapter 10). These details could be recorded by an annotated drawing or by writing in a fact file with relevant headings such as number of teeth, number of legs or toes, size, colour, body covering. The way in which these features allow the animal or plant to survive can then be considered. *Does the body covering or colour protect the animal from a particular predator? Are the teeth adapted to eat a particular food? Are the eyes adapted to be useful in particular conditions?* Other information such as lifespan, life cycle and natural habitat can be supplemented by reference to secondary sources. These fact files could be compiled by the class into a reference book and supplemented with all the features of a non-fiction text including table of contents, index and glossary.

One way to encourage children to think about adaptation is by giving a list of environmental features that an animal would have to cope with and by asking children to 'design' such an animal. For example, *If the animal preys on small invertebrates, lives in burrows in soil and is preyed upon by foxes, then what adaptations would it have to survive?* The animal might be nocturnal, have large eyes and sensitive nose to detect prey, strong front feet for digging and sharp teeth to eat and defend itself.

Children will find some animals inherently interesting and appealing. With other animals, such as bats and spiders, teachers may have to work harder to show that these animals too have needs and are valuable parts of an ecosystem. One approach to achieve a shift in attitude is to elicit children's beliefs about certain animals and ask them to research the truth behind them. A list of possible beliefs about bats is shown in the Battitude chart (Table 11.4). Younger children may wish to explore the lives of animals through role-play. For example, the teacher could construct with the class a story through which children can contrast their own behaviours and activities with those of nocturnal birds and animals.

Through studying the ways animals and plants are adapted to their environment and how these differences can be used to identify species, precise and accurate use of vocabulary can be encouraged. Children's initial responses about the variety of life before them can be refined by providing them with suitable identification keys so that 'lots of bits floating about in the pond' is more accurately expressed as 'water boatmen coming up to the surface then diving down' or 'the midge larvae are moving by wiggling their bodies from side to side'.

Food chains and webs

Children will find it easy to grasp the idea of a simple chain with one organism eating another. As we have seen above there are a number of alternative ideas that children may hold beyond this concept.

TABLE 11.4 A Battitude chart (adapted from Howe 2002)

Battitude	True or false?	Details
Bats are blind.	False.	Bats do have eyes but find their way mainly by using echoes (sonar).
Bats get caught in people's hair.	False.	Bats are very agile flyers and are very sensitive.
If a bat bites you, you will get rabies.	False.	Recent studies have shown bat populations in the UK do not have rabies. It is extremely unlikely that a bat will bite.
Bats need to be protected.	True.	All 16 UK bat species are rare and protected.
Bats drink blood.	True . . . but:	. . . no UK species drink blood.
Bats are flying mice.	False.	Bats are more closely related to primates than rodents.

The first task is to ensure children understand every food chain begins with plants (producers). This can be done through reference to the diet of any familiar animal (humans, for example, by looking at the contents of a lunchbox), and tracing back the source of all food. Food chains with two, three and four or more organisms can then be developed, ensuring the concept of food (and therefore energy) transfer from one level to the next is understood. A web can be constructed by assigning each child an animal to represent, or a population, in an ecosystem. A pond ecosystem could have populations of pond weed (algae), water fleas (that feed on algae) and stickleback (that feed on waterfleas) to begin with. Each population is joined to its predator by a length of wool. As other plants (duckweed, reeds) and animals (insect larvae, pond skaters, fish, ducks) are added, lengths of wool will criss-cross to show plants and animals providing food to populations higher up the trophic levels. While the details of exactly 'what eats what' may not be remembered, the kinaesthetic involvement of being part of a web may remain. A further development of the activity is to introduce a catastrophic event – perhaps all the pondweed is killed by pollution – which takes out one whole part of the web. The effect on the subsequent feeding levels will be drastic!

Micro-organisms

There are some activities that can be conducted safely (see chapter 9) in the classroom to demonstrate to children the presence of 'invisible' organisms. To focus only on micro-organisms that turn food 'bad' will be to give an impression that microbial activity is always unwanted. A key learning outcome in relation to ecology will be to understand that the micro-organisms involved in decay and rotting can be an important part of any ecosystem in that they recycle material by returning useful material to the soil. One way to do this is bury a range of items (e.g. apple core, stone, leaf, stick, paper, plastic bottle) in the soil at the edge of the school field and return to the spot at weekly intervals to take a photo. The children will see that some items are 'biodegradable' and some are not. In exploring ideas why some objects 'disappear' children may think an animal has eaten it or it has 'washed away'. To test this theory, similar items can be placed in jars with a little soil and sealed (they must not be reopened). Biodegradable materials will start to decompose within a few weeks. This works well with packaging: compare biodegradable starch packaging with polystyrene chips. The polystyrene will remain for years. This kind of activity will also help children realise that whatever we put into an ecosystem is likely to stay there: when we throw a plastic bottle 'away', it will still exist for years to come.

Using ICT to teach about living things in their environment

There is great scope for promoting learning thorough Information Technology when teaching about ecosystems. Rugged, hand-held PDAs (Personal Digital Assistants) can be taken into the 'field' and it is possible to load software on to them that helps children with plant and animal identification. Furthermore, the location of measurements can be accurately recorded on the PDA using a GPS (Global Positioning System) so that, for example, back in the classroom a profile of the physical environment can be produced, or the distribution of a population mapped.

We saw earlier in chapter 3 how data loggers can be used to record environmental measurements such as light or temperature, and similarly they can also support studies of ecosystems. Just leaving a logger outside, possibly in the school's conservation area, over a 24-hour period provides a wealth of fascinating data. How does the temperature change, and is it in step with light readings? Does the sound level remain constant, or do you notice a change at dawn? Children can be encouraged to tell the story of day and night-time activity through the readings taken. A woodland walk can be accurately mapped using a GPS and the level of light intensity recorded by a datalogger. Then back in the classroom it is even possible to produce a visual record of your position, sensor data and images from a digital camera, using Google Earth and Google Maps (see http://www.sciencescope.co.uk for further details about this).

It is obviously difficult to study at first-hand anything other than the local environment, but through webcams it is possible to look further afield so that, in real-time, an elephant can be seen coming down to its water hole in Africa, or an ostrich observed sheltering under the shade of a bush. One site that offers live pictures from Africa is the National Geographic's website (http://www9.nationalgeographic.com/ngm/wildcamafrica/). Webcams also allow us to intrude on a nesting box full of house sparrow chicks or pipistrelle bat pups. For example, the Eco-watch website (http://www.eco-watch/heligan/) offers live pictures of the animals from the Lost Gardens of Heligan in Cornwall that featured on BBC's Springwatch programme. All in all there is something rather magical about bringing these experiences to the classroom.

Finally it is possible for schools to be part of a national survey that records the changing of the seasons via the Nature's Calendar website (http://www.naturescalendar.org.uk/). Signs of spring, such as the date that frog spawn was first sighted in the school pond, can be recorded on a map of the UK, and over time, a picture built up of regional differences – watch the plots spread from South-West England to Scotland as spring proceeds.

Classroom management

Working outside is rewarding and it is also unpredictable. Teachers have a duty to consider the risks of any activity, to take action to minimise risk and to know what to do if children's health or safety is compromised. The Association for Science Education's (2001) publication *Be Safe!* is the definitive guide to health and safety.

Things for teachers to consider when working outside include the adult-to-child ratio, which should be around 1 : 6 if the class is outside the school. If you are in doubt, visit the site to make a risk assessment and seek advice from your headteacher. All adults should be briefed about the possible risks and how to control them. Children too should be briefed about potential risks and how to control them. Some of these risks are listed in Table 11.5.

The environment and the law

Many of Britain's wild plants and animals are legally protected, and although it is unlikely that teachers will transgress these laws they do need to be aware of them. The law most relevant to living things in their environment is the Wildlife and Countryside Act (1981). Parts of the Wildlife and Countryside Act and some other laws dealing with species protection are described briefly here.

Teachers should be aware of the legal aspects of collecting plants and animals. It is *not* normally an offence to pick the 'Four Fs' – fruit, foliage, fungi or flowers (assuming that none of them are protected) – especially if they are growing wild and are for personal use and not for sale. This is not

TABLE 11.5 Risks of working outside

Risk	Action
Sharp items/syringes in leaf litter/undergrowth	Teacher to check general condition of the site. Use disposable gloves for collecting from the ground. In the event of a cut, inform parents as soon as possible.
Falling into pond	Children to be taught about appropriate behaviour. Adult to control access to pond unless children are deemed responsible and capable of dealing with an accident. Consult doctor immediately in the event of children swallowing pond water.
Allergic reaction to found material/animal (most likely to manifest itself as hives/nettle rash or breathing difficulties)	Ensure data on children's known allergies is collected and checked and prescribed medication is available. Children at risk could use gloves and keep specimens in plastic bags.
Cuts caused by garden tools	Show children how to use tools properly. Clean tools afterwards. In the event of a cut, inform parents as soon as possible.
Animal bite	Show children how to handle the animal in question. In the event of a bite, inform parents as soon as possible.

part of any Act, but a part of common law. It covers such customs as blackberry-picking and taking ivy and holly at Christmas. To exercise this right you must be somewhere you have a legal right to be, such as on a public footpath or in a public park. Of course, if enough children exercise this right at the same time and in the same place it could cause a lot of damage to habitats and species. It is therefore worth considering some approaches to collection – such as the 'nature palette' activity (Box 11.1) that encourages children to gather only a tiny sample. In some places, such as parks or commons, local by-laws may prevent such activities altogether. The Wildlife and Countryside Act (1981) identifies measures for the protection of wild plants. It prohibits the unauthorised intentional uprooting of any wild plant species and forbids any picking, uprooting or destruction of listed plants. It provides certain defences, for example provision to cover incidental actions that are an unavoidable result of an otherwise lawful activity, so the chances that a teacher would fall foul of this law are minimal.

Some of the animals protected by law are listed here and should not be disturbed or collected:

- adders
- bats
- some beetles, for example the stag beetle
- some butterflies
- some crickets, for example the mole cricket
- common lizards
- dormice (also a European protected species)
- common frogs (in that they must not be sold)
- common toads (in that they must not be sold)
- grass snakes
- great-crested newts (also a European protected species)
- natterjack toads (also a European protected species)
- newts (in that they must not be sold)
- sand lizards (also a European protected species)
- slow worms (in that they must not be sold, killed or injured)
- smooth snakes (also a European protected species).

It is also against the law to take birds, their eggs or other protected wild animals from the wild, to intentionally kill or injure birds or other protected wild animals or to destroy or possess birds' eggs. The places these animals use for shelter and protection (for example a bird's nest when it is in use or being built, or a bat roost) are also protected.

If children do collect invertebrates (minibeasts) from the wild or the school conservation area, ensure that they are returned as soon as possible to the same spot. Do not take animals from the wild to keep for long periods in the classroom: they can quickly die from overheating.

Summary

In this chapter we have discussed how the science of living things in their environment relates to other concepts within the science curriculum and beyond it. We have shown how children can study local environments in a way that helps them appreciate the diversity and beauty of the natural world. These experiences can then be developed into systematic investigations of ecosystems that can be the basis for informed involvement in active citizenship. As children learn about the environment they will begin to learn skills and knowledge that are relevant to ESD.

Discussion points

1. How will an understanding of the needs of life help children understand the concept of sustainable development?
2. What animals and plants are children likely to have knowledge of, and which common groups of living things may children not know much about?
3. Is it best to begin with the local environment before embarking on a study of a rain forest?

Further reading

Children of the World (1994), *Rescue Mission Planet Earth: A Children's Edition of Agenda 21*
de Boo (2004), *Nature Detectives.*
Plimmer *et al.* (1996), *The Environment: A Primary Teacher's Guide.*

CHAPTER

12

The science subject leader

Purpose of this chapter

After reading this chapter you should have:

- an understanding of how class teachers can be supported by science subject leaders
- a general understanding of the wider role of the subject leader and how teachers can work with them to develop science teaching
- information about further sources of support for becoming a science subject leader.

Introduction

YOU ARE NOT ALONE! Nobody has all the answers, and the teaching of science will continue to evolve as teachers reflect on their practice in the light of new ideas. The purpose of this chapter is to consider how teachers can work together with science subject leaders within their own schools to develop teaching and learning in science. Science subject leaders in school have specific responsibilities, and we will outline and explain these, but the emphasis of this chapter is on how a relationship between teachers and subject leaders can be based on dialogue and collaboration.

Sometimes the science subject leader in a school will have particular expertise in science and/or science teaching, perhaps through their own education or previous work, but more often the role is taken on by a generalist primary teacher who then develops their expertise in the area of science teaching. This is one reason why it would not be appropriate to see science subject leaders as a source of authoritative answers, but it is not the main reason. In line with the social constructivist theory of learning on which the previous chapters are based, we see teachers as active learners, and argue that professional development is most likely to be successful when it is meaningful to the individual teachers concerned and when they are able to initiate changes themselves. Although subject leaders will find this chapter helpful, its main audience is primary class teachers in general. The insights of socio-cultural approaches to understanding learning mean that it is not helpful to consider individuals in isolation; other colleagues and the culture of the school are clearly also factors in how science teaching is developed. This chapter will help you to reflect on the following questions:

1. What can a science subject leader do for me?
2. How can I work with colleagues in school to develop science?
3. How might I get started in becoming a science subject leader?

What do subject leaders do?

The first task of this section is to explain why we have chosen to use the term 'subject leader' rather than 'coordinator', which is the term used in many schools. The term coordinator is often preferrred beacuse it implies a role in which one teacher supports colleagues in their work, without taking a position of power. The term 'leader' implies a sense of direction and purposefulness that the term 'coordinator' lacks; a coordinator keeps things ticking over smoothly whereas a leader makes judgements and takes things forward. The term leadership can seem threatening if it is associated with hierarchy and 'telling' others what to do. An alternative view is leadership distributed through a school, with colleagues taking on responsibility for leading different aspects of the school curriculum within an ethos of collaboration and culture of shared ownership.

The key areas of responsibility of a science subject leader are: the strategic direction of the subject, managing change and general issues of management. These broad areas are unpicked further in Box 12.1 and some aspects of these will be discussed in this chapter. (See Bell and Ritchie (1999) for a full discussion of the role of subject leadership in primary schools.)

BOX 12.1 Key responsibilities of the science subject leader

Strategic direction

- Leading the development of a vision for science in the school and approaches to teaching and learning
- Leading the writing of policies and long term plans, comunication beyond immediate colleagues, e.g. governors, Ofsted, LA, universities, ASE
- Promoting values; high expectations, inclusion

Managing change

- Supporting colleagues
- Arranging INSET monitoring and evalulating progress
- Listening to the pupil voice
- Data analysis
- Action planning – contributing to school development plans

Management

- Ordering and storage of resources
- Maintaining an overview of health and safety in science
- Providing a framework for implementing planning and record keeping for science
- Collating data.

Getting started on science in a school

The management role of the science subject leader is likely to be the first one that a class teacher encounters directly. The subject leader can provide help with locating existing planning documentation and resources. It might be helpful to discuss with them how much flexibility in planning there is in the school; to what extent are class teachers expected to follow existing medium-term planning, how can they introduce new ideas of their own and be responsive to the classes they are teaching? Science resources may be stored in classrooms or centrally and the science subject leader can explain procedures for borrowing and returning equipment, books, and ICT resources. They will be able to provide information on health and safety policies, although they may well need to direct teachers to further sources of information in order to answer specific questions. The class teacher needs to take responsibility for making judgments about managing risks within the context of their own classroom.

Beyond being a source of information, it may be helpful to seek out the science subject leader to discuss planning ideas, perhaps for teaching a year group that is unfamiliar, or to consider the pros and cons of different ways of introducing a new topic. Most schools have approaches to assessment that are related to the different subjects and as a core subject, science is likely to have particular assessment policies associated with it. These policies may be to do with assessment for learning, and will probably include some whole school systems for recording children's achievements. Making summative judgements about children's achievment in science is not easy and it may help to discuss the process or particular children with the subject leader.

As all teachers are very busy, asking others for their valuable time can sometimes seem like an unreasonable demand. However, colleagues coming forward with ideas and talking openly about the practice of teaching science actually helps the subject leader to monitor what is happening in classrooms and to maintain the profile of science. It contributes to a positive culture within a school in which teachers discuss how they are teaching in order to support children's learning. Of course, there are limits to available time, and subject leaders are not expected to do their colleagues' planning for them, but most will be only too pleased to discuss ideas with an interested colleague.

Beyond the immediate advice and support in getting started with teaching science in a school, the subject leader will be able to explain what is on the current agenda both nationally and for the development of science in the school and it is part of their role to support colleagues in the development of their practice. Different ways in which this might happen are considered in the next section.

Continued professional development within a staff team

An individal teacher seeking to develop their science teaching may find the science subject leader a useful source of support. Schools have to balance the development needs of individual teachers with maintaining a whole school approach to teaching and this means that the priorities of one teacher are sometimes in line with the plans for whole school development, but sometimes they are not. Particularly in the latter case it is important that teachers take responsibility for identifying their own needs, but recognise that time and budgets limit the kind of support that is available. The overriding focus for school development should be on supporting children's learning and the test for any investment in professional development is whether the outcomes will ultimately benefit the children, although the impact on pupils is often not immediately seen, making it difficult to track and attribute to particular action(s). Personal change and development can come within a whole school focus for development, such as improving assessment for learning, developing cross-curricular approaches or broadening children's reading. In these examples it is possible to see how there might be room to adjust the focus according to the interest of different teachers: e.g. assessment for learning in science, exploring links between science and art, or investigating the use of poetry texts within science teaching. Professional development can also be very much tailored to an individual and their needs. This might involve going on external courses, but making use of the expertise and experience of colleagues within school is a good option as they are able to give support over a longer period of time and have a good understanding of the context in which they are working.

There are different ways in which science subject leaders lead and manage change with their colleagues including:

- Introducing ideas or inviting discussion at staff meetings
- Leading or arranging INSET (In Service Training) days
- Observing others teach and feeding back
- Having other teachers observe their teaching
- Teaching alongside colleagues
- Setting up working groups to focus on an issue
- Informal discussions.

The success of these strategies for change depends on the attitudes of and relationships between the people concerned. Staff meetings can be a time for issuing instructions or a forum for open dicussions. There may be occasions when subject leaders are simply giving information or asking other teachers to carry out a task, perhaps completing a quick audit of resources in their room, or providing assessment information, but generally they are more productive if there is a dialogue between staff about an issue. By definition, the subject leader can't achieve a dialogue on their own and the thoughtful contributions of colleagues are vital. INSET days can be hugely enjoyable, but provide no lasting impact on teachers' practice unless they are really committed to implementing the changes. There are challenges here for the subject leader, but a teacher with a positive attitude and open mind will be able to gain more from the opportunities than one who disengages from debates or who resists all change as a matter of course.

Often subject leaders are required to observe teachers in the classroom as part of 'monitoring'. Although this can be very valuable for all parties if it is well focussed and everyone knows what the purpose of the observation is, and trusts that the information gained will be used constructively, it can sometimes be a rather threatening experience. Classteachers can regain some control of an unfocussed 'monitoring' visit by asking in advance for the observation to concentrate on some specific aspects of what is going on in the classroom. Arranging an exchange observation visit to the subject leader's class can help develop an approach in which two colleagues are discussing a matter of professional practice rather than one making an authoritative judgement on another.

Approaches to working directly with an indivdual to support their development can be labelled as coaching or mentoring. Coaching is focussed on a specific aspect of a job, often involving on-going feedback on the way an individual is carrying out a task and can be a collegial process between peers. In mentoring, one person is offering their expertise and experience to another, usually less experienced, colleague. In the context of a class teacher working with a science subject leader, either mentoring or coaching may be more appropriate, depending on the need that has been identified, and the relationship between the indviduals.

When being coached it may help to know that the coach will only give advice when asked to do so. You will be supported to explore the current situation and consider a range of options for yourself, and it will be you who will decide upon the actions you will take. Therefore you might expect to be asked about the first steps you are going to take towards a particular goal and what help you need, but not be told what that goal/support might be. In reality, the distinction between mentoring and coaching is often blurred so that you might expect to be given advice by colleagues as well as helped to find answers by yourself.

It is a requirement of the TDA core standards that mainscale teachers take an active role in their personal professional development and are involved in team working and collaboration (Table 12.1). This specifically notes that being open to mentoring and coaching is a professional responsibility.

TABLE 12.1 Professional standards related to working with subject leaders

	Professional attributes	**Professional knowledge and understanding**	**Professional skills**
	Personal professional development	**Subjects and curriculum**	**Team working and collaboration**
C Core standards for main scale teachers who have successfully completed their induction	C7 Evaluate their performance and be committed to improving their practice through appropriate professional development. C8 Have a creative and constructively critical approach towards innovation; being prepared to adapt their practice where benefits and improvements are identified. C9 Act upon advice and feedback and be open to coaching and mentoring.		C40 Work as a team member and identify opportunities for working with colleagues, managing their work where appropriate and sharing the development of effective practice with them.

P Post-threshold teachers on the upper pay scale	P1 Contribute significantly, where appropriate, to implementing workplace policies and practice and to promoting collective responsibility for their implementation.	P5 Have a more developed knowledge and understanding of their subjects/ curriculum areas and related pedagogy including how learning progresses within them.	P9 Promote collaboration and work effectively as a team member. P10 Contribute to the professional development of colleagues through coaching and mentoring, demonstrating effective practice, and providing advice and feedback
E Excellent teachers	E2 Research and evaluate innovative curricular practices and draw on research outcomes and other sources of external evidence to inform their own practice and that of colleagues.	E5 Have an extensive and deep knowledge and understanding of their subjects/ curriculum areas and related pedagogy gained for example through involvement in wider professional networks associated with their subjects/ curriculum areas.	E13 Work closely with leadership teams, taking a leading role in developing, implementing and evaluating policies and practice that contribute to school improvement. E14 Contribute to the professional development of colleagues using a broad range of techniques and skills appropriate to their needs so that they demonstrate enhanced and effective practice. E15 Make well-founded appraisals of situations upon which they are asked to advise, applying high-level skills in classroom observation to evaluate and advise colleagues on their work and devising and implementing effective strategies to meet the learning needs of children and young people leading to improvements in pupil outcomes.
A Advanced skills teachers (ASTs)	A1 Be willing to take on a strategic leadership role in developing workplace policies and practice and in promoting collective responsibility for their implementation in their own and other workplaces.		A2 Be part of or work closely with leadership teams, taking a leadership role in developing, implementing and evaluating policies and practice in their own and other workplaces that contribute to school improvement. A3 Possess the analytical, interpersonal and organisational skills necessary to work effectively with staff and leadership teams beyond their own school.

Source: www.tda.gov.uk/teachers/professionalstandards.

The first step in making any change is identifying needs. This may sound straightfoward and reflective practioners will generally have a good sense of where their practice can be developed, but it may be that someone else might be able to contribute a further insight into what is happening and come up with different ways of addressing the situation. For example, a teacher might identify support for high attaining children as an area for development, but through discussion with a colleague about the issue may conclude that presenting starting points for scientific enquiries in a more open-ended way would benefit not only the high attainers, but the whole class. Or, a teacher may want to improve the children's scientific language when 'writing up' investigations, and the science subject leader may initially be at a loss for ideas, but after talking to another colleague who is responsible for English in the school, all three teachers work together on strategies to improve oral work in science and alternative forms of recording outcomes. Or, a teacher might decide they want to improve their questioning skills when they work with a group of children and ask the science subject leader to video them teaching and reflect on it together later. In all of these cases the subject leader is likely to learn as much as the classteacher concerned. It is this sense of 'learning together' that is central to success.

Having analysed the situation, and planned some ways forward, it is a good idea to identify some success critera. How will everyone know that a change has been achieved and what its impact is? Again, subject leaders might be very helpful in gathering evidence to review changes and give some feedback. Successes are best shared! Where things haven't worked as hoped, having someone else to help think about why, can reduce feelings of failure and provide motivation to try something different. Fullan (2007) points out that having a clear sense of the particular change that should happen at the outset can actually present a barrier to productive development if it means that people are too rigid to listen and look at the evidence of what is really happening to everyone during a process of change. A summary of the processes this may involve is shown in Figure 12.1:

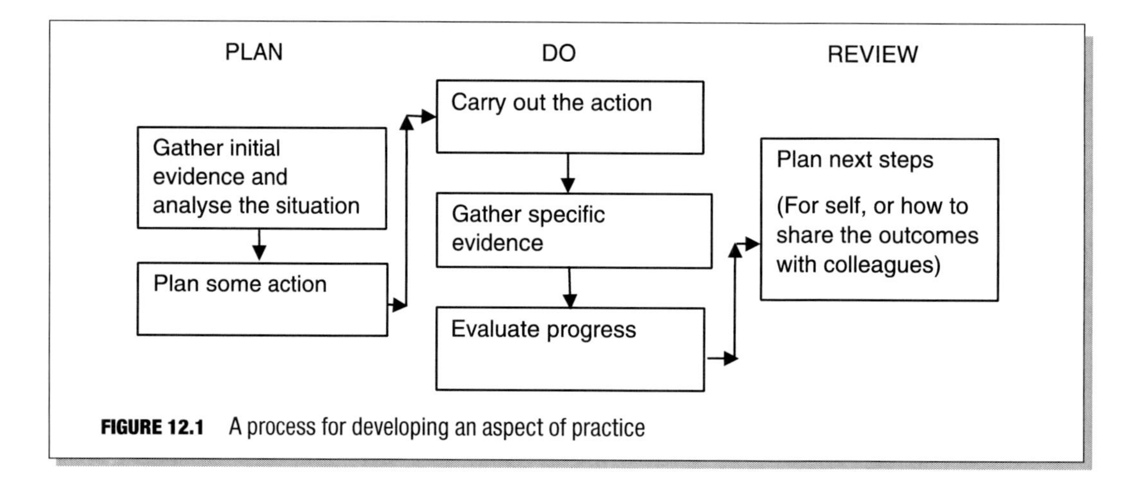

FIGURE 12.1 A process for developing an aspect of practice

A dialogic school culture?

> **Educational change is a process of coming to grips with the *multiple* realities of people, who are the main participants in implementing change.**
>
> **(Fullan 2007: 109)**

Fullan's (2007) view of educational change means that it is not something that leaders in schools can plan for without being open to the ideas and experiences of all the people involved. Although leaders with a clear vision and sense of purpose can be powerful in leading change, they cannot do it alone. Fullan also stresses the importance of understanding cultural contexts of schools and how the people within them will respond to any innovations. What does this mean for those teachers who do not have the labels of leadership?

One implication is that it gives a valid reason for individuals to voice their ideas; ideas matter because the way people understand things is central to what they actually do in practice. In the long run it is not actually helpful to 'go along with' innovations that are not fully understood or are disagreed with. Leaders are not in a position to understand all the different points of view and interpretations that their colleagues in a school will have of proposed change and are dependent on those ideas being voiced to understand all the implications. Leaders need our feedback! That doesn't mean that it is always easy to give, or that leaders find it easy to listen to responses that seem to be critical. It can help to find ways of expressing ideas that enable different opinions to be discussed without it becoming a personal conflict:

> *From my point of view, I am worried about doing that because . . .*
> *We might need to consider the impact of that on . . .*
> *To make that work I would need . . .*
> *For me that seems to conflict with our aim to . . .*

Differences between ideas can be constructive and creative. When taking part in discussions, as well as expressing your own ideas, there is a genuine opportunity to understand better those of others. It helps to develop a collaborative culture if all members of staff are aware of the wider roles and relationships of colleagues and support dialogues that are open and honest, but also caring and professional. (See Bell and Ritchie (1999) for further discussion about school cultures and subject leadership.)

In chapter 1 we introduced the term 'dialogic teaching' to explore how teachers can work with children's ideas and encourage children to use talk productively with each other. The central idea here is that people will have different ideas and we need to find out what they are and use them to develop a better shared understanding. Dialogic discussions are: collective, reciprocal, supportive, cumulative and purposeful (Alexander 2008). This concept can be usefully applied to discussions between colleagues as they work together with the common purpose of improving the learning of children in their school.

Fullan's ideas about leadership and change (Fullan 2007) also mean that it is not helpful to expect science subject leaders to be people with all the answers. In any time of change and development we all have to learn to tolerate periods of uncertainty and not demand instant solutions to problems. Ownership of outcomes requires an active involvement in developing them. A school that is going to continue to improve and meet the needs of the children in it needs all of its teachers to reflect on existing practices and be prepared to make changes. You don't have to be a science subject leader to have some good ideas about how science might be developed, but it would be sensible to work with them and foolish to exclude them. Below we list a few suggestions for start points for collectively developing science in schools with the intention of stimulating ideas that are relevant to your own context.

- If the school has rather rigid medium term planning ask if you can do a 'pilot' study on an alternative approach in your class with another teacher acting as a 'critical friend'

- If resources are inadequate for teaching a topic – say so, but then help fundraise, or try to develop imaginative alternative solutions
- If your own subject knowledge in a particular areas of the science curriculum is weak, ask if anyone else feels similarly and together set about addressing it in at least three completely different ways
- In a small working party, consider opportunites for a cross-curricular approach to developing the outdoor environment
- Conduct a small-scale study into the effective use of a new technology to support children's learning in science, e.g PDAs
- If being able to assess children's progress in scientific process skills is an issue, gather examples of children's scientific enquiry work for a key stage or whole-school work sampling meeting.

Becoming a science subject leader

It isn't obvious how to go about becoming a science subject leader. Sometimes job advertisements do include something about science subject leadership, but this is not common. The role is usually an internal appointment within a school, and is not always open to all, but a responsibility allocated by the headteacher. This means that the first step to becoming a subject leader for science is making your interest known in the school. This can be done in a professional way that does not threaten the position of the existing science subject leader, but is supportive, by offering to help out and perhaps 'shadowing' them in order to learn more about what the responsibilty entails. It is worth taking up available opportunites to lead other subjects, as there is much generic learning to be done about the leadership role and how to work with colleagues.

The desire to become a science subject leader may be rooted in a passion for the subject, or perhaps, having seen how positively children can respond to imaginative science lessons, a teacher may want to share this with others. It can also be seen within a wider view of career development as a teaching professional in which supporting colleagues and leadership become increasingly important. How science subject leadership fits within the model of career progression as set out in the TDA framework is considered in the next section.

TDA Professional Standards and Subject Leadership

The Training and Development Agency for Schools provides a framework of Professional Standards (for teachers in England from 2007) aimed at supporting career progression for teachers. After the standards that teachers in initial teacher training are required to meet in order to gain Qualified Teacher Status there are further standards they are required to meet at the end of their induction period and these become the Core standards for mainscale teachers (C). Further standards are set for teachers to 'cross the threshold', or to become 'excellent' or 'Advanced skills' teachers.

The standards are divided into three headings:

- professional attributes
- professional knowledge and understanding
- professional skills.

The TDA standards provide a means of demonstrating professional development, and rewarding it too. Using them as a starting point for discussion with a headteacher during performance management might be a good means of planning for your own professional development.

Although all the standards can be seen as having relevance to developing science teaching, such as assessment and monitoring, or communicating and working with others, aspects of these standards that have particular relevance to the issue of continued professional development and the role of the science subject leader have been selected and presented in Table 12.1.

In order to develop a specialist expertise in science teaching it is helpful to become involved with people beyond the school who share this interest and the next section makes some suggestions about where to look for this. The suggested further reading at the end of the chapter would also be a good next step.

Sources of help and professional development outside school

Although most of this chapter has emphasised the opportunities for development that exist within school, organisations outside schools have much to offer, and some of these are described in this section. All primary teachers may find them very useful, and science subject leaders will find them a particularly valuable source of expertise and ideas.

Science Learning centres: www.sciencelearningcentres.org.uk

There are ten Science Learning centres located in regions around the UK whose central purpose is to support the professional development of teachers of science, in both primary and secondary schools. They offer a variety of courses and one-off events as well as drop-in support and useful webpages with online resources and reports of innovative projects.

The Association for Science Education: www.ase.org.uk

The Assocication for Science Education (ASE) is the national professional association for teachers of science in the UK for primary and secondary teachers. It offers conferences and courses regionally and nationally, and publishes a range of teaching resources and books. Members can get involved in local and regional networks of other science educators and this is a really good way of getting to know some key national people at a personal level. Nationally it also acts as a political lobby group and frequently advises the government on matters concerned with science education.

The ASE is also the awarding body for CSciTeach, or Chartered Science Teacher, which is a chartered designation in line with other awards, such as Chartered Accountant or Chartered Surveyor, that recognises the professional standing of an individual working in that field. The awards are made under powers granted by the Privy Council.

Your local authority

Most local authorities offer some form of support for science teaching and for science subject leaders. They may offer courses of different lengths, sometimes in conjunction with local universities. There may be cluster groups, in which science subject leaders from different schools within a local area can meet on a regular basis and share ideas. Titles vary between authorities, but there is likely to be at least one primary science specialist who offers support to schools in different ways, often coming into the school to talk with the science subject leader, or work alongside a teacher, sometimes leading a whole school training day. Sometimes this role is carried out by advanced skills teachers (ASTs).

Hands-on science centres and technology centres

Around the country there are a large number of centres dedicated to developing the public understanding of science and technology, while giving people a good day out. Some examples are: 'Explore@Bristol', 'Inspire' in Norwich, 'Stratosphere' in Aberdeen, 'Centre for Alternative Technology' in Snowdonia and 'Investigate' in the London Natural History Museum. As well as being educational to visit, these centres often run courses for teachers and have useful websites reporting on their latest projects. Often, just reading what others have done is enough to stimulate creative ideas that could be tried in schools!

Higher education

Many universities have faculties of education that run courses for primary teachers, and some provide courses associated with teaching primary science or subject leadership. Usually these courses are accredited and can be used towards gaining a higher academic qualification such as a certificate or a master's degree. They may also be leading research projects locally and may be interested in hearing from local teachers who are keen to be involved with new initiatives.

Summary

In this chapter we have considered ways in which classteachers might get support in their work from science subject leaders in school. We have emphasised how a two-way, or dialogic, relationship with the subject leader is more productive than seeing them as an authoritative source of information. This supports our view of the importance of developing a collaborative culture in schools in which colleagues learn together. Through discussion of this we have introduced a view of the roles of the subject leader and finally provided information about how this could be developed further.

Discussion points

1. What are your priorities for developing your own teaching and how could you best go about it?
2. What opportunities can you identify (or create) for working with colleagues to develop science teaching in your school?

Further reading

Bell and Ritchie (1999), ***Towards Effective Subject Leadership in the Primary School*****:** this book provides a detailed and thoughtful discussion of the role of the subject leader in primary schools. It includes advice on how to go about leading and managing change exemplified with short case studies.

Fullan (2007), ***Planning, Doing and Coping with Change, The New Meaning of Educational Change*****, Chapter 6:** to gain a further understanding of the ideas of Michael Fullan that are briefly introduced in this chapter, read chapter 6 of his book for a realistic, but positive view of what is and isn't possible to achieve!

Garrett (1999), 'Managing Change' in Davies, B. and Ellison, L. (eds) School Leadership for the 21st Century, Chapter 8: this chapter provides a general discussion about the process of management of change in the context of schools.

Newton and Newton (1998), ***Coordinating Science across the Primary School*****:** this book provides a science-specific overview of the role of the subject leader and includes some useful sections on monitoring different aspects of science teaching and learning.

References

Adey, P., Nagy, F., Robertson, A., Serret, N. and Wadsworth, P. (2003) *Let's Think through Science: Developing Thinking with seven- and eight-year-olds*. London: nferNelson.

Adey, P., Robertson, A. and Venville, G. (2001) *Let's Think: A Programme for Developing Thinking with five and six year olds*. London: nferNelson.

Alexander, R.J. (2008) *Towards Dialogic Teaching: Rethinking classroom talk* (4th edn). Dialogos.

Arnold, N. (2006) *Earth and Beyond*. Leamington Spa: Scholastic.

Association for Science Education (ASE) (2001) *Be Safe! Health and Safety in Primary School Science and Technology* (3rd edn). Hatfield: ASE Publications.

Barlex, D. (2001) *Primary Solutions in D&T*. London: Nuffield Foundation.

Bell, D. and Ritchie, R. (1999) *Towards Effective Subject Leadership in the Primary School*. Buckingham: Open University Press.

Brown, R. (1992) *Dark, Dark Tale*. London: Red Fox.

Bruner, J.S. (1966) *Toward a Theory of Instruction*. New York: Norton.

Bruner, J. (1996) *The Culture of Education*. Cambridge, MA : Harvard University Press.

Carey, S. (1985) *Conceptual Change in Childhood*. Cambridge, MA: MIT Press.

Carlton, K. and Parkinson, E. (1994) *Physical Sciences; A Primary Teacher's Guide*. London: Cassell Education.

Carson, R. (2000) *Silent Spring*. London: Penguin Books.

Carson, R. (1998) *The Sense of Wonder*. London: HarperCollins.

Children of the World (1994) *Rescue Mission Planet Earth: A Children's Edition of Agenda 21*. London: Kingfisher Books.

Clegg, B. (2007) *Getting Science The teacher's guide to exciting and painless primary school science*. Oxon: Routledge Falmer.

Cole, B. (1995) *Mummy Laid an Egg*. London: Red Fox.

Cole, B. (1996) *Dr Dog*. London: Red Fox.

Cole, B. (2001) *Hair in Funny Places*. London: Red Fox.

Collins Educational (2003, 2004, 2005) Science Directions – Virtual Experiments Years 5 and 6 CD-ROM, Years 3 and 4 CD-ROM, Years 1 and 2 CD-ROM. Glasgow: Collins Educational.

Cox, M., Abbot, C., Webb, M., Blakely, B., Beauchamp, T. and Rhodes, V. (2004) *ICT and Attainment: A Review of the Research Literature*. London: DfES.

Dale Tunnicliffe, S. (1999) 'What's inside a tree?', *Primary Science & Technology Today*, **11**, Spring 1999, 3–5.

Davies, D. (2001) 'What kind of light will work for you?', in Barlex, D. (ed.) *Nuffield Primary Solutions in Design & Technology*. Wellesbourne: DATA.

Davies, D. and Heal, S. (2006) 'Ground Control to Moonbase': communications technology in primary D&T, in Norman, E., Spendlove, D. and Owen-Jackson, G. (eds) *Designing the Future: The D&T Association International Research Conference 2006*. Wellesbourne: DATA. 33–40.

Davies, D. and Howe, A. (2003) *Teaching Science and Design and Technology in the Early Years*. London: David Fulton.

Davies, D. and Ward, S. (2003) Young children as scientists and designers in Davies, D. and Howe, A. (2003) *Teaching Science and Design and Technology in the Early Years*, Chapter 1. London: David Fulton.

Davies, N. (2004) *Poo*. London: Walker Books.

de Boo, M. (2004) *Nature Detectives*. Hatfield: ASE Publications.

de Boo, M. and Asoko, H. (2001) *Analogies and Illustrations: Representing Ideas in Primary Science*. Hatfield: ASE Publications.

Department for Children, Schools and Families (DCSF) (2008) *Statutory Framework for the Early Years Foundation Stage*. London: DCSF.

Department for Education and Employment (DfEE) (2000) *Sex and Relationship Education Guidance*. London: DfEE.

Department for Education and Employment (DfEE)/Qualifications and Curriculum Authority (QCA) (1998) *A Scheme of Work for Key Stages 1 and 2 Science*. London: QCA Publications.

Department for Education and Employment (DfEE)/Qualifications and Curriculum Authority (QCA) (1999) *The National Curriculum for Science*. London: DfEE/QCA.

Department for Education and Skills (DfES) (2003) *Excellence and Enjoyment: A Strategy for Primary Schools*. Nottingham: DfES.

Department for Education and Skills (DfES) (2004) *Every Child Matters: Change for Children in Schools*. Nottingham: DfES.

Driver, R. (1983) *The Pupil as Scientist*. Milton Keynes: Open University Press.

Driver, R., Guesne, E. and Tiberghien, A. (1985) *Children's Ideas in Science*. Milton Keynes: Open University Press.

Farrow, S. (1999) *The Really Useful Science Book: A Framework for Primary Teachers* (2nd edn). London: Falmer.

Feasey, R., Goldsworthy, A., Phipps, R. and Stringer, J. (2000) *New Star Science Series*. Oxford: Ginn.

Fullan, M. (2007) *Planning, Doing and Coping with Change: The New Meaning of Educational Change*, Chapter 6, Oxon: Routledge.

Garrett, V. (1999) 'Managing Change' in Davies, B. and Ellison, L. (eds) *School Leadership for the 21st Century*, Chapter 8. London: Routledge.

Goldsworthy, A. and Feasey, R. (1998) *Making Sense of Primary Science Investigations* (2nd edn). Hatfield: ASE.

Goldsworthy, A. and Holmes, M. (1999) *Teach It, Do It, Let's Get To It*. Hatfield: ASE Publications.

Goldsworthy, A., Watson, R. and Wood-Robinson, V. (2000a) *Investigations: Developing Understanding*. Hatfield: ASE.

Goldsworthy, A., Watson, R. and Wood-Robinson, V. (2000b) *Investigations: Getting to Grips with Graphs*. Hatfield: ASE.

Goodall, J. (1996) *My Life with Chimpanzees*. New York: Aladdin.

Goodall, J. (2001) *The Chimpanzees I Love: Saving Their World and Ours*. New York: Scholastic.

Grace, M. (2000) *Ecosystems in SciCentre: Developing Primary Teachers' Science Knowledge – A Bank of Self-Study Materials*. Leicester: SciCentre.

Gregory, R. (1981) *Mind in Science*. London: Penguin.

Harlen, W. (2000) *The Teaching of Science in Primary Schools* (3rd edn). London: David Fulton.

Harlen, W. (2006) *Teaching, Learning and Assessing Science 5–12* (4th edn). London : Sage Publications.

Harlen, W. and Qualter, A. (2004) *The Teaching of Science in Primary Schools* (4th edn). London: David Fulton.

Hawley, D. (2002) 'Building Conceptual Understanding in Young Scientists', *Journal of Geoscience Education*, **50** (4), 363–371.

Health Education Authority (1998a) *A Parent's Guide to Drugs and Alcohol*. Abingdon: Health Education Authority.

Health Education Authority (1998b) *The Score. Facts about Drugs*. Abingdon: Health Education Authority.

Howe, A. (2002) 'Animal attitudes', *RSPCA Animal Focus: Nocturnal Animals*, **5**, October, 16.

Howe, A., Davies, D. and Ritchie, R. (2001) *Primary Design and Technology for the Future: Creativity, culture and citizenship*. London: David Fulton Publishers.

Howe, L. (1990) *Collins Primary Science Series*. London: Collins Educational.

Johnsey, R., Peacock, G., Sharp, J., Wright, D. (2000) 'Functioning of Organisms: Green Plants', in *Achieving QTS: Primary Science Knowledge and Understanding*. Exeter: Learning Matters.

Johnston, K. and Scott, P. (1990) *Children's Learning in Science Projects: Interactive Teaching in Science – Workshops for Training Courses*. Hatfield: ASE.

Kruger, C., Palacio, D. and Summers, M. (1991) *Understanding Forces: Understanding Science Concepts: Teacher Education Material for Primary School Science*. Oxford: Oxford University and Westminster College.

Leach, J. and Scott, P. (2002) 'Designing and evaluating science teaching sequences: an approach drawing upon the concept of learning demand and a social constructivist perspective on learning', *Studies in Science Education*, **38**, 115–142.

Leach, R., Driver, R., Scott, P. and Wood-Robinson, V. (1996) 'Children's ideas about ecology 3: ideas found in children 5–16 about the interdependency of organisms', *International Journal of Science Education*, **18** (2), 129–141.

Lipman, M. (2003) *Thinking in Education* (2nd edn). Cambridge and New York: Cambridge University Press.

McGough, R. (2003) *The Collected Poems*. London: Viking.

McGuigan, L. and Hughes, A. (1998) *Primary Science Processes and Concept Exploration (SPACE) Project Research Report: Forces*. Liverpool: Liverpool University Press.

McMahon, K. (2009) *Interactive whole class teaching in Key Stage Two Classrooms*. (PhD thesis – forthcoming)

McMahon, K. and Davies, D. (2003) 'Assessment for inquiry: supporting teaching and learning in primary science', *Science Education International*, **14** (4), 29–39.

Marshall, F. (2001) *Models and Analogies*, ideas presented during an Improving Science Together Project meeting.

Millar, R. and Osborne, J. (eds) (1998) *Beyond 2000: Science Education for the Future*. London: King's College.

Mortimer, E. and Scott, P. (2003) *Meaning Making in Secondary Science Classrooms*. Maidenhead: Open University Press.

Muijs, D. and Reynolds, D. (2001) *Effective Teaching: Evidence and Practice*. London: Paul Chapman.

Murphy, J. (1995a) *Peace At Last*. London: Macmillan.

Murphy, J. (1995b) *Whatever Next?* London: Macmillan.

Naylor, S. and Keogh, B. (2000) *Concept Cartoons in Science Education*. London: Millgate House.

Newton, L. and Newton, P. (1998) *Coordinating Science across the Primary School*. London: Falmer Press.

Nuffield Primary Science (1993) *Sound and Music Teachers' Guide*. London: Collins Educational.

Nuffield Primary Science (1995) *Living Things in Their Environment: Teachers' Guide*. London: Collins Educational.

Nussbaum, J. (1985) 'The Earth as a cosmic body, children's ideas in science', in Driver, R., Guesne, E. and Tiberghien, A. (eds) *Children's Ideas in Science*. Milton Keynes: Open University Press, pp. 170–192.

Office for Standards in Education (Ofsted) (2004) *Ofsted Subject Reports 2002/03: Science in Primary Schools*. London: Ofsted.

Office for Standards in Education (Ofsted) (2008) *Success in Science*. London: Ofsted.

Ollerenshaw, C. and Ritchie, R. (1997) *Primary Science: Making It Work* (2nd edn). London: David Fulton.

Osborne, J.F., Black, P.J., Smith, M. and Meadow, J. (1990) *SPACE Project Research Report: Light*. Liverpool: Liverpool University Press.

Osborne, J.F., Wadsworth, P. and Black, P.J. (1990) *SPACE Research Project Report: Life Processes*. Liverpool: Liverpool University Press.

Osborne, J.F., Wadsworth, P., Black, P.J. and Meadows, J. (1993) *SPACE Research Report: The Earth in Space*. Liverpool: Liverpool University Press.

Palmer, J. and Suggate, J. (2005) 'Children's reasoning about Global Environmental Issues: Deforestation and Global Warming', *Primary Science Review, 87*, 12–16.

Piaget, J. (1929) *The Child's Conception of the World*. New York: Harcourt Brace.

Plimmer, D., Parkinson, E. and Carlton, K. (1996) *The Environment: A Primary Teacher's Guide*. London: Cassell Education.

Poole, M. (1995) *Beliefs and Values in Science Education*. Milton Keynes: Open University Press.

Qualifications and Curriculum Authority and Department for Education and Employment (QCA/DfEE) (2000) *Curriculum Guidance for the Foundation Stage*. London: QCA.

Qualifications and Curriculum Authority (QCA) (2003a) *Assessing Progress in Science, Key Stages 1 and 2: Unit 3 Materials.* London: QCA.

Qualifications and Curriculum Authority (QCA) (2003b) *Assessing Progress in Science, Key Stages 1 and 2: Unit 6 Sound and Light.* London: QCA.

Qualifications and Curriculum Authority (QCA) (2003c) *Assessing Progress in Science, Key Stages 1 and 2: Unit 5 Electricity.* London: QCA.

Qualifications and Curriculum Authority (QCA) (2003d) *Changes to Assessment 2003: Sample Materials for Key Stages 1 and 2.* London: QCA.

Qualifications and Curriculum Authority (QCA) (2003e) *Assessing Progress in Science, Key Stage 1 (KS1) and 2: Unit 2 Living Things in Their Environment.* London: QCA.

Qualifications and Curriculum Authority (QCA) (2003g) *Assessing Progress in Science, Key Stage 2: Unit 8 Humans.* London: QCA.

Qualifications and Curriculum Authority (QCA) (2004) *National Curriculum (NC) Tests 2004: Implications for Teaching and Learning from the 2004 Tests, Ks2 Science.* Norwich: QCA.

Rogoff, B. (1990). *Apprenticeship in Thinking: Cognitive development in social context.* New York : Oxford University Press.

Russell, T. and Watt, D. (1990a) *Primary SPACE Project Research Report: Evaporation and Condensation.* Liverpool: Liverpool University Press.

Russell, T. and Watt, D. (1990b) *Primary Science Processes and Concept Exploration (SPACE) Project Research Report: Growth.* Liverpool: Liverpool University Press.

Russell, T., Bell, D., Longden, K. and McGuigan, L. (1993) *Primary SPACE Project Research Report: Rocks, Soil and Weather.* Liverpool: Liverpool University Press.

Russell, T., Longden, K. and McGuigan, L. (1991) *Primary Science Processes and Concept Exploration (SPACE) Project Research Report: Materials.* Liverpool: Liverpool University Press.

Russell, T., McGuigan, L. and Hughes, A. (1998) *Science Processes and Concept Exploration (SPACE) Project Research Report: Forces.* Liverpool: Liverpool University Press.

Rymell, R. (1999) 'What Defines a Plant?' *Primary Science Review,* **57**, 23–25.

Scott, P. (1987). *A Constructivist View of Teaching and Learning.* Leeds: Children's Learning in Science Project, University of Leeds.

Shulman, L. (1987) 'Knowledge and teaching: foundations of the new reform', *Harvard Educational Review,* **57**, 1–22.

Software Production Enterprises (SPE) (1995) *Making Sense of Science; Teacher's Notes.* London: SPE.

Summers, M., Kruger, C., Childs, A. and Mant, J. (2000) *One Small Step: Understanding the Science of Environmental Issues.* Hatfield: ASE.

Summers, M., Kruger, J. and Mant, J. (1997) *Teaching Electricity Effectively: a Research-Based Guide for Primary Science.* Hatfield: ASE.

Sylva, K., Melhuish, E., Sammons, P., Siraj-Blatchford, I., Taggart, B. and Elliot, K. (2004) *The Effective Provision of Pre-School Education (EPPE) Project: Findings from the Pre-school Period.* London: Institute of Education.

Tomlinson, J. (1988) *The Owl Who Was Afraid of the Dark.* Basingstoke: Macmillan.

Vygotsky, L.S. (1978). *Mind in Society: The development of higher psychological processes.* Cambridge, MA: Harvard University Press.

Waddell, M. (2001) *Can't You Sleep Little Bear?* London: Walker Books.

Watson, R., Wood-Robinson, V. and Goldsworthy, A. (2000) *AKSIS Investigations Targeted Learning.* Hatfield: ASE Publications.

Watt, D. and Russell, T. (1990) *Science Processes and Concept Exploration Project Research Report: Sound.* Liverpool: Liverpool University Press.

Wenham, M. (2005) *Understanding Primary Science: Ideas, Concepts and Explanations* (2nd edn). London: Paul Chapman.

Wray, D. and Lewis, M. (1997) *Extending Literacy: Children Reading and Writing Non-Fiction.* London: Routledge.

Websites

American Society for Nutrition: www.nutrition.org [last accessed 1 September 2008].

Association for Science Education: www.ase.org.uk [last accessed 1 September 2008].

AstraZeneca Science Teaching Trust: www.azteachscience.co.uk [last accessed 1 September 2008].

Astroventure: http://astroventure.arc.nasa.gov/DAP/DAP.html [last accessed 1 September 2008].

Barnardos (2004) http://www.barnardos.org.uk/burger_boy_report_1.pdf [last accessed 1 September 2008].

BBC: http://www.bbc.co.uk/climate/evidence/extreme.shtml [last accessed 1 September 2008].

http://www.bbc.co.uk/schools/ks2bitesize/science/activities/earth_sun_moon.shtml [last accessed 1 September 2008].

www.bbc.co.uk/science/humanbody [last accessed 1 September 2008].

www.bbc.co.uk/nature/animals/planetearth/hd [last accessed 1 September 2008].

Carymoor Environmental Trust: www.carymoor.org.uk [last accessed 1 September 2008].

Concept Cartoons: www.conceptcartoons.com [last accessed 1 September 2008].

Consortium of Local Education Authorities for the Provision of Science Services: www.cleapss.org.uk [last accessed 1 September 2008].

Earth Charter Initiative: www.earthcharter.org [last accessed 1 September 2008].

Eco-schools: www.eco-schools.org [last accessed 1 September 2008].

Fear of Physics: www.fearofphysics.com [last accessed 1 September 2008].

Healthy Schools: www.wiredforhealth.gov.uk [last accessed 1 September 2008].

International Web-cams: http://www.teleobjektiv.com/WebCam/index-webcam.htm [last accessed 1 September 2008].

Jane Goodall Institute: www.janegoodall.org [last accessed 1 August 2008].

Kids' Health: www.kidshealth.org [last accessed 1 September 2008]

National Geographic: http://www9.nationalgeographic.com/ngm/wildcamafrica [last accessed 1 September 2008].

Plants in Motion: http://plantsinmotion.bio.indiana.edu/plantmotion/starthere.html [last accessed 1 September 2008].

Qualifications and Curriculum Authority: http://www.standards.dfes.gov.uk/schemes2/ks1-2 citizenship/cit03/?view=get [last accessed 1 September 2008].

Science and Plants for Schools (SAPS): http://www-saps.plantsci.cam.ac.uk/ [last accessed 1 September 2008].

Science Learning Centres: www.sciencelearningcentres.org.uk. [last accessed 1 September 2008].

Teachernet: www.teachernet.gov.uk/PSHE [last accessed 1 September 2008].

Teachers TV: Science Tube – Green World: http://www.teachers.tv/video/12097 [last accessed 1 September 2008].

Index